THOMAS ATKINSON

EDITOR
The Crawford Messenger

and
Related Families
Stuart and Stebbins

Emily Pritchard Cary

HERITAGE BOOKS
2018

HERITAGE BOOKS

AN IMPRINT OF HERITAGE BOOKS, INC.

Books, CDs, and more—Worldwide

For our listing of thousands of titles see our website
at
www.HeritageBooks.com

Published 2018 by
HERITAGE BOOKS, INC.
Publishing Division
5810 Ruatan Street
Berwyn Heights, Md. 20740

Copyright © 2018 Emily Pritchard Cary

Heritage Books by the author:

The Pritchard Family History:
The Virginia Line from Thomas, Jamestown Immigrant
with Related Families of Tichenell, Nestor, and Meredith, Third Edition

The Pritchard/Pritchett Family History:
The Virginia Line from Thomas, Jamestown Immigrant
with Related Families of Tichenell, Nestor, and Meredith, Fourth Edition

Thomas Atkinson, Editor, The Crawford Messenger,
and Related Families Stuart and Stebbins

International Standard Book Numbers
Paperbound: 978-0-7884-5858-3

THOMAS ATKINSON, EDITOR,

THE CRAWFORD MESSENGER

AND RELATED FAMILIES STUART AND STEBBINS

EMILY PRITCHARD CARY

Table of Contents

SETTING THE STAGE

Meadville, Pennsylvania, was a microcosm of settlements which blossomed along the American frontier after the Revolutionary War. Because the Crawford Messenger is one of the few early American newspapers completely extant, its editor, Thomas Atkinson, unwittingly held a mirror into which succeeding generations might glimpse life during the nation's first few decades.

Not content with simply recording the best and worst events and trends of his time, Atkinson set for himself lofty personal goals so that he might inspire his family, associates and average citizens. In his zeal to accomplish all the tasks his heritage and God commanded, he played his roles in life to the hilt, becoming an expert in each of the professions he most admired.

To his wife, Sally Sommers Atkinson, Thomas was, first and last, a loving husband, parent and provider. To his countless admirers, this writer, editor, publisher, educator, businessman, and politician was the greatest of all humanitarians: a good citizen.

SARAH SOMMERS ATKINSON'S LETTER TO HER GREAT- GRANDDAUGHTER

Meadville, Pennsylvania
September 6, 1870

My darling Mary Adelaide,

How hard it is for me to realize that you have become such a big girl and are starting school today! Now you are forsaking your great-grandmother's knee for the wider world of education. Soon you will discover for yourself the blessings and mysteries of this miraculous gift called life. You will recite lessons, commit sums to memory, and marvel at the history of our nation, which has grown from thirteen tiny colonies that people traversed by foot, horseback, or cart, to this mighty land linked by thousands of railway miles.

The many hours you have spent at my side have been a blessing to me. I hope you have received from them the deep contentment I have felt while relating events of my own life. Often, I have smiled as you begged, "Tell me about when you were a little girl, Great Gamma," and I have cherished those happy moments spent with you, your brothers and sister, and your cousins.

Now that you have reached this auspicious milepost of your childhood and we no longer will have much time to spend together, I fear that I shall become a very old lady quite soon. Your presence has kept me young remembering my own youth and young womanhood. I came to Meadville when it was not the progressive, comfortable town it is today, but a tiny frontier village. You have heard my stories so many times I fear that they have become boring to you. But our minds fail in time, as I pray mine will not, and there may come a day when you will not recall some of the tales I have told you about Meadville and your ancestors, especially your great-great grandfather, who helped it grow into this lovely town.

Memory being a fragile thing, I shall spend the hours while you are in school writing down all the thoughts flooding my mind in the hope that when I am gone and my voice is silenced forever, my memories will be captured on paper so that you, your children, your children's children, and those beyond will know that those who came before were more than names carved on gravestones or entered into family Bibles. They were good citizens who took pride in building this fine community out of the wilderness.

How I regret that you never knew your great-grandfather! If I quote too much from his newspapers, please be patient with this old lady, Except for my children, these yellowed copies of the Crawford Messenger are all that remains of our life together and of Meadville when it was very young. My little world was so entwined with the newspaper that re-reading its pages opens for me a secret door into the past.

One day, when you are grown and married with children of your own, you may glance at this journal and consider casting it aside to make room on the shelf for a pretty trinket or a worldly book. But please, dear Mary Adelaide, think at that time upon the happy hours we have spent together and remember that another may follow you who dearly yearns to know about the people who preceded him. So, preserve it treasure it, and be assured that in honoring the past you are also blessing the future.

With deep fondness,

Sarah Sommers Atkinson

CHAPTER ONE

THE HERITAGE

Thomas Atkinson, my husband, was destined to be a leader. He bore his responsibilities nobly from his very first challenge. Not long after we met, he told me about it, very casually. I believe it was his account of the turning point in his life which made me realize that he was, not only a man whose love I would gladly share for eternity, but also a man who would earn respect from everyone whose life he touched.

Thomas had turned twelve a few months past. It was a sobering age for a young man in the year of our Lord 1793, and even more so for Thomas because, for the first time, he was replacing his father. It was only a temporary change, but just the same he felt obliged to exert all the bravery he could muster. I can picture it now, exactly as he described the scene.

Thomas's horse trotted at the vanguard of the little procession. His mother, Salome Weidner Atkinson, followed his lead. Behind her, his older sisters, Betsy and Sophia, shared a mount, while his brother, Mathew, brought up the rear clutching onto their younger sister who bounced and laughed in front of him on the saddle, as if anticipating an enchanted land around the next bend. Thomas was thankful that his little sister was amused. He knew the seriousness of their journey.

The Atkinsons were traveling northward along the Patapsco Road in Maryland, not far from Thomas Creek Valley where they had lived for four years before circumstances beckoned them first to Baltimore, then on to Alexandria, Virginia.

Despite the glorious October weather, the return journey through the Thomas Creek Valley was somber. Already the trees were turning marvelous shades of red and gold. The fresh air crackled, sweet with the aroma of hay newly mowed and of apples ripening in nearby orchards.

The trip by horseback through Maryland's mellow countryside would have been a treat beyond description under any other circumstances. Instead, it was fraught with melancholy. The Atkinsons were retreating from a happy life in Loudoun County, Virginia, hastening to outdistance the oncoming winter.

Salome Atkinson, now bravely retracing the route she had traveled in happier times nearly a decade earlier, frequently remarked how much busier the road was than she remembered it, for now more travelers and west-bound settlers were in view. As the young nation gathered strength after its independence, hardy men and their families were plunging into daring ventures, some into business or trades which required frequent long-distance travel, others abandoning the depleted soil of their farms or plantations to see new land and new futures in settlements springing up further west or in eastern towns expanding to meet the economic demands of a young country.

Wayfarers encountering the little family recognized Salome Atkinson as a gracious lady leading a well-mannered brood. They paused to tip their hats or bid the time of day, no matter how surly or thoughtless they might have behaved toward other fellow travelers.

Salome was a lady, just as Thomas knew his father was a gentleman. Thomas Atkinson Sr. was the grandson of Stephen Atkinson, who immigrated to America with William Penn and other members of the Society of Friends, or Quakers. This first Atkinson to arrive in Pennsylvania had a son, also named Stephen, who obtained property in Lancaster County. There he lived by the Conestoga Creek until his death.

He was buried in the Friends' Burial Grounds at Lancaster, leaving seven children by his second wife, Margaret. Thomas Sr., the first born, was well educated, for all Quakers were devoted to schooling. By the time he reached adulthood, he had acquired so compelling and pleasant a manner that he was well suited for business ventures.

As was the custom for the third born son of Quaker families, Thomas Sr. learned the art of masonry, a very precise and respectable occupation. Blessed with intelligence and manly good looks, the young mason set out for Reading, Pennsylvania where the jobs came as readily as he matched his promise of work well done with finished products worthy of praise.

One of his assignments brought him to the attention of an attorney named Whitehead. Mr. Whitehead was so impressed by the young man's skill that he invited him home to meet his stepdaughter, Salome Weidner. Salome's own father had willed her extensive property in Sinking Springs, a thousand acres of the most valuable land near Reading. Although he had died when she was only four years old, Salome was spared a fatherless childhood. So entranced was Mr. Whitehead by the three Weidner daughters he gained

3

upon marrying their mother, that he provided them with a free education comparable to that which any proper young man of the times would have desired. This education was to serve Salome well in the years to come.

At their very first meeting, Salome and Thomas fell hopelessly in love. Whitehead congratulated himself for engineering the match. Salome was only seventeen when she married the talented, dashing Thomas Atkinson Sr. in 1772. They lived happily in Reading until Thomas joined the Revolutionary army, serving two years as a second lieutenant. In 1777, he went directly into the thick of the Battle of Brandywine. At the same time, his farm team was forcibly impressed, or taken, into service by the government.

When Thomas's service ended in 1779, his horses were still gone, so he and Salome decided to strike out on a new venture. Even though the was still in progress in a few areas, the westward movement had begun. Pioneers moved across Pennsylvania by the hundreds daily. All were in need of lodging along the way. It seemed to Thomas an ideal time to open a public house to serve these travelers.

Salome offered to stake their venture by selling the Sinking Springs property she had inherited from her father. The buyer was General Mifflin, who later was to become a governor of Pennsylvania. With their assets, the Atkinsons were able to open a public hotel on a heavily traveled route in Silver Springs, Cumberland County, not far from Mechanicsburg.

Although the hotel was a profitable enterprise, after two years they grew weary of the constant petty demands made of an innkeeper and his wife. When then heard about rich land available on the state road from

4

Carlisle to Sunbury at the mouth of Raccoon Creek, they decided it would be an ideal spot to farm and raise their two daughters. Eagerly, they turned over the busy public house to another enterprising innkeeper and moved to their new home.

At the farm near Millersville, their two sons were born, first my husband, Thomas Jr, on July 11, 1781, then Mathew two years later. It was a wonderful place for children, and other new families moving into the area provided so much masonry business to Thomas Sr. that he did not have time to worry about the whereabouts of his farm team. The horses were used by General Washington's army until after the Battle of Yorktown in 1781, when Thomas and Salome expected their return. Instead, they learned that the team was totally ruined. No compensation was ever offered.

As his masonry business prospered, Thomas's desire to spread his wins surged. When word filtered back about the fertile farm lands and influx of families into the Thomas Creek Valley of Maryland, Thomas could not resist. He disposed of the farm and moved his family to Maryland.

There his reputation as an outstanding mason grew. Many of the sturdy stone farmhouses standing there today are the fruits of his labor. His fame spread, and within four years he was summoned to Baltimore, where he moved the family onto the estate of George Lux. Lux, a distant relative of Salome's, was an influential citizen who was subsequently instrumental in persuading city officials to consider Thomas for one phase of the new court house construction. After examining his credentials, they chose him over many other applicants.

The Baltimore Court House was a unique building designed to stand on pillars so that the public street ran beneath it. Thomas Atkinson's portion of the prestigious contract involved placing the pillars and excavating the passageway for the street beneath.

Shortly after he commenced work on the Court House Atkinson became ill. The malady was yellow fever, a disease common to low, swampy areas. The fever wracked his body for three months. He knew that he must complete his portion within the time specified so that the other contractors could begin their work, so he decided to hire others, or to sub-contract them to finish his job.

Atkinson feared that his failure to do the actual work himself would damage his reputation and career, but he planned so well and the men he hired carried out his instructions so well that the job brought him more work than he had ever dreamed.

His greatest surprise followed. He was asked to build the jail and marketplace in Alexandria, Virginia, a great honor for so young a mason.

While he worked on this contract for over five years, he moved his family to Alexandria. All went well until toward the end of the construction when he had a relapse. The yellow fever still gripped him.

Worried about her husband's health, Salome suggested that he curtail his masonry work and take a long rest in the country. Once he saw that the jail and market place were nearing completion, Thomas agreed that her idea had merit and so he rented a sprawling farm in Loudoun County, about twenty-three miles west of Alexandria.

THE BALTIMORE COURTHOUSE

It was a lovely peaceful spot. Salome was relieved that her husband would have time to regain his strength. Even though he had to oversee his tobacco and wheat crops, there were ample farm hands to do the labor. Young Thomas Jr. and his brothers and sisters, now totaling seven in number, were thriving in the country life. They fully expected their father to recuperate and be good as new within weeks.

But as the summer of 1793 wore on, it became apparent that the illness was stubborn. After deep discussion, Thomas, Sr. and Salome concluded that his health would never improve in Virginia's damp climate. Even though they regretted leaving, it seemed prudent to return to Pennsylvania where they had never been ill, and where yellow fever was not nearly so common as it was in the South.

Although he could not leave until he directed the tobacco and wheat harvest and saw his masonry contracts to their completion, an estimated two or three months hence, Thomas urged Salome and the children to begin the trip back to Pennsylvania before the weather became harsh.

They would stay with relatives in Lancaster County until he arrived. There they could establish a new home of their own. He was certain that his reputation as a master mason in Maryland and Virginia would stand him in good stead for future work in Pennsylvania. It was really a matter of making the move.

At length, it was decided that Salome, Thomas, Jr., Mathew, and the three older girls would travel together. The two youngest children would remain with their father and a housekeeper in Virginia and journey to Lancaster with him later. It would be too difficult for Salome to handle small children on a long trip by horseback, the only practical means of travel.

Overcoming Salome's argument that the two youngest children should accompany her instead of staying with their father, Thomas Sr. insisted that she needed all the support she could get, support which could come only from the older, more dependable children. He pointed out all the calamities that could befall small children on the trail, from accidents and illness to becoming lost or stolen.

In the end, Salome agreed reluctantly to the plan, and the little band set out.

As young Thomas Jr. jogged along on his mount, he became apprehensive about his father. They had never been parted for long, and he could not dismiss the memory of his father suffering from the fever. The more he dwelled upon it, the less likely it seemed to him that his father would recover enough to make the journey with the two small girls.

Thomas told me that he knew York was not far when traffic on the road increased noticeably, with Conestoga wagons by the dozens seeking an easy passage across the Allegheny Mountains. At York, there were several forks for travelers to contemplate. Most pioneers followed the Monocacy Road to Fort Cumberland and the booming Wills Creek settlement, but others took a northerly route over the mountains by way of Fort Littleton and Fort Ligonier.

The Atkinson family was headed in the opposite, or eastern, direction to Lancaster. Once they passed York, the villages increased in number. Quaker and Presbyterian meeting houses dotted the roadside. By the time they boarded Wright's Ferry for the ride across the Susquehanna River, Salome sensed that she was home, but to Thomas, Mathew, and the girls, it was a strange, new land. They had lived so many years in Maryland and Virginia that their birthplace was only a dream, a dream supported by stories their parents had told them of life before the nation earned its independence.

Arriving at last in Ephrata, they moved in with Salome's aunt to await word from their father. Each day, they hoped, would bring word that he and the two youngest children were setting forth from Virginia to join them,

As time elapsed, Salome became uneasy. Thomas Jr. sensed her worry as day after day he watched her stare out of the window awaiting the post, nervously twisting her hands.

Finally, the letter came. As her eyes scanned the words, Salome became deathly silent. Thomas and the other children studied her face, not daring to guess the awful news. At length, Salome spoke, her voice hollow with disbelief and desperate resignation, "Children, I am afraid that your father is dead."

The fever had consumed him. He was buried in a Virginia grave by strangers several weeks before his wife and children in far-off Pennsylvania knew what had happened. The long-awaited letter had been written by a Virginia neighbor who promised to care for the two young girls until spring,

At first, Salome had no idea what to do. Left with seven children to support, she despaired of being able to cope with the situation until my Thomas pointed out her great asset: an excellent education.

"Since you have taught us so well," he said, "why not teach others?"

The more Salome turned over her son's suggestion, the better it sounded. Learning of a teaching position in nearby Reamstown, she applied and was quickly accepted. The next step was to arrange proper situations for her oldest children.

Betsy and Sophia were no problem. Being lovely young ladies, willing and able to help in all matters, they were invited to move in with relatives to donate their time and efforts to teaching and amusing the younger children in return for learning the fine arts of sewing, cooking, and performing on the spinet, talents becoming genteel young ladies of their day.

As for the two children alone in Virginia, Salome ceased fretting about transporting them to Pennsylvania when Thomas conceived the ideal solution. "Mathew and I will ride back for them. We remember the way."

"But you cannot!" Salome protested. "You're much too young to make such a journey by yourselves."

"Don't worry, Mother," Thomas said. "Mathew and I are perfectly able. Truly, we are."

Salome smiled, recognizing a trace of her optimistic husband in her son. And so, in the spring, Thomas and Mathew traveled alone to Virginia to retrieve the younger girls who, with their sister a few years older, posed no problem for Salome. She could keep them with her and instruct them along with her students.

Thomas and Mathew, however, were special cases. Boys needed to study for a profession, and since they no longer had a father to emulate, they must be placed with master craftsmen in order to learn a trade.

Thomas had no problem deciding what he would like to do. Even though he could work with him hands in an acceptable manner, his greatest pleasure came from books. For years, his mother had told him about the eminent statesman, Benjamin Franklin. From the time he could read, Thomas devoured Poor Richard's Almanac and everything else written by Franklin that he could find. There was no question in his mind; he would become a printer, exactly like his idol, Franklin.

Being younger and having no burning desire to pursue any profession in particular, Mathew decided that printing was to his liking also. Salome could not have been more pleased. She located what she believed was an excellent situation for them both as printing apprentices with Benjamin Mayer, printer for the Ephrata Cloister community of which she had been a part as a young girl. There they would remain for seven years until they had learned every angle of the profession.

Thomas was elated. He knuckled down to his task, absorbing every facet of printing with all the zeal he could muster, because no matter how difficult his chores proved to be, he knew that he was advancing, day by day, step by step, toward his goal.

The seven years passed quickly for Thomas Atkinson. They were made all the happier by his mother's good fortune in marrying Mayer, who had been entranced by her beauty, charm, and intelligence. Even though Salome loved teaching, she was well suited to living the life of a prosperous matron and knowing that her older children had been carefully trained in respectable occupations and proper social graces. Had she held a crystal ball, she would learn that her children would become happy, responsible adults, no more than she would have blinked had she foreseen Thomas's accomplishments. After all, he was the namesake of the handsome, accomplished man who had swept her off her feet at their first meeting in reading.

And young Thomas had something more than his father's imposing personality and capacity for success: he had also inherited Salome's own strength and sheer perseverance.

CHAPTER TWO

WESTWARD TRAVEL

Upon graduating from his apprenticeship in Lancaster, Thomas Atkinson had no trouble finding work as a journeyman printer. Word of his ability spread from one printing shop to another in Lancaster County, and he quickly moved into a good position near Harrisburg.

Harrisburg was still a tiny country town compared with large cities like Philadelphia and Baltimore, but the neighboring village of Paxtang dated back for so many years that most of its residents were becoming eager to stretch their legs and more on to more virgin territory.

About the time that Thomas arrived in town, many people were beginning to pull up stakes and head for the French Creek Valley in western Pennsylvania near Mead's Crawford County settlement. Thomas listened attentively as prospective pioneers extolled the pleasures and possibilities of the beautiful rolling land beyond the Alleghany Mountains. When someone mentioned that the settlement lacked a newspaper, he listened even more intently.

In the meantime, he frequently visited his mother and her new husband, Benjamin Mayer, in nearby Lancaster County. During one of his visits, they introduced him to their new neighbors, the Leonard

Sommers family. Like Thomas's father, Sommers had served in the Revolutionary War and was now seeking his own fortune by developing some newly acquired acreage.

As far as I was concerned, the Sommers family's decision to forsake Germantown, north of Philadelphia, was fated in heaven. You see, I was the oldest Sommers daughter, and on one of Thomas's visits to his mother, he and I came face to face.

Never had I met anyone as handsome and self-reliant as Thomas Atkinson. His visits home seemed to increase, for which I was very thankful, and when I remarked that his mother surely was pleased to see him so often, he replied, with a smile, "To be sure, I take great pleasure in spending time with my family, but that is not my sole reason for coming." Growing very serious, he moved closer and took my hands. Earnestly, he said, "You, Sally, are the other reason."

I shivered involuntarily until he broke into a smile and continued, "From the moment I saw you., I believed that our futures were destined to be as one."

"You do?" I replied, both astounded and overjoyed. Paying no heed to the rules of decorum for young ladies, I cried, "Oh, Thomas, I feel exactly the same about you!"

"Well then, that's settled," he grinned, "We were meant to spend our lives together. I shall have my own print shop, and you will be my bride."

As he took me in his arms, I knew I would never question his determination to become a pioneer printer in the wild Indian country. He could accomplish anything he set his mind on doing.

On March 24, 1804, a little more than three months after I turned seventeen, we were married at Harrisburg. We spent our honeymoon and the first part of the summer preparing for our journey. Even though neither of us had seen Meadville, as the new settlement had come to be called, we both were drawn by a curious, compelling force to the town which was destined to be our home.

Thomas had encouragement from several early settlers of Meadville, particularly the Mead and Reynolds families, as well as others from Paxtang who were acquainted with his work. Having lived in Meadville for a period of time, they knew its problems and were aware that it would be difficult to lure an established printer to the frontier town, but they were certain that Thomas Atkinson was an exceptional young man. If anyone had the grit and skills demanded for one establishing a print shop in Meadville, Thomas did. The growing northwest territory of Pennsylvania desperately needed a newspaper. It could not come too soon.

By some remarkable dealing, Thomas managed to purchase a great mahogany screw-type printing press used for printing Continental currency in Lancaster County during the Revolution. It was exactly the type Benjamin Franklin had used. In fact, Thomas bought it because its owner assured him it had been used originally in one of Franklin's early printing shops in Philadelphia, all the more reason for its appeal.

Thomas was overjoyed with his prize, heavy and bulky though it was, and he saw to its careful loading in a sturdy horse-drawn wagon. The press took up so much room in the wagon, there was little left for our household goods, but both Thomas and I knew that the press was the critical link between our old and new lives. We guarded it fiercely.

Not so unique, but equally necessary for our purpose, was an enormous supply of paper, for the editor with nothing but a printing press was no better off than a writer with only a pen. Once the press and the paper were loaded into the wagon, we added the other necessities. We decided against taking a spinning wheel because we heard that Meadville had an able wheelwright who could build one for us after our arrival. Cooking utensils were another matter, however, and I was glad that my wedding dowry had included a reliable iron cooking kettle, a frying pan, and a coffee pot. My hope chest was well stocked with quilts and pretty cloth, and my sewing kit held a thimble, scissors, needles, and knitting needles, scarce items on the frontier. I also had a few pewter dishes, knives, and forks.

We carried the food staples of coffee, salt, sacks of cornmeal, and molasses. The rest of our diet was gathered along the way. For this reason, Thomas took along his gun, gun powder, and bullet bags, as well as knives for skinning game and lines for fishing in the well-stocked streams and rivers. Of course, there was a medicine kit containing herbs, such as penny-royal to repel ticks and chiggers, and rattlesnake oil for healing blisters.

We were just starting out in life, so it is no wonder that the trip promised us excitement, adventure, and reward at the end, but I often worried about wives of established men who gave up lovely homes and made do in the wilderness with much less than they had known in the East.

We set forth in September, just as the days were becoming golden, the nights nipped with autumn chill.

Crossing the Susquehanna River on Harris's Ferry, our caravan headed westward to Carlisle. Beyond that village, we paralleled Kittatinny, or Blue, Mountain in order to locate the pass around it. Some of the men in our group had made the journey earlier on horseback, so they could assure Thomas that the few extra days off course would more than make up for the time and hazards involved in a mountain crossing.

The roads, not much wider than they had been centuries ago when there were merely Indian trails, twisted in and around the bases of mountains for the first leg of the trip. But at Fort Loudoun, the pass narrowed, and Thomas warned me that our travel difficulties would increase as soon as we reached Fort Littleton just beyond the Tuscarora Mountains.

There we forced the heavy wagon up and across Sideling Hill Ridge. It was a laborious task, and I began to fret that the snows would be upon us before long. Already, the trees at higher altitudes were bare, the air was raw, and small animals were scurrying to lay in supplies for a long winter.

As we skirted the higher mountains through passes in Ray's Hill Ridge and the Allequippa Ridge, I pondered the imminent perils and earlier tragedies which gave Bloody Run its name. Many before us had perished near that spot from exhaustion – or from an Indian attack.

Our little group of pioneer families was completely worn out by the time we arrived at Bedford, the only town along the way. For several days, we remained there in the inn to recoup our energy. The first chore accomplished there was a visit to the blacksmith for new horseshoes.

While Thomas attended to that, I went to the miller for meal and flour. Later, I visited the small shops and chatted with other travelers in the stone inn where we lodged. It was a brief, but refreshing, respite from the long, arduous trail over steep mountain ridges.

After Bedford, there were miles of uninhabited hills to surmount. The horses and oxen struggled valiantly up each mountain, grateful, as we all were, for the cool, clear spring water plentiful everywhere. Thomas and I expected the downward course to be much easier, but we soon discovered that it was every bit as dangerous and slow as the climb, for both horses and hikers slipped over loose rocks.

Frequently, we passed pack trains on the narrow paths, and when we stopped to exchange greetings, we heard many a tale of broken limbs of both man and beast. The eastbound pack trains carried beaver skins to be traded for salt, a valuable commodity west of the mountains.

I recall a few times when Thomas and I fought back the temptation to turn around and return to the easy living and familiarity of Lancaster County, but the anticipation of realizing our dream defeated our fears. Onward we trudge across the wilderness trails in our wagon, bearing the precious printing press which was destined to be the first link of communication between the rest of the new nation and the settlers beyond the Alleghenies.

By the time we crossed Edmond's Swamp, we knew that we had reached the midpoint between Bedford and Fort Ligonier, where we would again pause for several days to revive and mark the halfway spot of our journey to Meadville.

19

Even though we never experienced trouble directly, we sensed it hovering near. At night, I slept in the wagon while Thomas joined the other men lying in a circle on the ground with their feet toward the fire. Taking turns staying awake, the men kept the fire going, alert for Indians or dangerous animals. Always they slept with guns at their sides.

Beyond Fort Ligonier was Laurel Hill, the highest ridge to cross. When we finally reached the summit and saw before us broad valleys and meadows, we knew that the rest of the trip would be easy in comparison.

We forded the Allegheny River at Fort Pitt, then turned directly northward along the road to Presque Isle, a trail once traced by such adventurers as the French explorers, Jesuit priests, and a major from Virginia named George Washington.

Now we breathed easier. We had mastered the western ridges of the Alleghany Mountains which already were fading into rolling, fertile sweeps of land fed by pristine streams. Astounded by the vast unspoiled beauty in all directions, I eagerly strained to capture a glimpse of my future home on the distant horizon.

Six weeks after leaving Lancaster County, our weary caravan rolled into a tiny frontier town, and my apprehension vanished when Thomas took my hand and grinned down at me, "We're home, Sally. This is Meadville."

Thomas and I moved into a two-story log house with a clapboard roof located in the north side of Center street near Water. The printing press was the first piece of furniture unloaded from the wagon. A half-dozen strong men helped Thomas move it into our new home.

On one side of the press, we stacked several cases of type; on the other, we placed a large stone table. The rest of our furnishings were rustic, freshly hewn from logs, but I made the dwelling as homey as I could, never missing the finery I had known in Philadelphia and Lancaster County.

Despite the hardships and the fear of not knowing what strange adventures each day had in store, Thomas and I were filled with such enthusiasm for our magnificent enterprise that, within two months after arriving in Meadville, Thomas hired a helper, Mr. W. Brendle. Now he was ready to strike off the town's first newspaper!

CHAPTER THREE

BIRTH OF THE MESSENGER

On a chilly Wednesday, the second day of the new year 1805, Thomas Atkinson became a newspaper editor and publisher. From necessity he was also the paper's principal writer and reporter.

The Crawford Weekly Messenger was born in a very public setting. A host of Meadville citizens stuffed themselves into the small room so as to be present at what they believed would be an historic event. After all, the Messenger, as everyone called it, was the first newspaper in Pennsylvania west of the Allegheny mountains, and only the fourth in all of America west of Pittsburgh. The others with that distinction were in Ohio, two in Cincinnati and another in Chillicothe.

Brendle smeared the stone with ink, and with two stuffed ink balls which some people thought resembled amputated camel's feet. With many a flourish he beat the inky stone and, rolling the pads together, beat the form, or type, with the black skin cushions.

Then Thomas spread a sheet of dampened paper on its frame and with a crank brought it down with a crash on the blackened type. Rolling it halfway under the suspended press, he grasped the lever with his right hand, and with a backward movement of his body, released the lever.

Next, he rolled in the other half, rolled it all back, with another crash unfolded the frame, and lifted off the printed sheet. Laughing heartily, he tossed to the expectant crowd the first number of the Crawford Weekly Messenger.

The crowd cheered, not only for Thomas Atkinson's newspaper, but also for the miracle of modern transportation which would bring the news across the mountains, and even across the ocean, with incredible speed. A competent carrier could transport papers to Meadville from the city of Philadelphia in only fourteen days!

There were even more breathtaking statistics to consider. Meadville was only eighteen days from New York, twenty-one days from Washington, twenty-two days from Boston, and – wonder of wonders! – only sixty days from London. This was little more time than it had taken us to trudge to Meadville from Lancaster County.

The first issue of the Messenger carried the results of the presidential election. Thomas Jefferson was elected President over Charles Pinckney, and George Clinton became our Vice-President, elected over Rufus King. There was also the notice of a subscription offering for the Waterford and Erie Turnpike Road, a list of letters unclaimed in the Meadville post office, the U.S. Senate appointments, an advertisement by Samuel Mead, saddle-maker, and a report on the situation in Algiers.

In his editorial Thomas told his new readers that the purpose of his paper was to introduce "the READER INTO THE THEATRE OF THE WORLD AND SHOW HIM THE GREAT ACTORS ON THE STAGE OF TIME, while it leads him into the cabinet…the field...the senate...the courts of justice...the circles of the busy and the learned...it promotes in a very important degree the grand interest of Trade, Commerce, Agriculture, Literature, and almost everything that adorns and dignifies mankind.

He did not overlook the essential bit of news. Below the editorial he inserted a statement of his terms: "The Messenger will be published every Wednesday morning and delivered to subscribers at two dollars a year, one dollar to be paid upon receiving the first number, and the remainder in six months."

In this way, Thomas made it clear to his readers that he could not exist on good will alone; both he and I needed sustenance and he was not timid about requesting prompt payment. After all, he had performed a noble deed; he had linked the village of Meadville to the outside world. So certain was he that potential readers would hasten forth with their subscription money, or goods of equal value, that he issued an ultimatum: no money, no paper.

"In order that further means may be adopted to facilitate the distribution of the Messenger, and to give patrons an opportunity of coming forward to throw in their mite, the editor proposes suspending the publication of the second number until Wednesday the 16th inst."

True to his word, Thomas did not issue the next paper until January 16th. Instead, he sat in his office peering out of the frosty windows for sight of a huge queue of prospective readers trudging through the snow bearing subscription money. Alas, not all readers were forthcoming with their shares. In fact, for as long as he published the paper, Thomas issued warnings to stragglers, impressing on them the fact that his family and the newspaper could not exist without every cent due him. In truth, this was a slight exaggeration. The first few months were precarious financially, but it soon became apparent to Thomas and me that we were rich compared with our neighbors. In less than a year, the Messenger was doing well enough for Thomas to take on an apprentice. The November 27, 1805 issue had a 'Wanted' ad: "An active lad between 12 and 14 years of age as an apprentice to the printing business."

He himself had responded to such an ad several years earlier. Now it was his opportunity to prepare another lad for a fine career.

The boy he hired, as was the custom, was given lodging in our home so long as he agreed to work for Thomas, the master printer. With some helping hands in the printing office, it did not take Thomas long to begin following the advice of his hero, Franklin.

I often laughed when he thrust his fingers – sometimes his nose – into everything going on around us. He loved new business ventures, especially if they promised a profit, so he began (and often ended) one after another. Although land was cheap when we moved to Meadville, it continually increased in value. It was fortunate for me and our children that he took advantage of local land development…but I am getting ahead of my story.

CHAPTER FOUR

FRONTIER HAZARDS

A year after we arrived in Meadville, Henrietta was born. She was the first of our nine children: Salome, named for my brave mother-in law, Eliza, Sarah Ann, Augusta, Thomas Jr., Adelaide, Monroe, and William. Darling little Lehman, our tenth child, died at childbirth.

You can well imagine how busy I was caring for our family and home and preparing all our food and clothing. I was more fortunate than most women on the frontier, however, because Thomas was a devoted father. He loved taking our children for a daily stroll and always set aside time in the afternoon to be with them.

While he and the children were out, I had several hours to myself. Then I could pen letters to my family back in Lancaster County, read, wash my hair, or pretty myself. But most of that precious time was spent baking, sewing, washing, and doing all the chores that were difficult to complete with children underfoot.

We lived on food and raw goods which many Messenger readers paid instead of cash for their subscriptions. These bartered goods were every bit as valuable as cash. Unfortunately, many people with good intentions subscribed to the paper even though they could not meet the payment. In his editorials, Thomas frequently reminded readers of their obligation. He even drew a pointing finger in the margin to attract their attention.

When Thomas was not knocking on doors dunning subscribers who were slow to pay either cash or goods, he kept company with the town leaders. He hoped to sway their political decisions and, at the same time, to learn other ways of increasing his income.

One evening, while Thomas was attending a town meeting at the courthouse, Indians struck our print shop. They had always been a worry to me. particularly when they drank hard liquor traded to them by some of the settlers for furs or trinkets. On this occasion, I was reading to the children in the small sitting room adjacent to the shop. Henrietta, Salome, and Eliza were perched at my feet, while the baby, Sally Ann, lay on my lap.

Something, perhaps a faint noise, made me pause in the middle of a sentence. It seemed to come from the shop, but I knew I must be mistaken because Thomas was out of the house and all the children were with me.

Then the sound came again, ever so slightly. Stealthily, I arose and tip-toed to the door. I pushed it open a crack. In the muted half-light shining in from the street lamp, I beheld a terrible sight: drunken Indians had entered the shop. They were inspecting the printing press.

I did not recognize them, but I knew that they must live nearby and be familiar with the "strange beast that talks on paper." Even though Meadville had known little trouble from Indians, I had heard many tales of settlers in other communities being scalped or murdered by Indians who did not remember what they had done by the time the effects of the whiskey wore off the next day.

27

I knew that I had to reach Thomas at once. I also knew that I could travel much faster without a baby in my arms. Cautioning the three older girls to be quiet, I placed Sally Ann on a blanket under a large kettle by the hearth, then motioned to the others to follow me. Before creeping out the front door, we made sure there were no Indians outside to block our way. Then we raced as fast as we could to the courthouse. We burst in upon an orderly meeting of the town's most dignified and prominent men. Seeing me and the girls enter, Thomas was so shocked that he leaped up to silence the speaker. No sooner had I gasped out the frightful message than the room full of men grabbed their guns, which had been resting near the door, and sped down the street to the print shop.

The Indians were very drunk, but not so drunk that they did not know trouble when they heard it roaring down the street. They fled from the shop just in time to escape the furious townsmen.

When Thomas entered his shop, he found it in total disarray.

"Oh Tom! Whatever will you do?" I cried.

"Do? What else but clean it up and begin again," he replied. "We're fortunate they didn't get into the living quarters to harm you and the children."

The moment he said that, I remembered Sally Ann. I dashed into the sitting room, my heart pounding in terror, and lifted the overturned kettle. There lay Sally Ann cooing contentedly. Sweeping her into my arms, I cried, "O thank you, God!"

Somehow the destruction of the print shop seemed unimportant. Our children had been spared, and I had complete confidence that my wonderful husband would succeed in repairing the print shop exactly as he promised.

That was not the last of our troubles with the Indians, but Thomas was better prepared the next time because the town grew rapidly, attracting more men who were to become his allies in defense.

Running the newspaper was only part of Thomas's work day. Like most men of Meadville and other villages along our new nation's frontier, he was a farmer with sheep and cattle to tend, and he faced the hazards of that occupation. On September 25, 1805, he placed a notice in the paper asking for word of his stray red milk cow and offering a reward for her return.

The most frequent hazard he faced, however, was the weather. Because those who supplied him with paper frequently could not get through the snow, ice, rains, and mud, deliveries from early fall until late spring were infrequent. Often Thomas did not know if he would be able to strike a Messenger.

The paper Thomas used had to be drawn by horse and wagon over narrow trails from as far east as Lancaster County. It was not uncommon for a driver to face danger while crossing a swollen stream. In one issue, Thomas told his readers that he had been informed by several persons that Mr. Tucker, one of the carriers of the U.S. mail between Pittsburgh and Erie, had been drowned in attempting to cross Slippery Rock Creek.

At other times, he received no word, only silence. When an expected delivery failed to arrive, Thomas concluded that a similar tragedy had occurred. or that the driver had been captured and done away with by hostile Indians who still roamed the forests and trails of western Pennsylvania.

The Crawford Messenger was issued as often as conditions permitted. There were times when Thomas was so busy attending court to collect delinquent accounts that he put out but half a sheet. He was confident that Meadville residents would read his newspaper no matter its size because of the important role it played in their lives. He also knew that he would not be paid for his efforts if he did not continually demand payment from his debtors. Although he never formally studied for the law, he had read so extensively in that field that he could represent himself in court. Before matters reached that extreme, most readers heeded his notices. One he placed in the Messenger on January 30, 1818 was typical:

"As the 'scarcity of money' is almost universally given as a plea for non-payment...I am willing, indeed I shall be happy, to receive from such any one of the following articles: Wheat, Corn, Oats, Tallow, Bacon, Butter, Bags, Flax, Linen Cloth, Etc. Etc. at market price. Those who have neither money nor produce of any kind to spare had better be off."

There were other pressing demands which pulled Thomas away from his printing office. One of the most dreadful was the call to arms for the War of 1812. A captain in the army by that time, he always placed his country before his personal and business duties. He apologized to his readers when he was compelled to suspend publication from December 29, 1813 until February 16, 1814. The children and I were comforted knowing that he was keeping watch over our small community, a precious few miles from Lake Erie and the fearsome British warships.

CHAPTER FIVE

PATRIOTISM

We, the pioneers who settled western Pennsylvania, were separated from much of our country by the Allegheny Mountains. Nevertheless, we loved our new nation and the men of our town, led by my beloved Thomas, answered their patriotic obligations with the zeal of men who love their country more than selves.

The War of 1812 was their greatest test. It disrupted the lives of every family, ours perhaps more than most. As an officer in the Pennsylvania militia, Thomas gravely accepted the responsibility of training troops, for the British were at times as close by as our neighboring town of Erie.

Each time his duties took him away from Meadville for periods of several weeks, Thomas voluntarily ceased publication of the Messenger. When he had time to compose an issue for press, he gave front page coverage to the efforts of our brave local volunteers. On Tuesday, July 20, 1813, he printed what proved to be the largest headline ever to appear in the paper:

CITIZENS TO ARMS!

For years afterward, readers remembered the emotional editorial of that day, and many told Thomas that the words he wrote had spurred them to enlist.

"Your state is invaded! The enemy has arrived at Erie threatening to destroy our Navy and the town. His course, hitherto marked with rapine and fire wherever he touched our shore, must be arrested. The cries of infants and women, of the aged and infirm the devoted victims of the enemy and his savage allies, call on you for defense and protection. Your services to be useful must be rendered immediately! The delay of an hour may be fatal to your country in securing the enemy in his plunder and favoring his escape."

A few weeks later, the men of Meadville were routed from their harvesting chores, leaving their women and children to complete the job. We rallied bravely, disregarding the burning sun and the rough corn stalks and implements which tore our skin. Much as Thomas disliked leaving me with that responsibility, he was secretly proud to be able to serve his country so nobly.

The death of Captain James Lawrence during the Battle of Lake Erie brought great sorrow to patriots everywhere, but his dying words gave hope to our brave men. In the September 22nd issue of the Messenger, Thomas described Captain Lawrence's funeral services and his inspiring message, "Don't Give Up the Ship,". emblazoned on a flag sewn by Margaret Stuart, the wife of a naval officer on Commodore Oliver Hazard Perry's staff. Thomas believed that the flag was the single most valuable contribution to America's victory.

After the war, Meadville settled down once more to the task of becoming a pleasant place to live, trade, and prosper, her citizens proud that their united war efforts had frightened and discouraged the British troops bent on marauding the lake shore communities. As always, Thomas Atkinson was the local hero, the man everyone looked up to in those trying times. How proud I was of him!

Throughout his life, Thomas was twice as busy as most men because he pursued a career as an army officer while engaged in many other endeavors. He was a true patriot over and above all other considerations, and he so valued the memories the militia aroused in his heart that he cheerfully contributed countless hours to its service. Each time the ranks convened for training or celebration, he spread the good news. On May 12, 1832, he described the annual training ritual.

"We have two days of bustle and animated movement in our village this week. The precision, order, and celerity which marked the various movements and evolutions yielded satisfactory indications of improvement with both officers and men, compared with past years.

"The presence of Brigadier General Dick, in full uniform, seemed to impart life and animation to the exercises. Only one individual was observed in a state of intoxication on the first day; he had the appearance of being an old toper. On the second not even one could be found. Men are becoming ashamed to get drunk."

CHAPTER SIX

THOMAS ATKINSON, BUSINESSMAN

"That young man will be successful in every enterprise he undertakes," my father, Leonard Sommers, often said of Thomas. He was right.

The Crawford Messenger quickly became one of the most popular businesses in the county. Even though Thomas had some difficulties encouraging his subscribers to meet their payments, his newspaper was successful because everyone clamored to read it. The leading topics of conversation in the shops and on the streets of our little town were invariably what folks had read in the latest edition.

Still, Thomas was not satisfied. He wanted to be involved in everything going on in Meadville, and he was!

He was appointed the first secretary of the Meadville Chamber of Commerce on February 9, 1807, just two years after he arrived with little else but a bride, a press, and enough spunk for an entire army. As his fine reputation spread throughout the country, citizens urged him to take more responsibilities. He was the county commissioner from 1810 to 1813, and on May 4, 1814, he was named as a commissioner for the North Western Bank of Pennsylvania, the first bank to serve Erie, Crawford, Mercer, and Warren Counties.

Even though Thomas worked harder than any three men combined, he always found precious moments to devote to me and our children. I often cautioned him to rest more and guard his health, but he would throw back his head and laugh. "Don't you want a successful husband, Sally?" he would chide me.

I had to smile at his enthusiasm because he was becoming far more successful than neither I nor my father had ever dreamed. As for Thomas, he never doubted his own ability. Perhaps his own fierce belief in himself is what made this handsome, vibrant man special to me, and to our community.

Thomas was not the only businessman in Meadville who had difficulty wresting payment from customers. Because of his intelligence and honesty, numerous citizens engaged his services as an intermediary or collecting agent.

As he pursued his various vocations, he was all the while an avid student of law, literature and politics. He believed that education is life's most valuable commodity. That is why he was invited to join a small group of prominent Meadville citizens who met at the courthouse in order to establish a college in our town. The college, duly founded, became known as Allegheny College. It has grown each year, and I firmly believe that it will one day be regarded as one of the finest such institutions in the nation.

Although Thomas never attended law school, he studied as much as any practicing lawyer of his day. When he came home to the noon meal, he often pored over a volume as I set the table and prepared the main dish. His friends and associates respected his knowledge, and soon began to refer to him as "Esquire."

His other love was transportation. After establishing a college in our community, he plunged into the task of developing roads so that travelers could reach our town with ease. He was especially excited about the proposed Susquehanna and Waterford Turnpike Road which would greatly shorten and improve the travel conditions from Harrisburg to Meadville. How well Thomas and I knew that need!

The opportunity arose on August 19, 1815 when Thomas was appointed to a committee of thirteen men to raise money for the turnpike by selling stock. It was three years before construction began, but during that time the laborers managed to clear hundreds of miles of tree stumps for the road and to build bridges across small streams along the way.

In the meantime, Thomas was not content to limit his efforts to one turnpike. He forged ahead to create a better road system for our entire state. On April 25, 1817, the Messenger proudly announced that stock would be sold for the Mercer Meadville Turnpike Company. Naturally, Thomas was one of the four commissioners.

By 1824, less than a decade after Thomas and his associates commenced their campaign for turnpikes, it was possible to travel directly from Erie to Philadelphia. This success thrilled him, and he began thinking about the future of another form of transportation: canals.

From the beginning, the Messenger was Thomas's first business love because it enabled him to publicize his strong beliefs about everything from patriotism to farming methods. When his newspaper was not rolling off the press, other publications were. Several local organizations used his services. He regularly printed a magazine edited by local Unitarians, but he served his own church with equal zeal.

In 1814, Thomas was one of the founders of the Crawford County Sabbath School Union, and later he was among the prominent movers of the Protestant Episcopal Church. "My great-grandfather would roll over in his grave," he often chuckled, referring to the immigrant Quaker who came to America to worship far from the pressure of the Church of England.

I must confess that Thomas's busy schedule kept me on my toes. I had to care for our growing family and plan meals, as well, to fit into his plans. It seemed to me that my husband was everywhere at once, but I was grateful to God that he was so busy and successful.

His business had expanded so well by 1810 that he was able to move the print shop into a new building on land he purchased in the center of town. Although he said that his main reason for doing this was to give me the privacy I needed for raising our family, I knew that he was pleased to have his shop right in the center of Meadville's affair, exactly where he wanted to be.

Thomas had so many business interests, I had trouble keeping track of them all. They ranged from the establishment of a fire company to a cattle registry. One of his most ambitious projects was the paper mill which formed in his mind when he decided that enough was enough!

Each time the bad weather and difficult road conditions prevented the mail from delivering the large rolls of paper that he needed in order to publish the Messenger, he fussed and fumed and declared he would find a way of overcoming that continual problem. At long last, that dream came true in 1820, when he entered into partnership with William Magaw and David Carr for the express purpose of erecting a mill. As manufacturer of his own paper for the Messenger and other printed matter, Thomas could become his own master. He jumped into the challenge of his own paper mill with both feet.

The plant finally got underway in 1821, the same year Thomas broke up his partnership with James Buchanan. Had he known what future was in store for James, he might not have been so quick to send away that partner.

If Thomas had one fault, it was his need to be a perfectionist. This explains why he became dissatisfied with so many partners. W. Brendle, his first partner on the Messenger, was gone by July of the first year of publication. Other partners came and went so rapidly that I recall their names and faces in a blur, but in 1820 an old friendship blossomed into a business relationship that Thomas believed would be the best and the last.

One of my close friends Mrs. Charles M. Yates, was the wife of our town's most distinguished doctor. She and I were very companionable because we both came from Lancaster County, where our parents still resided. When Mrs. Yates invited Thomas and me to a special dinner party for her brother and niece from back home, Thomas was astonished to discover that the brother was none other than James Buchanan, a young man whom he had known in Lancaster when he was still a young apprentice in the print shop and James was a fledgling attorney with offices just around the corner.

Thomas recognized a promising business arrangement when he saw one. James Buchanan was already making a name for himself in the Pennsylvania state legislature. He also had inherited a sizable fortune.

Even though he would be a silent partner, his name and reputation were so respected that Thomas knew his readers would be impressed.

The proposition Thomas put to James Buchanan was appealing. Recognizing that Meadville was an up-and-coming town and that Thomas was an enterprising young man with many talents, Buchanan agreed to the investment. If Thomas had any thoughts about Buchanan serving as a stepping stone for his own aspirations, he never uttered a hint. But knowing my husband, I felt certain that Thomas was already manufacturing a dream in the most secret parlor of his mind—a dream of entering politics.

Perhaps the Atkinson-Buchanan venture was unsuccessful because two such out-spoken and brilliant men are apt to resent each other. For the next six months, Thomas busied himself tirelessly between the newspaper and the task of embarking upon the paper mill. His patience finally gave out when, for the first time in his life, he discovered that the newspaper was getting in the way for his own advancement. James Buchanan was scant help, being at too great a distance for regular communication. Although Thomas discussed the problem with me, I was almost as surprised as were his readers upon seeing the editorial on Tuesday morning, February 6, 1821. The Messenger had been the force which drove Thomas for so long that it was difficult for me to accept the fact that he truly had decided to forsake it.

"TO OUR PATRONS: this day closes, by agreement, the co-partnership between Mr. J Buchanan and myself, and with it the publication of the Messenger…In coming to this determination, I have been influenced by several considerations. Among the most prominent, however, is an anxious desire to remedy the serious difficulty experienced in this region from want of books for our schools and seminaries. These, at present, can only be had from a distance; and the absence of almost every kind of currency that will purchase them is such as to place it literally out of the power of nine-tenths of the community to supply themselves. Expecting our paper works to be in operation early the ensuing season, my labor and attention will then be exclusively devoted to that object...The printing office will be removed to the old stand on the public square in the course of a few days, where printing of every description will continue to be done with neatness and dispatch. THOS. ATKINSON."

My Thomas's aims were noble. He hoped to bring the joy of books to every single child and adult in Crawford County. If he could not establish his very own university, as did his idol, Benjamin Franklin, he at least could supply books for everyone in his community and take part in a group engaged in chartering a school.

At home, I busied myself with teaching handiwork to our lovely daughters, now growing into charming young women. I knew my Thomas inside and out, and I knew that he could not stay away from publishing and editing a newspaper any more than I could have left my wonderful family.

Of course, I did not utter a word of encouragement. I merely bided my days until September 3, 1922 when the Crawford Messenger was reborn, Thomas's editorial that day explained:

"Released in a great measure from a variety of duties and engagements which interfered with the attention due my printing establishment and encouraged by the solicitations of many of my late patrons, I have been led to resume the publication of a weekly journal…with the assurance that no attention or industry shall be wanting on my part to render its columns interesting and instructive."

The same issue of the Messenger told of a new business enterprise at Alleghany College, which was fast becoming Meadville's center of culture.

"President Alden has politely favored the editor with a pleasing specimen of cocoons, formed by about 2,000 silk worms, under his management, this season, in the college edifice. This, we believe, is the first essay which has ever been made to introduce the silk worm into this section of Pennsylvania. The fact is demonstrated that silk may be manufactured in this, as well as in other regions of the republic. The cocoons weight at the rate of 400 to a pound. Ten pounds of cocoons will make a pound of raw, or three quarters of a pound of finished, silk. The cocoons may be seen at this office."

The silk worm cocoons were but one example of strange items which crossed Thomas Atkinson's desk. He was forever on the watch for new fields to conquer and new businesses to benefit Meadville. When he learned that coal had been found in the area he became excited about beginning a large mining operation, and his editorial of April 21, 1832 called for readers to bring him evidence of its presence in Crawford County.

"COAL. Favorable indications of coal have been discovered at various points, so much so as to lead to the belief that it exists in large bodies. Persons who have found coal in detached pieces or otherwise within three or four miles of this village, will confer a favor by communicating this fact, and designating the place where to the editor."

41

For my part, I never said a word in opposition to Thomas, but I feel blest that he never saw fit to open a coal mine.

CHAPTER SEVEN

A FAIR AND AGREEABLE VILLAGE

Within the thirty years that Thomas published the Messenger, Meadville, Pennsylvania grew from a tiny cluster of log cabins to a flourishing town with attractive, comfortable homes suitable for large, happy families like ours.

Thomas never ceased to marvel at our agreeable geographical location. Meadville's weather was warm enough in the spring and summer to permit successful farming throughout the countryside, while it was cool enough to discourage the rampant fevers and damaging insects which plagued southern settlements. Each time Thomas dutifully reported deaths from yellow fever and crop destruction elsewhere in the nation, the Messenger readers gave thanks that our home town was so well situated.

Like most citizens of Meadville, we always kept animals, or livestock, of some sort. We had chickens for eggs, sheep for wool (and cutting our lawn), horses for transportation, cows for milk, and hogs for bacon and ham.

With such a multitude of livestock within the town limits, fences were constantly nudged over, and strays roamed the village. More than likely, they headed for the outlying districts, so in most issues of the Messenger, Thomas ran at least one notice about stray animals. If a subscriber was not pondering the whereabouts of his own prize beast, he was testily begging an owner to retrieve a wanderer. Such was the notice from Nicholas Charleston on December 31, 1806.

"Came to the plantation of the subscriber living on French Creek, Crawford County, sometime in September or October, four sows and one barrow, with a crop and a hole in the left ear. The owner or owners are requested to come, prove property, pay charges, and take them away."

Stray animals were not the only improper items regularly seen in and around Meadville. The town supervisor, S. Lord, placed a public notice in the Messenger on March 28, 1818.

"The citizens of Meadville are requested to remove their wood out of the streets. A reasonable time will be given, and if not attended to, it will be removed with costs to the owners."

The offensive wood was firewood, chopped by the citizens in great quantities for both fireplace and oven. As spring arrived, stray logs began poking from beneath the thawing snow, becoming hazards for horses, carts, and pedestrians.

All types of people continually moved into Meadville seeking fresh opportunities. As in all towns, there were some undesirable residents, but they were more than balanced by welcome professionals – physicians, clergymen, professors, and businessmen like Thomas – who grasped the opportunity to live and work among other literate, ambitious people.

Life in Meadville was dependent upon these fine people and the quality of services they offered. But, while we could choose those with whom we wished to associate, we were not able to choose the weather. We were beholden to its vagaries. The continual progress in building, transportation, and care of the ill and elderly in our fair village came to a standstill with each storm. Thomas regularly commented on the weather in his editorials. The winter of 1818 was especially devastating. Meadville was buried in snow, and it did not melt away with the advent of spring. The rest of the nation was suffering, too. Thomas published weather reports from newspapers printed in other states to show readers that we were not the only ones experiencing hardships which would cause future hunger because of the late planting season.

"PETERSBURG, VIRGINIA, April 21, 1818. Winter returned. On Saturday, we had a fall of snow and hail. On Sunday, it snowed considerable; and yesterday morning a severe frost spread destruction throughout the vegetable kingdom.

NORTHERN DELAWARE, April 24, 1828. In consequence of the late frosts and high winds, our prospects of a favorable wheat crop are entirely destroyed,

SAVANNAH, GEORGIA, April 20, 1818. On Friday night last we experienced a very sudden and severe change of the weather. The thermometer stood at the freezing point…The cotton crop which was up is completely destroyed.

CHARLESTON, SOUTH CAROLINA, April 20, 1818. Unseasonable frost has, we fear, done incalculable mischief."

Unlike the wretched summer of 1818, the summer of 1827 was unusually splendid. Thomas's editorial of August 16th told of the joyous activity which accompanied the beautiful weather. "Our village has been all life and bustle for some days past. The presence of a respectable company of theatricals and another of horsemanship, all, as we are assured, favored by full houses, a host of lawyers, jurors, parties in suit, witnesses attending court, candidates for office without number and tho' "last and least," between 70 and 100 applicants for contracts on the canal, has imparted an unusual degree of life and animation to our village."

Even the typically harsh Meadville winters were not without life's small pleasures, as Thomas observed in his editorial of January 14, 1823.

"GOOD ROADS. We begin to feel many of the benefits arising from good roads. Sledding is now excellent. We have noticed numerous sleds pass within a day or two laden with pork, butter, cheese, flax, linen, etc. for Phillipsburg and Bellfonte to barter for that article."

Weather continued to interest Thomas immensely, for his life as a farmer was built around it. The midsummer of 1830 marked the beginning of a fine harvest, as he mentioned in his editorial of July 22nd.

"THE HARVEST has commenced. Wheat and rye in general good. Corn and oats bid fair. Meadows yield bountifully. Our farmers in general, so far as we can learn, carry on their work without the use of ardent spirits. A squirrel hunt took place a week or two since. The number of scalps taken, we learn, amounted to eight hundred and ninety-one."

CHAPTER EIGHT

SOLEMN RITES OF PASSAGE

Happy though we citizens of Meadville may have been, we were never free from worry. Weather, disease, and death repeatedly taunted us, and my Thomas reported each lamented event in the Messenger. I particularly remember the coming of the dreaded disease, cholera, which Thomas attributed to our nation's newcomers. On June 23, 1832, he wrote:

"THE CHOLERA has at length found its way to the American continent. The fact of its existence, with details of its fatality and rapid progress at Quebec, Montreal, etc. have reached us within the last two days both by the southern and eastern mails. That it will in like manner pass over this continent can no longer be doubted. It is universally conceded that the cholera feeds with peculiar veracity upon the subjects of extreme Poverty, Fifth, and Intemperance. Much of this description of population has doubtless been found among the mass of emigrants from Europe, already cast upon the shores of the St. Lawrence this season, and hence the extreme fatality which has marked the early progress of the disease. The line of emigration being westward from the infected region, we may consequently look for its onward movement in that direction. Let every precautionary measure be put in requisition to meet its approach...Officers have been sent to inspect all the northern canal boats and those away from the juncture of the two canals, nine miles from Albany."

Thomas's fears were realized when New York and Philadelphia reported severe cases of cholera. Meadville was not spared. On July 20th, 1832, Mr. Cornelius Vanhorn, one of the first settlers on French Creek, was stricken, but recovered. Thomas wrote:

"LAST SATURDAY, our worthy old friend, aged about 75 years, who resides two miles south of the village, called at the office for his paper. We took occasion to enquire of him as to the particulars of his case, and we give his own words,

'I was taken with violent vomiting and purging about 3 o'clock in the morning. The cramp seized me in the legs and abdomen. It drew up knots on my legs as big as my fist and cramped me in the belly up to my heart. My sight and my hearing had almost entirely left me.'

"Fortunately for Mr. Vanhorn, it so happened that the Rev. Mr. Barris of the Methodist church lodged at his house that night…Mr. B. lost no time in administering a strong dose of the Oil of Hemlock which he happened to have with him, and applied strong vinegar, well heated, with severe friction, to the body and limbs. In about 10 minutes after the oil was administered, the vomiting ceased, which was soon followed by perspiration, and as the day wore on, the old gentleman was able to get up."

Thomas himself was taken ill that summer, and I spent much time making him comfortable and administering to his needs. Some days he was completely indisposed, and others he made his way out

48

of bed and down to the printing office, but he believed that the quality of his work suffered because of his distress. He, therefore, apologized to his readers on October 27, 1832.

"SICKNESS has prevented the editor for some time past from bestowing the attention which he desired on the columns of his paper."

By Thanksgiving time, Thomas had rallied and returned to his busy ways. How he hated to be slowed down by bad weather! On December 22, 1832, he grumbled, "WINTER has made its appearance in earnest. The snow is from 16 to 18 inches deep and, preceded by much rain, rests upon a very soft foundation. The roads are consequently deep, and the stages rendered uncertain in their movements. We look to old father Frost for a speedy reform."

Quaking before Thomas's furious fist, the elements became agreeable, and on January 5, 1833, he marveled, "JANUARY has made his appearance altogether divested of his icy locks and has for two or three days past assumed the smiling aspect of May. Grass is beginning to vegetate, Our Neighbor, Judge Shippen, who delights in taking 'time by the fore-top' put his plough in motion yesterday in an adjoining field. All looks fair when penning this paragraph but we know not what an hour, much less a day, may bring forth."

On that same day Thomas wrote of a calamity which was precipitated by the warm weather and melting ice. "Mr. Isaac Kelly, an old and respectable citizen...left home on Sunday morning last with the view of attending religious services on the west side of French Creek. Not returning home at the time expected, his family became alarmed, and went in search of him. His track was readily found, and traced to the creek, at a

49

point on the Dead Water, and for some distance on the ice where, from evident appearances, he must have fallen through and perished under the ice."

The mystery of Isaac Kelly's disappearance was solved and reported in the Messenger on Saturday morning, January 19, 1833: "The body of Mr. Isaac Kelly, whose death by drowning in French Creek we noticed week before last, was found a few days since in a body of drift wood, about two miles below where the accident occurred."

By that time, winter had returned, as Thomas reported: "THE EARTH is now covered with a heavy bed of snow, resting upon a well frozen foundation, giving fair promise of excellent roads for the sled of business and the SLEIGH of pleasure."

No sooner had Meadville recovered from the sad occasion of Mr. Isaac Kelly's death by drowning than another tragedy took place. Thomas's editorial on January 26, 1833, was headlined: SHOCKING!

"On the morning of Tuesday last, Mr. Thompson, merchant unfortunately mistook the keg he was accustomed to use in conveying ashes from the stove for one that contained about two pounds of damaged powder. While in the act of discharging the ashes from the keg, his body leaning over it into the street, the powder exploded and killed him instantaneously. His face was literally torn off. Mr. T. was in the prime of life and much esteemed."

As tragedy roamed across the American frontier, it seized its victims with little regard to age or station in life. It was in our pleasant village of Meadville where my Thomas solemnly accepted his calling as the herald of major events in our citizens' lives, from the births and marriages to the final gasps. One of our neighbor boys met an unseemly end, as Thomas reported on September 7, 1814.

"DIED on Monday last, a son of John Brooks, Esq. in the 11th year of his age, occasioned by the bite of a rattlesnake."

Thomas's pet project, the construction of canals throughout our bountiful state, was plagued by both slow advancement and occasional sorrow. The issue of September 1, 1825 contained mute evidence that progress in western Pennsylvania was in partnership with hazards.

"Was drowned on Saturday the 27th inst. In Lake Erie near the mouth of the Elk Creek, Richard Cranch, Esq., a gentleman attached to the Brigade of Topographical Engineers now occupied on locating the rout for a canal between Lake Erie and Pittsburgh...General sympathy is felt in this community with the untimely fate of this estimable young man."

Thomas believed that God gave us earth's bounties to use to our good and the good of all mankind. He admired the Indian's way of hunting only for need, not for pleasure, and he reminded his readers of their obligation to nature every time an unhappy example was brought to his attention. On January 24, 1821, he wrote:

"SHOCKING ACCIDENT. On the 6th inst., two brothers by the name of English went in pursuit of a wolf, but not being successful in their search, returned in the evening to the house of one of the brothers, who was in the act of putting up his gun, when she went off, and, shocking to relate, killed his brother on the spot and wounded his wife and two children! The gun was loaded with five bullets, two of which passed through the head

51

and neck of the deceased. The woman was shot through the body, and the ball lodged in the opposite side, and one of her arms broken in such a manner as to render amputation necessary. It is doubtful whether she will recover. One of the children had its finger shot off the hand, and the other was wounded in the head, supposedly not mortally. The above is a solemn warning to those who are fond of the chase, the sports of the field, or who are in the habit of using or exercising with firearms."

Such freak accidents were commonplace on the frontier. On January 15, 1829, the Messenger related the sad death of a son of Mr. Andrew Radle, of Randolph Township, about ten years of age, who was killed by a falling tree, and on August 15, 1835, Thomas reported that Stephen Curtis of Centreville in our county was killed by the kick of a horse, dying twelve hours after the accident. One calamity after another befell residents of our community, many of whom merely happened to be at the wrong place at the wrong time doing the wrong thing. Such was Mr. John Pratt, who lost his life, as reported in the Messenger of February 18, 1832, by the fall of a tree while chopping it down, leaving a wife and eight children.

My Thomas, I am proud to declare, was a highly moral man, who often remarked that the rewards a person reaps in thus life and the circumstances of his death reflect his character. He set high standards for himself and for others as well, and he believed that God had entrusted him with the ability to write in order to teach proper morals to others by reporting the consequences of sin, according to the Bible.

To Thomas, one of the most despicable sins of all was drunkenness, and he frequently published article supporting his views. When he ran a news item about the fate of a man who was dragged to destruction by drink, he never failed to emphasize that the sad state of affairs was caused by a powerful evil. On July 9, 1824, he ran a "Cure for Drunkenness," which was written as if it had been delivered to him for publication by an anonymous donor. The author, Benevolus, was none other than Thomas himself.

"Mr. Atkinson, Be so good as to insert the following in your Messenger. Possibly some among that unhappy and numerous class of human being, who are sinking fast into the grave from a seemingly endless thirst for the intoxicating draught, may have philosophy enough to make one effort for a deliverance from a vice more destructive of life than war in its most bloody form and more prolific of evil to the world than the curse of Pandora's box.

Baron Bruch Crammer, a celebrated German, has found a method of making the most confirmed tippler have the greatest loathing and repugnance to all sorts of spirits and strong liquor. Take one teaspoonful of the tincture of Columbo, one teaspoonful of the compound tincture of gentian, a wine glassful of the infusion of quassia, and 20 drops of elixir of vitriol. Mix and take twice or thrice a day and have a jug of cold water dashed over the head every morning coming out of bed, and the feet bathed in warm water every night. Continue this for 6 or 8 weeks. Dr. Rath of Sinemunde has succeeded with this remedy in curing many poor creatures, both men and women, who were killing themselves by continual tippling and drunkenness.   BENEVOLUS."

If a local fatality was precipitated by liquor, I always knew that Thomas would cluck his tongue verbally at the unfortunate, misled victim, as in the item appearing on March 30, 1826.

"John Rake was found dead near Flemington. Verdict, by intoxication. He had been to what is called a chopping frolic and had drunk too much, the fate of many of his namesakes.

Drunkenness continued to worry Thomas, who knew many such sad tales through conversations with the men of our town. His contribution to temperance was "The Drunkard's Tree" which he constructed with exquisite care as a lesson to all lovers of nature and life. It appeared in the Messenger on April 8, 1820.

When the townspeople read Thomas's words, many felt obligated to heed his warning. One of his last editorials on February 23, 1823, heralded a meeting of the Temperance Society. So strong was my husband's personality and his influence on members of the community that one year later, on January 23, 1824, he was elected President of the Meadville Temperance Society.

Forgetting the proper use of the Sabbath was to Thomas equally as sinful as drink. He used his newspaper to spread his convictions on this matter.

"MELANCHOLY ACCIDENT. As several persons were engaged in the erection of a building in this village on Sunday past, a piece of timber fell and struck the head of a young man by the name of Henry Towne, and it also broke his arm. His skull was injured so much that he survived until Thursday in extreme agony when death terminated his suffering. A young man by the name of Bruner in Cranberry Township, accidentally shot his father on Sunday morning the 2nd inst. They were watching a deer lick, and the father having wandered from the course agreed upon, the son perceived something moving in the bushes, which he supposed was a buck, and fired; then conceive his astonishment upon coming up to find, instead of a buck, the almost lifeless remains of his father. Awful warning to Sabbath breakers."

THE DRUNKARD'S TREE

The Sin of

DRUNKENNESS

Expels reason,   drowns memory
Distempers the body,   defaces beauty
Diminishes strength, corrupts the blood.
Inflames the liver,   weakens the brain
Turns men into walking hospitals,   causes
Internal, external, and incurable wounds: is a
witch to the senses,   a devil to the soul, a
Thief to the purse, the beggar's associate.
A wife's woe,   and children's sorrow
Makes man become a beast   and a
Self-Murderer,   who drinks to
others' good health, And robs
himself of his own!   Nor
is this all; it serves
for the

DIVINE DISPLEASURE
HERE AND HEREAFTER
ETERNAL DAMNATION.

Such are
some of
the evils
springing
from the
Root of
DRUNKENNESS

Even though Thomas believed Meadville to be the most perfect town in the nation, it was not without crime. As for himself, he took great pride in working fervently at being good and preparing his soul for the hereafter. He could not understand how anyone could falter from the straight and narrow path. On Saturday morning, July 4, 1818, he termed a local event ATROCIOUS!

"On the evening of Saturday last, John Wade, Dominick McBride, and Edward Sweeney left this village in company to return to their homes in Cussewago Township, all three somewhat intoxicated. On the way a dispute took place between McBride and Sweeney. Wade interfered to prevent them from coming to blows. McBride immediately turned upon him and gave him six or eight shocking stabs with a knife, by one of which a large portion of his intestines were let out; and in this truly distressing situation the unfortunate sufferer remained for several hours before medical aid could be got to rescue him. But notwithstanding the severity of his wounds, we are happy to learn that his physician, Dr. Bemus, begins to entertain a faint hope of his recovery. Active means have been taken to apprehend the aggressor, but he has so far eluded every attempt."

A less violent crime, the local mail robbery conceived by one of the mail drivers, was quickly solved. This pleased Thomas greatly because his mail had been damaged and certain communications lost by the thieves. He disliked using the Messenger as a forum for publicizing crime, giving criminals just enough mention to assure himself that his readers were aware of the transgressions and would conduct themselves appropriately to instill good citizenship in their own families. Nevertheless, as the community grew, so grew the number of undesirable residents and unhappy events he was obliged to report.

The Messenger of March 30, 1826 contained an abundance of ugly stories which so outraged Thomas that he had great difficulty writing about them.

"HORRID AND BRUTAL OUTRAGE. We have been informed that on Wednesday evening the 8th inst. A young woman, the daughter of a respectable man in this county, left her father's house about dusk for the purpose of going to her brother-in-law's, who lived about a quarter of a mile from her father. On the way she was seized by 3 or 4 ruffians who it seems were lying in wait, blindfolded her with a handkerchief and stopped her mouth to prevent her shrieks from being heard. After their brutal desires were satiated, they wounded her in the neck and arms with a knife and left her with her hands tied behind her back, her feet tied together across a log. In this wretched situation she was found a short time after the perpetration of this horrid crime. It is stated that she did not see any of them as they seized her suddenly and blindfolded her before she could distinguish their features, but from their voices she believes she knows who they were. Three persons have been arrested on suspicion of being the perpetrators of the hellish deed."

"HORRIBLE CIRCUMSTANCES. A few days ago, a man died in this county of small pox; on the same day the body was put into a coffin and placed in the church yard while the grave was made. Some children who stood near the coffin, thinking they heard a groan, mentioned the circumstance to the grave digger who however took no notice of it and the body was interred. The children having talked of what they heard attention was excited, and the following morning, the body was taken up, when dreadful to relate, the torn state of the shroud left no doubt that the poor wretch had been buried alive."

"MELANCHOLY DISASTER. On Thursday last, Joseph and Wheeler Buffum, sons of Richard

Buffum, Esq., accompanied by a guide by the name of Quigley, of Chatauqua County, left Chippewa Creek, upon the Canada side of the Niagara River, in a large open boat. The wind was strong, directly up the river, but the current was increased by a freshet. On being struck by the stream, they were driven a little down the river, and the man at the helm so lost his presence of mind that he headed the boat directly for Niagara Falls, which are but a short distance below. At the boat entered the Rapids, the three persons jumped out and swam for the shore, but Wheeler Buffum only was fortunate enough to reach it. The other two were seen struggling for some minutes against the surge, but no help could be given from the shore and they were precipitated into the abyss below. The boat lodged upon a small island in the rapid a short distance above the precipice."

As the year 1832 closed, Thomas sadly wrote about another local tragedy which shocked the citizens of Meadville as they perused the December 28th issue of the Messenger.

"DIED. At Franklin Furnace, Garrett Lucas, Jr., in the 16th year of his age, deeply lamented by all his friends and acquaintances. The deceased was bitten on the hand by a rabid fox on October the 30th last; the animal was not known to be mad, and no danger being apprehended the wound was permitted to heal until the 26th ult. when symptoms of Hydrophobia made their appearance, Medical aid was called in, but he remained insensible of the nature of his disease or the peril of his situation. The disease having already made rapid advances his case was pronounced hopeless by his physician. The symptom continued to increase rapidly and steadily until about 12 o'clock on the 30th when his system sank under the 'pressure of misery' nearly two months after he received the wound."

This was the last account of its kind reported by Thomas Atkinson in his Messenger. Three months later, he sold his newspaper to Joseph Kennedy. However, tragedy in Meadville was not to subside for – as in all places where humans tarry – it was ever an unhappy companion. The issue of February 13, 1835 mentioned another melancholy accident which visited one of our neighbors.

"On Saturday evening last, a daughter of Brazilla Goodrich. Aged about 4 years, was so scalded that she died on Monday morning at 2 o'clock. The child was lying asleep by a stove which by some means was upset. On it was a teakettle of boiling water, the contents of which fell directly on the unfortunate child."

For the nearly thirty years that Thomas published and edited the Messenger, he always printed the local death notices edged in black. The saddest of these for our family was the one appearing in the issue of September 4, 1828.

"DEPARTED this life on Monday last, Lehman, infant son of the editor of this paper. Of such is the kingdom of Heaven."

Thomas had named our tiny babe Lehman after his good friend, Dr. William Lehman, of Philadelphia, a member of the Pennsylvania House of Representatives who shared his political views, especially the fond hope of connecting the cities, towns, and villages of our state by canals.

The sad moments of life in Meadville were softened by times of great joy, and as Justice of the Peace, Thomas was continually in the midst of the festivities as he officiated at many local marriages which he duly recorded in the pages of the Messenger. Among them were the unions of the daughters of many of our friends.

"September 13, 1816, MARRIED on Tuesday last, by T. Atkinson, Esq., Mr. Daniel Shryock, of Beaver Township, to Miss Eliza McNamara, of Meadville."

"May 2, 1817. MARRIED yesterday evening, by T. Atkinson, Esq., Mr. Thomas Bloomfield, of Bloomfield Township, Crawford County, to the agreeable Miss Fanny Wyeman, of Meadville."

The high and low points of life in Meadville were frequently separated by very few days. On June 24, 1823, Thomas published one particular wedding announcement:

"MARRIED on Thursday last by the Rev. T. Alden, Mr. Edward Stebbins to Miss Delilah Ellis, both of Meadville."

The August 18, 1823 issue, less than two months later, carried a notice edged in black:

"DIED on Sunday last in Mead Township Mrs. Delilah Stebbins."

Joy of joys, six year later, Edward Stebbins, widower, took a second bride, one dear to all of our hearts!

"December 3, 1829. MARRIED. Yesterday evening by the Rev. Mr. James, Mr. Edward Stebbins to Miss Sally Ann Atkinson, all of this borough."

Thomas and I highly approved the match. Edward Stebbins, a distinguished, gracious gentleman, was also a printer. He had come to Thomas's attention

60

when he was elected to the Board of Managers of Christ Church of Meadville. I never knew if Thomas selected Edward for Sally, or if Edward sought Thomas's attention by becoming active in our church in the fond hope that he would qualify for Sally's hand.

Like Thomas, Edward Stebbins was a man of many virtues. He was the Captain of the Meadville Light artillery, a worthy pastime indeed, in the eyes of Thomas, who had also led the group. Thomas was filled with pride at acquiring a son-in-law cut from such admirable cloth. The happy occasion of the marriage of our Sally and Edward Stebbins helped subdue some of the sorrow we felt a year earlier at the death of our dear little Lehman. Sally Ann was attended by Salome, whose marriage to John McFarland had been announced in the issue of September 1, 1825.

Although most of the God-fearing citizens of Meadville disliked admitting that some local marriages were not happy, there were many families in our vicinity who led unpleasant existences. Thomas regularly published notices placed by husbands or wives whose mates were disagreeable for one reason or another On January 2, 1813, James Smith placed the following:

"CAUTION: The public is cautioned against trusting my wife Ruth on my account as I will no longer pay any debts of her contracting. She is not in her right senses"

Ruth Smith never complained about the notice her husband placed, but Deborah Thurston was a spunkier girl. On October 17, 1817, her husband, David Thurston, placed a caution, warning readers not to trust Deborah because she had left his bed and board without any reasonable cause. Deborah replied on November 14, 1817, her notice appearing directly beneath that of her

61

husband, which Thomas was running for the fourth week in a row.

"DAVID THURSTON, sorry I am that you pay no respect to decency; for you have proven yourself a liar, my dear, by advertising me."

On July 28, 1825, George McKnight placed his caution notice for all in our town to behold.

"WHEREAS my wife Esther has left my bed and board, I hereby forbid all persons from harboring her, as they will be dealt with according to law."

Esther, carved from the same brave mold as Deborah Thurston, replied to George in the August 4th issue:

"WHEREAS George McKnight had cautioned the public against harboring me, inasmuch as I have left his bed and board, it has been my misfortune, through the advice of others, to unite my destiny with a man who is utterly insensible of the respect due a wife. He has neither home, bed, nor board, excepting what I have furnished, He left me, and I am exceedingly thankful for it. He has no property, and is too indolent to acquire any, I must therefore caution the public against trusting him on my account."

Family finances and lack of marital love were the reasons cited in most of the advertises separations, but sometimes frontier wives became weary of their hardships and fled westward with men traveling through our town who offered vague promises of seeking new fortunes in the western wilderness. At those time, the unhappy husband would place a caution such as the one J. Rockwell submitted to Thomas for the issue of February 28, 1817.

"WHEREAS Hetty, my wife, after robbing me of my children and property, with the assistance of a worthless vagabond who called himself George Holland, hath eloped from my bed and board, this is to forewarn all persons from trusting or harboring her on their peril."

Thomas was happy to provide his services for Meadville citizens whose sad, joyous, and sometimes amusing announcements needed to be placed before the public. His chief delight however, was in eulogizing distinguished men after his own heart. For him, the most memorable moment occurred during the brief visit by the celebrated Marquis de Lafayette. As one of our fair town's foremost citizens, Thomas was among those welcoming Lafayette on his passage through the village on June 2, 1815. Thomas reported the event in detail in his June 9th editorial.

"THE VENERABLE LAYAFETTE and suite arrived at Mr. Bigson's hotel on Thursday last between the hours of 1 and 2 o'clock, on his route from Pittsburg to Erie…He appeared evidently fatigued. His arrival was announced by the thunder of cannon. A numberless assemblage had collected at an early hour, but the moment the first gun was fired – old and young, maid and matron, one and all – hastened with rapid strides to get a sight of 'the General.'

The throng of persons collected…were soon given to understand that he meant to pay his personal respects to them. They were accordingly formed in lines, when the 'man of the people' made his appearance, passing each line from right to left, exchanging a kind and familiar shake of the hand with each and every individual…The ceremony being over, he was conducted to Mr. Torbett's Hotel, where he paid his respects to, and was received with the most marked attention by, a numerous assemblage of ladies…Many of our revolutionary worthies attended, who were invariably received by the General with expressions of peculiar kindness, followed by several extra cordial shakes of the hand.

A public dinner had been proffered to the good man by the citizens of the village; but lest it might retard his progress, and thereby interfere with the solemn duty which had been assigned him, of assisting in laying the cornerstone of the monument about to be erected at Boston to the memory of General Warren on the 17 inst. he was under the necessity of declining it…He took his departure between 3 and 4 o'clock amid the cheers and blessings of hundreds whose hearts were warmed with gratitude and who had felt an intense anxiety to behold the distinguished companion in arms of Washington, and the gallant champion of the freedom and independence."

So thrilled was Thomas to gaze upon and greet this great humanitarian that he spoke warmly of those few hours until his dying day.

CHAPTER NINE

EXCITING EVENTS AND CURIOSITIES

Thomas Atkinson was not a provincial editor who limited his news to local events. For as long as he published the Messenger, he remained true to his early vow to introduce his readers to 'the theater of the world and...the great actors on the stage of time.'

If it appeared to him that little of interest or value was happening in Meadville, Crawford Count, or the wider scope of western Pennsylvania during a typical week, he selected prominent news items from his many national and international sources. This was the reason for his deep concern that the mail delivery from the eastern side of the mountains must go through daily without fail.

Many lead articles in the Messenger were datelined several weeks earlier from a Philadelphia, New York, Baltimore, Boston, or London newspaper. Believing that the educated man (and woman) must be aware of world and national happenings, Thomas tried to include snatches of politics, science and literature in every issue.

Above all, Thomas loved the unusual. If a natural disaster, a strange event, or a remarkable discovery was reported elsewhere he gave it a prominent column. Typical of these unique stories which whetted his appetite was one which he recounted on April 7l 1813.

"As a person was digging after saltpeter in the summer of 1811 on the waters of Dutch River, Smith County, state of Tennessee, he discovered a large stone set against the mouth of a cave, and curiosity led him to move the stone. On entering the cave which appeared natural in a limestone rock, something resembling a vault, or ancient sepulcher, he discovered in the cave the bodies of two human persons, a male and a female, each in a curious wrought basket made of splits of cane.

The bodies were in a sitting position. Around each body was wrapped a kind of large shroud of plaid seemingly wrought with the fingers made of lint, or something resembling wild nettles of Indian hemp. Both bodies and shrouds were entire. The bodies were consolidated.

A number of doctors and the curious from several states visited the cave. The body of the male was dissected into hundreds of pieces, every person desirous of having a small piece of both body and shroud. In dissecting the flesh, it cut resembling leather. The man appeared old and grey-headed. The female appeared a child about several years old. She was transported entire with her shroud to Peal's museum in Philadelphia. The baskets still remain in the cave consolidated fast to the rock."

Thomas firmly believed that one of the most valuable discoveries made during the early years of our new nation, and indeed during our lifetime, was the development of small pox vaccination. Although Dr. Edward Jenner introduced his vaccine, derived from cowpox, to England in the last years of the 18th century, it was several years before all respected doctors truly accepted it and most citizens overcame their objections to it. How difficult it now is to realize that one of the most popularly held theories in those days was that people who were inoculated would commence resembling cows.

Thomas learned that Dr. Benjamin Waterhouse of Harvard University experimented on his own children and later on some American Indians. The results of his work were encouraging, and he was later acclaimed for introducing the vaccination to America. However, other American physicians were experimenting with equally gratifying results. One of these men, Dr. Sylvanus Fansher, visited Meadville in October of 1811 to lecture before Thomas and other leading men of our village about the results of his experiments. Thomas reported these in the Messenger on October 23, 1811.

"DR. FANSHER first experimented at Connecticut Farms, New Jersey in 1802, giving the Kine Pock I (cowpox) to five children and then inoculating them with matter warm from the pustules of victims of small pox. In two or three days, a small red spot appeared where the matter was inserted, similar to a mosquito bite, and the inflammation was like the sting of a bee, but soon disappeared.

At Scotch Plains, New Jersey, he vaccinated five more children and then placed them in an infectious room and inoculated them with fresh smallpox matter; but to the inexpressible joy of their fond parents, they were found to be invulnerable to that contagious disease.

Dr. Fansher continued experimenting throughout New Jersey, Connecticut, and New Hampshire. His most conclusive experiment ever performed took place in Randolph, Vermont where seventy-five persons – men, women, and children – who had been vaccinated with

Kine Pock, were all inoculated with fresh smallpox matter at the pest house. At the same pest house, he reported, Mrs. Moulton suckled her child which had the Kine Pock, while she herself had the smallpox, and although it was judged that Mrs. Moulton had a thousand pustules, yet the child continued at the breast and was as healthy through the whole process as if it had been nursed by a well person."

Thomas was so impressed by Dr. Fansher that he insisted we all agree to the Kine pock vaccination. Most of the gentle people of Meadville agreed that this was a wondrous discovery and they followed our family's lead when Dr. Fancher set up a temporary clinic in the town hall. Meadville has indeed been fortunate in being one of the few towns in the nation which has not suffered the loss of great numbers of its citizens from the dreaded smallpox, as have many other communities. Thomas was certain that this good fortune is directly attributed to the large number of people who followed our example.

One of the most exciting events of those early years was the sighting of a great sea serpent off the New England coast. Thomas was thrilled by the accounts reaching him from Boston newspapers, and he published stories of the creature's appearance on and off throughout the summer of 1818. The initial account out of Boston on May 14, 1818 was publication of an affidavit signed by Joseph Woodward, master of the schooner Adamant, at Hingham on May 12th.

"DURING a passage from Penobscot to Hingham on the previous Saturday at two o'clock p.m., a crew member observed something on the surface of the water. Supposing it to be the wreck of some vessel, I made toward it, and on approaching it, to my surprise and that of my crew, discovered it to be a monstrous sea serpent. As we approached him he threw himself into a coil and came across our bow at not more than sixty feet distance with amazing velocity Having a gun charged with a ball and shot, I discharged the contents of it at his head. The ball and shot were distinctly heard to strike him and rebound as though fired against a rock.

He, however, shook his head and tail most terribly. He again threw himself into a coil and came toward us with his mouth wide open. In the meantime, I had charged my gun again and intended to discharge the contents of it into his mouth, but he came so near I was fearful of the consequences and withheld it. He came close under the bows of the schooner, and had she not been kept away, must have come on board of us. He sunk down under the vessel, his head a considerable distance on one side of the vessel and his tail on the other.

He played around us about five hours. My crew and I had probably the best opportunity of seeing him that has occurred. I judge him to be, at the least, twice the length of my schooner, say one hundred thirty feet. His head was about the size of a ship's long boat, say fourteen feet. His body, below the neck, at least six feet in diameter. His head was large in proportion to his body. His tail was formed like a squid's and his body was of a dark color and resembled the joints of a shark's back bone. His gills were about twelve feet from the end of his head, and his whole appearance was most terrific.

His manner of throwing himself into a coil appeared to be done by contracting his body in a number of places in perpendicular directions and placing his tail so as to throw himself forward with great force. He could contract and throw himself in any direction desired with apparently the greatest ease and most astonishing celerity."

Many other affidavits about the sea serpent appeared in the Messenger, including one from Captain Richard Rick of Plymouth, another from Samuel Dexter of Gloucester, and an account from the Paladium, which bore on September 6th the headline: 'THE SEA SERPENT – CAUGHT!' The animal was dissected by a jury of doctors and naturalists.

This was not the end of sea serpents in the news. The strange beasts continued to trouble sailors all up and down the Atlantic coast. Twelve years later, the Messenger was still carrying account of serpents. One was dated August 15, 1830 from the Kennebunk Gazette.

"OUR BELIEF is strengthened that it was a sea serpent which destroyed Mr. Blaney of Lynn, an account of whose melancholy fate we lately published.

The coast in our immediate vicinity has at last received a visit from the far-famed Sea Serpent. He was seen by three men who were fishing a few miles distant from the short on Thursday afternoon last. Two of the men were so alarmed at his nearness to the boat that they went below. The third, however, Mr. Gooch, a man whose statements can be relied on, remained on deck and returned the glances of the serpent for a considerable length of time.

The fish was first seen a short distance from them and shortly after he turned about and came within six feet of the boat, when he raised his head about four feet from the water and looked directly into the boat, and so remained for several minutes. Mr. Gooch noted him attentively, and thinks he was sixty feet in length and about six feet in circumference. His head, he says, was about the size of a ten-gallon keg, having long flaps or ears hanging down, and his eyes about the size of those of an ox, bright and projecting from his head. His skin was dark grey and covered with scales. He had no bunches on his back.

When he disappeared, he made no effort to swim, but sunk down apparently without any exertion. Mr. Gooch says he could have struck the fish very easily with his oar, but he was willing to let the serpent alone, if the serpent would not molest him."

Isolated as Meadville was from the rest of the nation, great events did occur here too, and Thomas always placed them on the front page. On October 1, 1819, he announced the visit of LIVING AFRICAN LION.

"NATURAL CURIOSITY. For two days only. The Lion will be seen at the inn of S. Torbett, on Saturday and Monday, the 2nd and 4th of October…from 9 o'clock in the morning until 6 in the evening.

The form of this LION is strikingly majestic, his figure is very respectable, his looks are determined, his gait is stately, and his voice is tremendous. He is the largest in America, and the only one of his kind. This LION is the surviving one of a pair which were on board the brig William, from the river Senegal bound to Liverpool, and were intended as a present to the Prince Regent of Great Britain. He is perfectly docile and obedient to his keeper, will lick his hand and permit him to handle his paws, to play with him, and often manifests great fondness and affection for him. Those wishing to gratify their curiosity had better avail themselves of the present opportunity.

Admittance, 25 cents – children half price."

Thomas, all our children, and I were at the unveiling of this, the first lion to visit Meadville. Fourteen years later, our town was thrilled by the arrival of an entire Menagerie and Circus on August 7th and 8th 1823.

MENAGERIE. Among the collection of animals will be found the following:

The beautiful young Elephant RUNJECT SING,

Two African LIONESSES in one cage,

The GNU, a fierce and untamable animal from the Desert of Zahara, the only one ever imported to this country,

The ETHIOPEAN ZEBRA,

Two KANGAROOS, Male and Female from New Holland,

BRAZILIAN TIGRESS,

HUANICUS, Or Peruvian Camel.

HUNTING LEOPARD, from Senegal,

Two NORTH AMERICAN PANTHERS,

The EUROPEAN BADGER,

Together with a variety of other animals worthy the attention of the lovers of Natural History.

CAPTAIN DICK AND DANDY JACK with the two Shetland ponies will go through a variety of pleasing performances and conclude with the pony races.

THE CIRCUS

The performance of this celebrated company will consist in part of Horsemanship, most astonishing feats of Tumbling, Vaulting, Grecian juggling, etc.

Mr. Sergeant, the unrivalled equestrian, will appear in the circle and go through his much-admired act of the Flying Indian, portraying the Indian customs with Paddle, Spear, and Tomahawk.

Mr. Burt will go through the acts of Horsemanship, Leap his Whip, and conclude by throwing a lofty somerset from his horse while at full speed.

Mr. Jennings, the celebrated Juggler, will go through his performance with the GOLDEN BALL, CUPS, DAGGERS, etc. in which he will throw them in 90 different changes, such as rainbows, waterfalls, triangles, etc.

CARPET LEAPS. By the whole company. A band of good music accompanies the exhibition; good and comfortable seats will be prepared.

Meadville's thirst for unusual theatrics was sated again on the evening of September 1, 1825, when our entire family, together with the rest of the town, flocked to the Thespian Hall to enjoy Mr. Taylor, the Dramatic VENTRILOQUIST. Front seats were reserved for the ladies. Thomas believed that the entertainment we welcomed to Meadville was every bit as elegant as that which the citizens of Philadelphia, New York, or Boston attended. I know that no audience was filled with greater delight than ours.

CHAPTER TEN

CLASSIFIEDS: RUNAWAYS

The roads of Pennsylvania became the main links between our new nation of the United States and the vast territories opening to the west. My Thomas's Messenger, the first newspaper beyond the Allegheny Mountains, was soon followed by other newspapers. Together, the editors formed a chain of information on matters great and small.

One of the responsibilities they accepted was advertising runaways. When a runaway notice appeared in one paper the editors of others very kindly ran the information so that their readers would be on the lookout for annoying, dastardly, even murderous runaways. Each notice ran for at least three weeks, some much longer.

The Pennsylvania printers' link was very important because, once a runaway reached Ohio, the towns were so far apart, the roadways so primitive, and the communication so intermittent and inadequate that it was difficult to find the culprit. As Meadville was near the Ohio border, the Messenger readers offered the last hope for capturing many of the runaways.

The editor of the Susquehanna Sentinel, an old friend, asked Thomas to run the following notice for the return of three apprentice printers. It appeared in the Messenger on May 16, 1818.

74

"PRINTERS! LOOK OUT FOR ROGUES. Elihu Chamberlain, Ebenezer Ferry, and Joseph Matterson have absconded from this place indebted to me.

"I warn all persons, printers especially, not to trust said runaways as they are persons in whom no dependence can be placed, who have forfeited all claims upon society, and will cheat all persons who deal with them. It is supposed they have gone to Ohio."

Robert Fee, the editor of the western Register in Brownsville, Pennsylvania, had a remarkable sense of humor. Thomas ran Mr. Fee's reward notice on October 21, 1822.

"TWENTY DOLLARS REWARD. Absconded on Friday night, the 11th inst. An indentured apprentice to the Printing business, named WILLIAM ALLINDER. He is between 19 and 20 years of age, 5 feet 7 or 8 inches high, fair complexioned and thin visaged; is remarkable sulky in his disposition and generally speaks in a muttering kind of tone. He had on when he went away a roram hat (made of wool with a fur face) nearly new, a blue broadcloth coat and vest, and green linen pantaloons. The above reward with all reasonable charges will be paid for apprehending and securing him in any jail, so that I may get him again. All persons are cautioned against harboring him.

"The above described runaway was seen near Wheeling since his departure, traveling west with a scape-gallows fellow named John H. Caulfield, whom I some time since turned out of my employ for misconduct. Caulfield is about 21 years of age, 5 feet 6 or 7 inches high, of a heavy clumsy make, was born in Ireland, county of Donegall, and by some means found

75

his way to this country in 1813 and attempted to learn the printing business, at which he is very deficient.

"He is near-sighted, and his eyes goggle wonderfully when he is fixing them on an object, especially if he is surprised. This defect was occasioned (he says) by an explosion of gunpowder in his face, with which he had been playing in Ireland when a lad, and which gives him the appearance of being pock-marked. He formerly professed to be a Roman Catholic but has since renounced his religion and is now Nothing That's Good. He seldom tells the truth, even when there is nothing to be gained by lying."

Thomas did not understand why Mr. Fee offered so much reward to Allinder, who seemed worth little, until I suggested that it may have been his own clothes he wanted to retrieve, not the rascal who stole them. A. White and Daniel Quigly were not so generous. They offered only ten dollars reward for the return of their tailor apprentice to the Pittsburgh tailor shop. Thomas ran their notice on February 21, 1827.

"STRAYED AWAY as fast as his legs would conveniently carry him, a full-grown Dandy Tailor, in bodily appearance, at least, by the name of Alexander Baird. He is about five feet, 5 or 6 inches high, with rather a downcast sour-looking countenance until become acquainted with – pretty high cheek bones, moderately large nose, somewhat sucker-mouthed, black hair and black eyes; had on a few hours before he decamped a dark grey, standing collar, Frock Coat with silver hooks and eyes, a Hat of Kramer's make, and a pair of boots, one of which was pretty much run down in the Heel; as he could not obtain a better pair by fraud, he was forced to proceed with his crooked Boots, although it was not for want of trying that he missed them; he took good care, however, to furnish a couple of his brother chips in trade and rascality (who were destitute of means themselves, and had not so good an opportunity of picking honest people's pockets as he had) with shoes handkerchiefs, hats, etc. in order to deceive by appearance, honest unsuspecting people in their travels, and escape from law and justice. The name of these two 'respectable brethren' are John J. Wells and Patrick Murray, who no doubt Baird will continue as his traveling companions, provided Murray's foot does not give out in his race, as he let a 'goose' fall on it a few weeks before he absconded. Being also pretty much addicted to dissipation, he may probably be found sleeping in a fence corner or in some tavern without his bail being paid. He is a slim, straight, pock-marked, black haired man (pardon the expression 'man,' when you become acquainted with him), generally wears a half-worn suit, consisting of a tight body coat (blue) and blue pantaloons and vest. Wells is tolerably round-faced, has dark brown hair, and has a slight scar on the right cheek, his speech rather slow, and he wishes to pass for a gentleman so long as his conduct will support it.

"Whoever returns the above-named Baird shall have Ten Dollars; or either of the other two, Five Dollars; or if they will send us word where they reside, we will send them a 'goose' (a kind of tailor's iron with a long handle resembling a goose's neck), as it was the only article they could not conveniently carry. Boss Tailors are cautioned against employing the above-named persons; if you do employ them, look out that they do not 'Cabbage' the whole job. As Baird took with him from here clothes belonging to other persons, no doubt he will try it again. Widows, who keep Boarding houses, are cautioned against them as they all three have left a poor widow in this place with her fatherless children to seek their just demands from people possessed of more honor and honesty than they."

Some of the devilish runaways Thomas advertised began their flights from our very own town, One, apprenticed to a carpenter in our village, fooled many who often saw him tripping around the ballroom floor with some of our town's most respectable young ladies. Thomas published this notice for his apprehension on April 14, 1825.

"BEWARE OF A VILLAIN! A supposed Double Flutter' to the North. Shasshhe'd from the borough of Meadville on Saturday evening the 9th inst. after having taken his 'five positions,' the accomplished ANDREW CASLER, high journeyman carpenter, and docile pupil of the Graces. This Adonis has 'contratem'd backwards' as is presumed, to have a more spacious 'Ballantzez' from his creditors, who have generously decorated him with 'spring heeled pumps, black hose, and white kid gloves,' in which he has for some two months past

'Kicked up such fantastic tricks

Beneath tin chandeliers,

That make even ladies weep.'

"To say that this young man has 'shuffled himself off' to avoid the odium of his 'sins committed,' were to say much; but let works bear witness.'

"ANDREW CASLER is by trade a carpenter, originally from the state of New York, resided in Warren, Pennsylvania some time previous to his coming to this place. He is about 5 feet, 6 or 7 inches high – tight, square built – wears a singular smiling countenance (especially in the presence of the fair),

78

aquiline nose, black fierce eyes, and dark curled hair. Possessing this exterior together with a double portion of assurance, he obtained credit to a considerable amount in several of our shops. But what is damnable in itself, he practiced upon the ingenuousness of many of the fine young gentlemen or our town, who loaned him small sums of cash, being assured that it should be returned in a day or two – and this the day and evening of his exit.

"Whoever will apprehend of give information of this 'vile standing tuck' to the Chief Burgess or High Constable of Meadville, shall receive the freedom of this borough in a leaden box."

The War of 1812 encouraged a special kind of runaway, the soldier who joined up only long enough to secure the bounty given to each volunteer. Thomas carried many notices of men who deserted from the nearby 4th rifle regiment in Franklin. One notice on October 5, 1814 was typical.

"ROBERT A. PHILLIPS is 39 years of age, dark complexion, blue eyes, dark hair, and by profession a Millwright. He enlisted on the 20th of August, and on the 22nd obtained a furlough for a few days to visit his family about twelve miles away.

"His furlough being out, and he not returning enquiries were made after him, and it appears he has decamped. He was seen going through Harmony a few days ago. It is supposed that he and his family will go down the Ohio River, as it is said to have been his intention to do so for a length of time, but for want of cash (being a poor man), he could not go until he took the bounty with the double intention of assisting himself and family to get away, and cheating the government."

In the same issue, Thomas published a notice offering 100 dollars reward for Silas Parker and Alpheas Holcomb, deserters from New Jersey, who married two of our Meadville girls taken by their gentlemanly ways, then stole their clothing and escaped dressed as women.

Rogues of other persuasions found their way through western Pennsylvania, duping good citizens in their wake. Among them were swindlers, horse thieves, and escaped prisoners. But there were some runaways for whom our hearts ached. These were the slaves.

Slaves who had escaped from cruel masters in the South often passed through Pennsylvania and Ohio on their way to freedom in Canada. Like his Quaker forefathers, Thomas was strongly opposed to slavery and abhorred the ability of one man to have total power over the destiny of another.

His ideals were the same as those of most pioneers on the western slopes of the Alleghenies. Even though the Virginia border was close at that hand, with that state's Ohio County just a few miles from Pittsburgh, most Pennsylvania citizen were too fond of liberty themselves to let freedom-seeking slaves be returned to masters in nearby Wheeling or Weirton. The only danger to slaves passing through Pennsylvania was from those for whom the temptation of the reward money was too great to resist.

On December 8, 1813, W. P. Anderson, a slave holder residing in the Virginia panhandle, offered a reward of 100 dollars in the Messenger for the return of a man named Harry.

"RAN AWAY from this place on the night of the 20th inst., a negro man slave named Harry. He is near 30 years of age, about 5 feet 8 or 9 inches high, rather slipped shouldered, speaks remarkably slow and with a smile on his fact; he is inclined to be polite, but is awkwardly so.

"He had on when he went off a pair of buckskin leather pantaloons, a common hunting shirt and a large drab colored great coat. He also took with him a Missouri Buffalo robe, neatly dressed and painted on the fleshy side, as well as sundry articles of clothing and blankets, and from 50 to 100 dollars in cash. He frequently wears a large butcher knife, fastened and exposed on his side. He is an excellent hostler and a tolerable good blacksmith and will doubtless make attempts to be employed in one of those professions.

"Since I am confident this negro man has been enticed by some hope of reward, such as his freedom, etc. to desert from me, I will give the above reward o any person who will apprehend and send him in irons to Major Butler in Pittsburgh, or one half that sum if confined in any jail where I can obtain him."

Upon reading that notice in the Messenger, I became furious and I marched down the street to the print shop to confront my husband. "Why," I demanded, "are you participating in this poor man's demise?"

Thomas grinned and winked at me, not saying a word in the event the wrong person overheard our exchange. I, too, dissolved into a relieved smile, realizing from his expression that Thomas already knew that Harry was happily in the company of some kindly westward travelers who needed a good blacksmith and hostler to attend to their needs during a journey through the wilderness. How could I have doubted Thomas's good intentions! We never heard where Harry went, but I am certain that he made for himself a useful life in the land beyond the Ohio.

One of the most vicious of all criminals to escape from a Pennsylvania prison was James Jameson. Three hundred dollars, a handsome sum, were offered for his apprehension It was believed that he was headed in the direction of Meadville and Erie with the intent of escaping into Canada.

"BROKE THE JAIL of Dauphin County between the hours of 6 and 7, on the evening of December 20, 1806, a certain JAMES JAMESON under sentence of death for the murder of Jacob Eshilman. Said Jameson is about 30 years of age, about 5 feet 5 or 6 inches high, sandy complexion, long sandy hair which he generally wears up with a comb.

"Had on when he broke jail, a brownish colored Coat, dark colored Jacket and Pantaloons, light- blue woolen Stockings, calf-skin Shoes, tied with silk strings, and a fur Hat; but, as he has heretofore changed his dress to women's clothes, it is probable he may appear in that apparel.

"At the time he made his escape, he had an iron collar round his neck, which he can easily conceal with his handkerchief. By trade a tailor, speaks both the English and German languages correctly. It is said that on one of his feet part of three toes are missing, and on the other foot, two – which he lost by getting his feet frozen. He is noted as a villain in every state of the union."

For many weeks, we feared that each day might bring the dreaded James Jameson to our village, but the cruel winter storms that ravaged the mountains protected us from that harm. In mid-winter, one of the mail carriers brought word that a skeleton of a traveler frozen to death on the pathway was singularly distinct for its iron collar.

CHAPTER ELEVEN

ADVERTISEMENTS

My husband, Thomas Atkinson, offered residents of Meadville and surrounding Crawford County a vital community service through the advertisements he solicited from local merchants. The advertising fees he received provided his main source of revenue for publishing the Messenger, assuring us a steady income. It was true that many subscribers were not dependable about paying on time because of their fluctuating financial situations, but the advertisers paid for Thomas's services promptly, knowing that their businesses were dependent upon his readers.

As young merchants moved into Crawford County, they rapidly discovered that the Messenger was the most expedient and dependable means of spreading their reputations throughout the community. William Magaw, our town's first dry goods merchant, never failed to advise the public of his constantly changing merchandise. Such was the advertisement appearing on January 23, 1818 which invited customers to avail themselves of his varied and unusual wares.

"FRESH GOODS. William Magaw has just received from Philadelphia a large and general assortment of Fall, Winter, and Fancy Goods, among which are the following: Superfine blue, black, brown, and mix'd cloths. Blue, mix'd and drab coarse cloths, blankets, coatings, flannels, etc. Black, purple, green, and brown Calicoes, Ginghams, Blue Vestings, Shawls, Handkerchiefs, etc. Silk, cotton and worsted hose. Domestic cottons, coarse muslins, cords and velvets. Black Florence double satin and silks. Fancy coloured silks for bonnets and dresses. Italian and Canton black fancy crapes, etc. W. J. (Wheat, rye, oats, all kinds of furs, deer, and bearskins taken in payment.)"

Like all the Meadville merchants, Mr. Magaw knew that our folks had little cash, but enough supplies to barter for his goods. By accepting raw goods in place of cash, he earned more than enough food to fill his pantry. We ladies thought his store to be the finest in town. How we loved to examine the beautiful bolts of silks and satins which he always carried in abundance at those times of the year when we devoted ourselves to sewing rather than tending the gardens.

His first competitor was James Herriott who arrived in town with a new idea. Realizing that Magaw already had a steady clientele, Mr. Herriott inserted advertisements which would appeal to those who could rarely afford Mr. Magaw's fine goods. He caught their attention with this unusual heading in the Messenger:

"CHEAP CASH STORE! Dry goods, Ironmongery, Jewelry, Groceries. All which will be sold at very reduced prices for CASH of approved notes at a short credit."

William Magaw did not fret about competition from Herriott because he did not limit his wares to dry goods. He also was the purveyor of most medicines sold in Meadville. One of his most popular brands was Lee's, which manufactured medicines to appeal to sufferers of every persuasion. Each advertisement included mention of many varieties of products. At least one was sure to interest a reader.

"LEE'S ANTI-BILIOUS PILLS

The operation of these highly esteemed pill is perfectly mild, and the experience of thousands has proved that they may be used in every situation in live without the least inconvenience. They are admirably adapted to carry off superfluous bile, etc.

"LEE'S SOVEREIGN OINTMENT FOR THE ITCH

Warranted to cure by one application free from Mercury or any pernicious ingredient. The vegetable remedy is so mild, yet efficacious, that it may be used with the utmost safety, on the most delicate pregnant lady, or on a child of a week old.

"LEE'S GENUINE PERSIAN LOTION

The Persian Lotion operates mildly rendering the skin delicately soft and smooth – improving the complexion.

"LEE'S RESTORATIVE TOOTH POWDER

This excellent preparation comforts and strengthens the gums and preserved the enamel from decay.

"LEE'S GENUINE ESSENCE AND EXTRACT OF MUSTARD

A safe and effectual remedy for Gout and Chronic Rheumatism, Rheumatic Gout, Palsy, Sprains, Bruises, pains in the face, neck, etc. The experience of many ages and the testimony of the best medical practitioners from the early period to the present time agree in ascribing to Mustard's very powerful and singular virtues."

One of William Magaw's most popular drug items was Lee's Worm Lozenges. His advertisement inserted in the Messenger on November 14, 1817 carried his own testimonial.

"The proprietor has now the pleasure of stating that the following case came under his immediate observation., His little daughter, about five years old, appeared very visibly to lose her flesh. No particular cause could be given for her thus pining away. She was at length taken with fevers which, with other symptoms, led him to believe she had worms.

He gave her a dose of Lee's Lozenges, which brought away, incredible as it may appear, two worms, the one 15 and the other 13 inches in length, each three-fourth of an inch round; he has given the Lozenges to another of his children, which brought away a vast quantity of very small worms.

The proprietor is now in possession of the large worms. Those inclined to see them will be gratified by calling at his Dispensary."

Thomas went at once to view the remarkable worms and reported back to me that they were indeed amazing. We were thankful that none of our children suffered from a case of worms as the symptoms in a small child are distressing to behold.

What William Magaw and other shopkeepers in Meadville did not stock for immediate use could be obtained by mail if one were inclined to pay in advance for articles offered. Thomas regularly ran advertisements for distant pharmacists. They were published once a month for a year, at which time Thomas would submit his bill for payment. One of the most popular products was Swain's Panacea, sold by J. Shinn, a Philadelphia chemist. His advertisement of March 2, 1824 was similar to those he sent Thomas from year to year.

"This medicine is celebrated for the cure of the following diseases: 'Scrofula, or King's evil; ulcerated or putrid soar (sic) throat, long standing rheumatic affections, cutaneous diseases, swelling, and diseases of the bones, and all cases of an ulcerous character, and chronic diseases, generally arising in debilitated constitutions, but more especially from syphilis, or affections arising therefrom: ulcers in the larynx, nodes, etc. And that dreadful disease occasioned by a long and excessive use of mercury. It is also useful in diseases of the liver."

The advertisement included testimonials from two University of Pennsylvania physicians, N. Chapman, Professor of the Institutes and Practice of Physic, and W. Gibson, Professor of Surgery,

Several people from Meadville traveled to Virginia to avail themselves of a cancer cure discovered by William Lily of Prince Edward County, which he advertised in the Messenger on February 3, 1812.

"I wish to inform the public that through the good providence of God, I have it in my power to cure Cancers of all kinds, on any part of the human body, whether it be broke or not; by applying the medicine once only. The Cancer will be dead in less than eight hours, at which time the pain will subside. I can discharge the patient in one quarter of an hour, and they may go where they please, and by my directions nurse the sore until well.

"There are witnesses enough to certify the salutary and happy effects it has had on those who have been cured in this part of the world. If I do not cure the Cancer, I will oblige myself to return every cent of money they pay me when I undertake to cure them and will have nothing. I live six miles above Prince Edward court house on the north side of Spring Creek."

Deafness was another common ailment suffered by our townsfolk both old and young. When Thomas heard of a physician in New York who had come across a very simple method for its cure, he ran the directions in the January 30, 1816 issue of the Messenger in the hope that it would serve his readers suffering from lack of hearing.

"The method is to fill the mouth with smoke of the strongest tobacco and instantly to close the mouth and nose by holding the nostrils very tight and force the smoke through the back passage into the ear. The efforts are to be repeated until one or both ears make a crack, when the hearing returns."

Some of our good citizens reported to Thomas that this method was truly beneficial. A few others availed themselves of a remedy prepared by Dr. D. Green of Reading, Pennsylvania which that gentleman advertised in the Messenger of February 24, 1817.

"Knowing that Providence had permitted a remedy to grow for every disease, Dr. Green flatters himself of being successful, more so than any other man yet. The remedy generally gives help except to very old people who begin to lose their eyesight about the time that the hearing becomes weakened. To all others, as yet, has seldom failed of restoring the great blessing of hearing.

"The medicine, with directions, can be sent to the patient by post to any place, however distant. At the same time, it may be somewhat satisfactory to those distressed to know that they may pursue their usual business, and to eat and drink what tastes best.

"The preparing transmission, postage, etc. of the remedy will come to about five dollars. This enclosed in a letter will cover all expenses to the patient."

Thomas received no payment from Dr. Green for inserting his advertisement, but he did receive a free sample of the elixir, which he tried. There was no effect, as his hearing was quite good, so he passed it along to several friends who in turn recommended it to others afflicted with failing hearing.

The spring of 1817 was notable for a great number of mad dogs reported running through parts of Virginia, Thomas thought this was significant enough to run two columns on the symptoms and treatment of hydrophobia in the issue of May 30th.

"Never meddle with strange dogs or cats because the feline may inflict a wound and insert the poison by its claws, owing to the habit of these animals licking their paws. There are two species of madness in dogs: the raging and the moping madness.

"Under the first, dogs become lank and thin, their eyes are of a red fiery hue, the tongue is discolored; they froth or foam, and slaver; unexpectedly they start, run against anything in their way, and will bite indiscriminately. They know no home or master, and thus are frequently wandering about. They howl and bark hoarsely, bite the ground, gnaw their flesh, and die in convulsions.

"In moping madness, dogs are seen moping under chairs and tables, as if sleepy and stupid. They have dull eyes and countenances, hanging head and tail, ears flabby, curved back, they shake and tremble, rarely bark, and die trembling and tossing.

"Destroy, as soon as possible, the bitten part by caustic or fire, keep the wound suppurating or discharging for a few weeks, and the patient is safe."

Dr. John Crow, of the state of New York, had earlier submitted to Thomas a recipe for curing the bite of a Mad Dog. It ran in the Messenger on March 6, 1806.

"Take the under jaw of a Dog, burnt and powdered one half teacup full. Sulphur of Venice (Rust of Copper), one half teaspoon full; one third of a Colt's tongue; a small quantity of blind root and snake root; reduce them to compound and give the patient one half of a teaspoonful in water. In half an hour give the filing of half a copper. Repeat the application on the following day."

Thomas was somewhat hesitant to publish that remedy, wondering aloud where the sufferer, or his family, was to obtain the strange ingredients. "If the patient dies: he remarked, "there may be some controversy over the cause of death: the bite or the remedy."

The horse-radish was his favorite among useful crops. He used it abundantly himself and recommended it to his readers in the March 18, 1830 issue as a good remedy for hoarseness, coughs, colds, and cases of incipient consumption when cut into small pieces. He also believed it to be a valuable substitute for tobacco.

As Meadville grew, so did the number of merchants in our town, By 1830, we had a fine new pharmacist in the community, James Hamilton, who had been trained for his profession in Philadelphia. He offered a fresh supply of goods for sale at a cheaper rate than we were accustomed to paying, and he kept on hand such items as Acid Muriatic, Aqua Ammonia, Balsam Copaiba, Bark Lima, Gum Suiscum, Oil Succini, Red Precipitate, Squills, and Ippocacuanna.

Thomas and I became very fond of the Hamiltons, so we were particularly distressed when both of their precious children were suddenly taken. Despite all the fine medical help in our town, nothing could be done to quell the ravages of scarlet fever. It was a sad Christmas time for us all when Thomas was obliged to report in the Messenger of December 20, 1833 the unhappy news of their deaths.

"DIED on Wednesday the 11th inst. Of scarlet fever, Mary, aged three years and 11 months, and John W. aged 2 years and four months, interesting children of Mr. James Hamilton."

CHAPTER TWELVE

HOUSEHOLD HINTS FOR THE LADIES

On his daily rounds through the village of Meadville, Thomas sought out his readers to learn their interests. By including their favorite kinds of columns in the Messenger, he knew that he could increase his newspaper's circulation.

The ladies of Meadville loved recipes, poetry, and love stories, while the gentlemen welcomed practical suggestions for easing their farming chores, political commentary, and humor.

Thomas was always on the lookout for helpful hints for his lady readers and for the girls and me, as well. Being a frugal man, he aimed to teach his readers to make do with common objects. Since the potato was a popular crop in Crawford County, it seemed logical to him to devote two columns of the November 27. 1805 issue to the various ways a settler might use the potato.

He reported that it can be roasted, boiled, or mashed for eating. Potato pie, bread, and pudding are also tasty. Other ways of using it are in potato yeast, potato starch, potato hair powder, as a coffee substitute, and to fatten cows and horses. Years later, some of my good lady friends remarked to me that it was the most useful column they had ever read, and they clipped the information and kept it in a special drawer along with a column for painting with milk which appeared in the issue of Thursday, February 25, 1808. As a farmer, Thomas became enthusiastic when he first heard of a new method for milking and felt obliged to alert his friends by posting it in the issue of July 23, 1824.

"IMPORTANT DISCOVERY. I have had the satisfaction of witnessing in the presence of a number of gentlemen a cow evacuating the whole of her milk by the following simple contrivance. A rye straw was introduced into the orifice of each teat, through which the milk flowed spontaneously in a full and uninterrupted stream until the udder was completely emptied. In exactly five minutes between five and six quarts were thus drawn off.

"...The straws are introduced about half an inch, which is done with great facility, the cow discovered not the least impatience, but in withdrawing the straw a little force is required...Small quills made entirely smooth at the end would be preferable, but milking tubes may be made of silver or tin, and it is not improbable that these articles will soon be numbered among our indispensable utensils. This method has the following advantages:

Ist. The whole business may be performed in one third of the time and with greater ease for the milker and the animal.

2nd. We may be relieved from the unpleasant apprehension of dirty hands employed in milking.

3rd. The animal may be milked without pain.

4th. Fractious, kicking cows may in this way be milked with less trouble and danger."

This new, easy method of milking sounded marvelous to Thomas. He even instructed me in the method so I could use it with our own cow and, in turn, teach our children. On July 30, 1824, just one week after

Thomas's article appeared (and just before I was about to try it at milking time), an irate reader replied,

"DEAR EDITOR,

The 'important discovery of a new and expeditious method of milking cows" may lead to very pernicious consequences if put into practice, and I hope the good housewives and lively maids of Crawford County will not consider the CASE OF MILKING THEIR COWS FOR ONE TIME can be put in competition with the loss of their milk altogether. After reading your article, the children of a lady, unknown to her, made the experiment with straws as recommended. The milk, to be sure, was drawn off very freely in a short time. From the time the cow has been milked with the straws, she has not given one drop of milk neither could any be extracted from her in either the old or new way. The udder had been considerably swelled. The lady also informed me that the children of one of her neighbors made the same experiment on their cow at the same time, and the effect was precisely similar…In my opinion…it ought to be called that of a 'new and expeditious method of rendering our cows useless.'"

Thomas was mortified that readers found this piece of advice so inaccurate. After that, he was very careful about publishing advice which he himself had not tested over a period of time. On November 10, 1825, unbeknownst to me, he printed some of my favorite recipes, all ones that he particularly enjoyed. I had paid no attention when he asked me this and that about the cakes I had prepared, merely supposing that he wanted to know what was in the slice he was eating. That is why the directions for combining the ingredients was missing in the published recipes. No doubt he surmised that all ladies would know what to do with them.

Before I could bite my tongue, I cried, "Oh, Thomas! You've forgotten the…" and then I ceased talking, not wishing to disappoint him. He was so pleased at having shared my delicious cakes with his readers.

"Is something wrong?" he asked, looking very worried.

"No," I assured him, smiling to allay his fears. "I see that everything is here after all."

This is the way my favorite recipes appeared in the Messenger:

"Composition cake. One pound of flour, one of sugar, half a pound of butter, seven eggs, half a pint of cream and a gill of brandy.

Tea cake. Three cups of sugar, three eggs, one cup of butter, one cup of milk, a small lump of pearlash, and make it not quite as stiff as the pound cake.

Soft gingerbread. Six teacups of flour, three of molasses, one of butter, one tablespoonful of ginger, and one of pearlash.

Diely bread. One pound of flour, one of sugar nine eggs, leaving out some of the whites, a little mace, and rose water.

Pound cake. Three eggs, nine spoonsful of butter, three of sugar, and three hands full of flour.

Clove cake. Three pounds of flour, one of butter, one of sugar, three eggs, two spoonsful of cloves; mix it with molasses.

Bread pudding. One pound of soft bread or biscuit, soaked in one quart of milk, run through a sieve or colander; add seven eggs, three quarters of a pound of sugar, one quarter of a pound of butter, nutmeg, cinnamon, one gill of rose water, one pound of raisins, half a pint of milk; bake three quarters of an hour, middling hot oven."

Thomas had such good responses from my recipes, even though the directions left something to be desired, that he printed my rule for boiled ham the following week.

"Ham should be boiled in a large quantity of water, and that for a very long time – one quarter of an hour for each pound – the rind to be taken off when warm. The ham is most palatable when cold, and should be sent to the table with eggs, horseradish, and mustard. This affords a cheap repast at any time of day."

Before long, Thomas discovered that many of his readers eagerly awaited editions of the Messenger in the hope they would contain more of my recipes. After he had printed all my favorite rules for preparing food which I thought worthy of passing on to others, he began to share many other hints for the household we had learned over the years. Some appeared in the Messenger on September 27, 1827.

"To take mildew out of linen – Rub it well with soap, then scrape some fine chalk, and rub that into the linen; lay it on the grass, and as it dries wet it a little. Repeat the operation.

"To prevent cider bottles from bursting – When you bottle cider, place the bottles on the ground in the northerly part of the cellar and cover them with moss which you must keep constantly wet with cold water.

"To destroy flies – Dissolve 2 drachms of the extract of quassia in a half pint of boiling water, add a little sugar or syrup, pour the mixture on plates, and set them in places infested by flies.

"Plums, peaches, etc. How kept fresh through the year – Beat well together equal quantities of honey and spring water, pour it into an earthen vessel, put in the fruits, all freshly gathered, and cover them quite close. When any of the fruit is taken out, wash it in cold water, and it is fit for immediate use.

"To clean the teeth and improve the breath – To 4 cups of fresh prepared lime water, add a drachm of Peruvian bark and wash the teeth with this water in the morning before breakfast and after supper. It will effectually destroy the tartar and remove the offensive small from those which have most decayed.

"Care for the sting of Wasps – It has been found that the best remedy is an application of salt moistened with a little water, and even in a case where a person has been stung in the windpipe by accidentally swallowing one in a draught of any kind of liquor, the alarming symptoms that often ensue may be almost instantly relieved by swallowing repeated doses of water saturated with salt."

A cure for dysentery, a very common ailment at certain times of the year in our town, appeared in the Messenger on July 28, 1830.

"Take two glasses sweet oil, two glasses West Indian Molasses, two glasses West Indian rum. Simmer them together over a fire till it becomes the thickness of honey so that the oil may not separate from the rest. While on the fire, keep it well stirred, and when taken off continue the same till it is cold. Then the patient should take a spoonful once an hour until he finds the disease abating, thence once in two hours until cured."

One of the most common afflictions of young mothers was hysterics. I believe that mothers today do not suffer so regularly with this most distressing ailment. Perhaps that is because young mothers now have much more help and many more luxuries than we did in those early days on the frontier. Even though Meadville was a growing and lively town when Thomas and I moved here, we had to endure hardships that my own mother had never known in Philadelphia where she was a young bride, or even in Lancaster, her later home.

Like other young mothers in Meadville, I was forever weary from the hard work, long hours, and large numbers of children we had to bear. Even though Thomas was a wonderful, helpful husband, there were many days when I felt I could not lift another cooking vessel. Today, I am amazed as I look around and see all the helpful inventions my daughters and granddaughters have at their beck and call. How I would have delighted in them when Meadville was young.

Dr. Charles W. Colsen, one of our town's most worthy doctors, prescribed for me his special remedy for the hysterics when I was suffering under its yoke. It did me so much good that Thomas felt obliged to benefit other ladies in Crawford County by publishing Dr. Colsen's dignified announcement in the Messenger on July 20, 1816.

"POSSET DRINK. Many worthy mothers, afflicted with hysterical complaints, have, by means of this prescription been restored to health; and where the complaint has been found too deeply fixed, it has had the happy effect of ameliorating it and thereby prolonging life. Knowing how to prepare the above valuable drink as this is the only season of the year when it can be used to advantage, I respectfully tender my services to those afflicted with the complaint."

I encouraged Thomas to publish information to benefit other young mothers who scarcely had time to visit a doctor. I was especially pleased by the results of the recipe he ran on December 16, 1823 for preventing the Female Breasts from gathering, or to cure them after they are gathered.

"To the yellow of one egg add one tablespoon full of brown sugar, one of honey, and one of rum, a small teaspoonful of powdered alum and as much of rosin; this mixture should be put over a slow fire and stirred with the finger, until it comes to a consistency that will easily spread on lint, or order to keep the salve alive. It must never be made too hot to bear your finger in.

A plaster of this spread over the breasts before the child is put to them will prevent their gathering; and should fever at any time fall in them, a plaster of this salve should immediately be applied and it will certainly improve gathering; should matter be formed before the application of the salve, the breast should be kept covered with a thick brown paper made wet with rum, and the salve over the diseased part only; when it breaks, there should be a tent kept on it and the salve spread on linen, the salve side next to the udder; the child should be taken from the breast as soon as matter is discovered, which may be done without the least danger of losing the breast, as is too often the case, by the skin cleaving to the bones; after a cure is made, the child may be allowed to suck. The milk will soon return."

Cholera was one of the deadly diseases we feared. Thomas's concern about its spread to our little corner of Pennsylvania inspired him to print rules for its prevention which he had collected from doctors and survivors of cholera attacks. The rules appeared on

August 4, 1832 with recommendations for heavy clothing and a fire in the house despite the heat of the summer season:

"1. Wear a flannel garment next to the skin, large enough to cover the chest and the abdomen.

2. Wear woolen or thick worsted stockings.

3. Bathe or wash the whole body in warm water twice or thrice a week.

4. Keep a little fire in sitting rooms mornings and evenings.

5. Avoid fatigue, exposure to the sun, night air, and rain. If caught in a shower or rain, change the whole of the dress as soon as possible.

6. Abstain from the use of spirited liquors, acid drinks, tobacco (especially smoking), peas. beans, cucumbers, fruit, and pastry.

7. Use fresh mutton, beef or lamb daily, and take a liberal allowance of salt at every meal.

8. Keep an extra supply of woolen bed coverings at hand, made for immediate use, should a change of temperature during the night render it necessary.

9, Keep in the house a supply of good vinegar and mustard and have a supply of hot water available at all times.

10. If attacked by cholera, send for your physician and apply large poultices of mustard and hot vinegar to the pit of the stomach, to the back, opposite to the stomach, and to the calves of the legs, and bottles of hot water to the feet."

We were blessed to see most of our children live to become adults. God most surely gave us a fine family, and a large supply of daughters who required our constant attention to make certain that they developed into proper young ladies. After our daughters were grown, Thomas published on May 13, 1830 his own "Rules for a Young Lady" which he had personally tested in our home during the years, and which produced a very admirable product.

"1. Let her go to bed at ten o'clock, nine if she pleases. She must not grumble or be disheartened because she may not sleep the first night or two, and thus lay ruminating on the pleasures from which she has cut herself off; but persist steadily for a few nights, when she will find the habit will produce a far more pleasant repost than that which follows a late ball or assembly. She will also rise in the morning more refreshed with better spirits, and a more blooming complexion.

2. Let her rise about six o'clock in summer, and about eight in winter – immediately wash her face and hands with pure water- cool or tepid, according to the season of the year; and if she could by any means be induced to sweep her room, or bustle about some other domestic concerns for about an hour, she would be the gainer, as well in health as in beauty by the practice.

3. Her breakfast should be something more substantial than a cup of slips whether denominated tea or coffee, and a thin slice of bread and butter. She should take a soft-boiled egg or two, a little cold meat, a draught of milk or a cup or two of pure chocolate.

4. She should not lounge all day by the fire, reading novels, nor indulge herself in thinking of the perfidy of false swains, or the despair of a pining damsel; but bustle about – walk or ride in the open air, rub the furniture, or make puddings – and when she feels hungry eat a custard or something equally light, in place

101

of a fashionable morning treat or a slice of pound cake and a glass of wine or cordial.

5. Let her dine upon mutton or beef plainly cooked, and not too fat - but she need not turn away occasionally from a fowl or anything equally good; let her only observe to partake of it in moderation, and to drink sparing of water during the repast.

6. In place of three or four cups of strong tea for supper, she may eat a custard, a bowl of bread and milk, or similar articles, and in a few hours afterward let her retire to bed.

7. At other periods of the day which are occupied by business or exercise, let her read – no sickly love tales – but good humored and instructive works – calculated, while they keep the mind unencumbered with heavy thought to augment its store of ideas, and to guard it against the injury which will ever result from false perceptions of mankind and of the concerns of life."

Thomas was always interested in my activities at home, and he frequently made suggestions for easing my work. I believe that our young ladies turned out so well because he insisted that they help me at home. But my greatest help came long after my children were grown. It was my washing machine!

When the first washing machine arrived at the shop of Mr. David Philips, he placed one at my disposal, knowing that Thomas enjoyed learning about every new invention that came to town. He also knew that, if Thomas liked the results, he would encourage his readers to avail themselves of Mr. Philips's services. He knew Thomas very well. Thomas was so impressed by both the machine and my happy disposition at the end of the washday that he celebrated the machine's benefits in his editorial of May 2, 1832.

"LADIES, if you desire to be relieved from the laborious and unpleasant toil of the wash tub, let us advise you, by all means, to call upon Mr. David Philips for one of his excellent washing machines. We have obtained one and find on trial that it performs most admirably. The work which would require a day's labor in the ordinary way, may be dispatched in an hour or two, with a saving of soap, and without the slightest injury to the linen, however coarse or fine. Try the machine."

Thanks to Thomas's whole-hearted recommendation, Mr. Philips had more orders than he could fill, and very soon he became a prosperous man as more and more of the pleased ladies of Meadville were released from drudgery.

CHAPTER THIRTEEN

POLITICS

It was inevitable that Thomas became involved in politics. First of all, he had complete faith in his own opinions and he believed himself to be well informed in all matters and correct in his social graces.

Secondly, he was a fine figure of a man. He captured the eye and held the attention of everyone who knew him. Had the ladies been allowed to vote I am certain that he would have become governor of Pennsylvania, perhaps even President of these United States.

Thomas had his nose and hand in every important event that happened in Meadville and surrounding Crawford County, and when he was not directly involved in a matter, he volunteered his opinion about it in his editorials. By the close of the War of 1812, he began to advise his readers about various candidates, and many a local gentleman has confessed to me that Thomas enlightened him and changed his viewpoint on this or that political matter.

Not only did Thomas set his political views down on paper, but he also was an admirable physical presence at every political gathering in our town. Each Fourth of July he presided at Meadville's gala celebrations, and while he and his compatriots toasted and discussed America's heroes, the other ladies and I were busy preparing tasty treats for the worthy gentlemen.

The first politician Thomas actively supported was General Heister who was running for Governor of Pennsylvania. Impressed with the general's military experience during the Revolution, Thomas explained his reasons for switching his support from Findley in the hope that his readers would join him in voting for Heister. On September 5, 1817, he wrote:

"When I contrast the claims of Mr. Findley . . . with the long, faithful and important services of General Heister, the preponderance of merit, to my mind, appears most clearly and decidedly in favor of the latter . . . The man who aided and assisted, at the hazard of life and property, in securing to me (in common with my fellow citizens) those religious and political blessings which I enjoy, has a strong claim upon my gratitude.

"The most foul and cruel efforts have been made, by falsehoods, to blast the reputation of General Heister as a soldier of the Revolution – a reputation acquired through toil, danger, and hardships. As the descendant of one who partook with General Heister in the struggles of that memorable epoch, I cannot sanction those falsehoods by giving my vote to Mr. Findley."

Heister won the governorship because of backing from the western counties and such outspoken editors as my husband, Thomas Atkinson.

Thomas was usually on the winning side in politics. On December 23, 1822, he became the first Pennsylvania editor to suggest Andrew Jackson for President. He admired Jackson's military ability and was absolutely certain of Old Hickory's personal honesty and freedom from binding connections or intrigues.

How Thomas rued his support to that side when the banks of America fell into disgrace during Jackson's administration.

When an unknown candidate named John A. Shulze won the nomination for Governor of Pennsylvania six years after Findley took office, Thomas was furious. He could not understand how Shulze had beaten the popular George Bryan. "The result goes down with confounded bad grace in this quarter," he smarted in his editorial of May 18, 1823. "Beym donner un blitzen, we cannot divine how it has happened. ALL, we suspect, was not Fair Play."

Nevertheless, Thomas honored his obligations, and on August 12, 1823, he devoted his editorial to explaining his decision to vote for Shulze in spite of his personal reservations about the man.

"T. Atkinson was disappointed and mortified at the nomination of Mr. Shulze – really he is scarcely in a good humor about it yet. Nothing but a sense of political duty urges him to support that nomination."

Thomas was appalled to think that men who were less than remarkable could aspire to – and win! – high political offices. I was not surprised when he asked me to sit a bit after supper one evening, for I knew him like a book. Often, I would steal a glance at him when he was pondering, deep in thought, and I sensed that he was thinking about offering himself to the citizens of our state.

He was very serious as he began, "Sally, what would you say to having a politician in the family?"

"I would say life would be no different than it is today," I replied. "The only change would be that you would be speaking from a platform instead of your editor's soapbox."

He caught the twinkle in my eyes, for he threw back his head and roared, "So you don't object?"

"On the contrary, I'm delighted and honored to think that my husband is well qualified for public service."

We both knew that he would be among the finest in the land.

"Just for that, I'll nominate you for First Lady," he grinned.

"I'll accept that nomination only on the condition that I can name a very special gentleman as my running mate.:

"Agreed!" he said, putting his arms around me and giving me that hug I knew and loved so well. "However, he cautioned, "I believe in starting from the bottom if you don't mind."

"Not at all. I can wait. We've a long life ahead of us." I smiled and squeezed his hand.

Thomas has watched our state and nation grow, and the little voice in the back of his mind which had begun softly was now shouting to him that his experience and good judgment were needed to insure continued expansion. By Thursday morning, September 23, 1824, everyone in Meadville knew our secret; Thomas was throwing his hat into the political ring by running as Crawford County's Representative to the Pennsylvania State Assembly.

When the results of the election were published on October 16, there was no doubt that Thomas had won handily over the two other prominent residents of

Meadville, the Reverend Timothy Alden and Samuel Hays. Haye received 188 votes, Alden had 488, and Thomas had nearly twice their combined votes with 632.

And so, destiny catapulted Thomas from his tiny editorial desk in Meadville to a prominent office in Harrisburg for the 1824-25 session. Nevertheless, he kept the Messenger operating with the help of his assistant, Mr. Christopher Blystone, who saw that each deadline was met while Thomas was out of town.

I chose to remain in our fair village rather than endure a long, hard journey to Harrisburg, where my lodging would have been a modest rooming house. After all, the session lasted only a few months during the harshest weather, for the men were needed at home during the planting season. Then, too, Harrisburg, scarcely more than a tiny town with muddy streets, was not nearly so pleasant as our own city of Meadville. I had no desire to leave the company of my friends and the comfort of our home.

During his term, Thomas listened and learned, and he prepared himself for the next election. It had been an exhilarating experience for him, one which he yearned to repeat. In anticipation of being elected to serve another year, he decided to dispose of some of his property. By turning fifty acres of land with a small mill into cash, he would be able to provide me with the means of running our house comfortably while he was away for the winter.

If most Pennsylvania voters had never heard of Thomas Atkinson prior to December 4, 1826, the opening day of the 1826-27 state legislature in Harrisburg, they sat up and took notice. He had learned his earlier lessons well and he was duly rewarded. He was placed on the standing committee on Ways and

Means and was added to the committee on Accounts on December 6th when he was also given the responsibility of tending to a piece of unfinished business from the previous session, the erection of an academy in the town of Clearfield.

Like all county representatives, he had obligations to some of his constituents back home, particularly to the Revolutionary War veterans and their widows. He sought financial relief for Adam Owry, our most elderly local veteran, as well as for others who needed aid.

Within a week, Thomas requested legislative aid for Allegheny College, a project close to his heart. His enthusiasm and his proud bearing made him stand out among the men gathered at Harrisburg. On Thursday, December 14, he was appointed, on a motion, as teller of the House. This meant that he, and another appointed member of the Senate, opened the returns and counted the votes of the election for Governor. Already his honesty and integrity were being rewarded, and two full weeks of the session had not elapsed.

For two months, Thomas spread his authority around the capitol, impressing his fellow politicians by voting yes to vital motions and bills, and voting nay to those he sincerely believed were wrong. By Monday, February 5, 1827, he was ready for his first major act: presenting a petition from Crawford County citizens requesting incorporation of a company for the purpose of making a canal from the state line down the Conewango Creek to intersect the Pennsylvania canal. With that, Thomas Atkinson's great transportation project was launched!

Prodded by the lingering memories of his uncomfortable journey overland, Thomas was convinced that water offered the state of Pennsylvania the best form of public transportation. Construction of canals was just one phase of his vision for rapid and convenient travel for our state's citizens and visitors. He also believed that existing streams should be utilized for moving goods and people. For this reason, he presented a petition on February 12th to declare Muddy Creek in Crawford County a public highway and to appropriate money for improving its navigation.

A month later, on March 8, 1828, he brought to the attention of the legislature the proceedings of a convention of delegates from several counties who wished to extend the proposed Pennsylvania Canal to Lake Erie. That idea interested many of his associates, but the slow wheels of Harrisburg's legislative system held back the canal projects he was so eager to begin.

Even though his bills were not enacted promptly, and Thomas became frustrated because he could not accomplish the projects he yearned to complete, he was recognized by Governor Shulze and those who really mattered in the state government. Proof of this came when G. B. Porter, the Pennsylvania Adjutant General, submitted his report to the governor on March 10, 1827. In the report was a glowing commendation of the Meadville Arsenal and of Thomas, the appointed keeper of the Arsenal, described as "so respectable and competent a person."

At the close of the session, Thomas returned home to us, saddened by his annoyance at the slow moving legislative system, yet cheered by the recognition and support he had received from important politicians.

Quickly he turned his attention back to his newspaper, his farm fields, and the many community projects he had missed while in Harrisburg. By the time the spring of 1828 arrived, he had resumed the duties of Justice of the Peace, and he cheerfully used his editorials to admonish certain townspeople for not having gotten the Pennsylvania canal off the ground, or – more aptly – into the ground. Responding to his old friend, Colonel Moore, he denied that the explorations and surveys and contracts made for the canal between the Allegheny River and Lake Erie were permitted by the Easterners, Philadelphians in particular, as a temporary means of oppressing the western counties. He wrote:

"Enough, Col. - Forbear! In mercy, withhold the remaining thunderbolts which you assure us you hold in reserve. Seriously, Colonel, the task which you have imposed upon yourself reminds us of the case of the old lady who undertook to sweep sunbeams from her floor with the wing of a turkey. You have mounted a wrong hobby."

Instead of faltering for lack of support, Thomas eagerly accepted the chairmanship of the citizens' committee for the Allegheny, French Creek, and Waterford Canal. He was determined to overcome the obstacles and deliver his favorite transportation project to his fellow citizens. "Mark my word, Sally," he told me, "we'll see that finished canal within five years."

His spare hours were devoted to working for the Presidential election of 1828, driven by a personal commitment to deliver every eligible voter to the polls. The years had altered his opinion of General Andrew Jackson, and he now worked vigorously to keep John Quincy Adams in the White House. His feelings were reflected in his editorial of Thursday, October 30, 1828, which read in part:

111

"Tomorrow, as members of the only free government on earth, we have a sacred duty to discharge, not only to the present, but to future generations. The neglect of that duty, or a misapplication of our votes, may prove a curse or a blessing to our beloved country,

"An individual vote may continue the inestimable advantages which we enjoy, civil, religious, and political, under the guidance of our present enlightened Chief Magistrate, for another term of four years – or consign them into the hands of Gen. Jackson, the military candidate, without talents of civil acquirements – merciless in his nature, and with hands stained by the blood of his fellow man!"

The subsequent election of General Jackson saddened Thomas. The canals, which President Adams had favored, were rejected by Jackson. His election also prevented Thomas from winning his bid for Congress in 1830. Voters succumbed to the profound Jackson influence and stayed with the faction in the White House.

Thomas was quietly pleased that the President moved from one difficulty to another. His editorial of April 28, 1831 revealed some of the problems.

"TROUBLE AT HEADQUARTERS. A political explosion has taken place at Washington. The Secretaries of State, of War, of the Treasury, and of the Navy have simultaneously thrown up their commissions. That a bad state of feeling existed among the Heads of Departments for some time back was pretty well understood. But this general blow up will be witnessed with astonishment. Indeed the Jackson party seems to be crumbling to pieces in every quarter."

Trouble brewed everywhere. The July Fourth celebrations were a good excuse for toting in Philadelphia, as Thomas reported on July 21, 1831.

"The harmony of the Jackson men, who met to honor the occasion, although few in number, was sadly interrupted by contrariety of political feeling growing out of recent events and ended in a spirited interchange of bottles at each other's heads."

Despite the trouble they were causing throughout the nation the Jackson forces gathered enough support everywhere to dismay Thomas. He chose sides with Henry Clay for President and John Sergeant for Vice President, but he was pessimistic about their chance for success. On December 31, 1831, he wrote:

"A stranger to reward of every kind, during an editorial course of nearly thirty years...we have nothing now to hope for or expect from the coming presidential contest other than 'hard knocks' from political opponents, and of these, God knows, we have in times past received a most bountiful share."

The knowledge that his candidate, Clay, would lose to Jackson, was shadowed by Thomas's own personal disappointment. 'THE JIG'S AT AN END,' he blasted in his editorial of March 31, 1832. His fond dream of building a network of canals throughout Pennsylvania died when the funding of all branches was struck out of the bill on March 24th. Only a main line from Philadelphia to Pittsburgh was approved. "This is truly a sad state of things," he wrote.

He was not appeased the following week when an act was submitted to "stanch the wounds and tie up the broken limbs of the Branches," and he lamented in his editorial, "It reminds us of the case of a doctor and his hopeless patient – the administering of the last opiate in order to allay the pains of the sufferer."

Like his once-healthy canal bill, Thomas, too, suffered. He began to decline during the summer of 1832, and by August, Dr. Yates confirmed that he had contracted yellow fever, the very ailment which had taken his father so many years earlier in Virginia. At times, he could scarcely lift his hand to write, but he forced himself to keep up with his editorial duties. For days, he was unable to write the endorsements his candidates deserved, but on August 4th, he pushed himself to the limit to write:

"That Pennsylvania is lost to General Jackson no observant man can doubt, and it could not be otherwise, unless she were lost to herself, to her own interests, to her sense of consistency, and to her self-respect. Twice, during the last session, did both branches of the Legislature and her Governor declare that the Tariff, and the Bank must be preserved; and did require her members of Congress so to vote. The people also, in almost every section of the state, in public meetings, passed resolutions of similar purport. But General Jackson has destroyed the one and has done all he could to destroy the other...As might be expected, most of the cool, reflecting, and unprejudiced men who formerly supported him do so no longer."

Slowly, but surely, Thomas's health improved. By February, he was actively heading citizens' meetings to protest "high handed measures on the part of South Carolina" which he felt were destructive to our nation's Constitution.

Peeved that he had not been re-elected to the Legislature that year because of the Jackson influence everywhere, he busied himself by restyling the

114

Messenger with new type and selling more land. Almost thirty years earlier, he had purchased two hundred acres of land at very low cost from the state, but prices had risen considerably, and he was able to realize a very nice profit on that investment. All of a sudden, he acquired renewed courage to give up his business and rest on financial assets.

I was perfectly happy to remain in Meadville, but Thomas believed that we would benefit by moving away from town, and so he invested some of his money in a lovely farm about nine miles outside the city limits.

At first, I was apprehensive. Thomas loved talking to the citizens through his editorials, but he also loved life, and he knew that the strain of maintaining the weekly publication was becoming too much for his weakened constitution. Convinced that the full-time job of gentleman farmer would hasten his recuperation, he sold the Crawford Messenger to Joseph G. G. Kennedy on April 3, 1833, and we moved to life's next adventure at Woodcock.

"Don't fret, Sally," he pleaded. "After all, Woodcock is only seven miles from the center of Meadville, near enough to visit, and far enough away to block out all the cares of running a business in town."

I should have known that Thomas would not be content to live a leisurely life at Woodcock. Oh yes, he did regain his strength there, but it wasn't long before he was working full time for his pet projects. Most importantly, he became deeply involved once more in politics.

His happiest day came when, despite its many setbacks, the Pennsylvania Canal finally became a reality. On opening day, June 1, 1835, users learned that they need not have cash in order to pay toll. Such items as hay, straw, leaches ashes, manure, and steam engines were also welcome.

Thomas was overjoyed! His health improved almost overnight, and by the middle of August, the Crawford County committee passed a resolution stating that Thomas Atkinson of Woodcock was a suitable person to represent Crawford County in the next Legislature. On August 22, 1835, the masthead of the Messenger (now owned by Kennedy) ran these endorsements:

For President – Gen Wm. H. Harrison

For Governor – Joseph Ritner

Assembly – Thomas Atkinson

In his editorial, Kennedy said of Thomas:

"The citizens of the county know full well his qualifications to be much superior to any other man before the people for the office, and they are sensible that he will jot violate the pledge he has so publicly given, that he will yield all sectional partialities and sacrifice them to the public good."

Just prior to the election, on October 10, 1835, Kennedy again endorsed Thomas.

"The friends of the Canal system have placed the name of THOMAS ATKINSON before the public…as an individual who possesses in an eminent degree all the necessary qualifications for a prudent and a skillful legislator. With his commanding influence and great experience, he will be more able to unite and combine all parties in the great measure of the extension of the canal to Lake Erie than any of his competitors."

116

The citizens of Crawford County heeded the Messenger's endorsement of its former editor. When the November 7, 1835 edition rolled off the press, the name of their first choice for the Pennsylvania State House of Representatives was my own distinguished husband, Thomas Atkinson.

For the third time, he went to Harrisburg for the winter months, content in the knowledge that he was finally on his way to an important political future. On the first day of the 1835-36 session, he sprang from his seat to nominate a printer for the German Journal. The following Friday, he was appointed to the Education Committee. During that first month, he presented petitions for several war pensions, but he did not accomplish his major chore until January 4, 1836, when he presented three petitions from residents of Crawford, Erie, and Venango Counties wishing the construction of turnpike roads. These roads, Thomas thought, were poor substitutes for his beloved canals, but he realized that a statewide means of reliable transportation was essential. How he would have rejoiced to see the railroads which today crisscross our state! He could not have envisioned their success.

During the 1835-37 legislative session, Thomas became involved in banking interests, but very little was accomplished because of Henry Conrad. Conrad, a member of the House, was the subject of hearings because it was said that he had tried to bribe a member of the Senate. Thomas was among the majority of members who voted to discharge Conrad, but the defendant protested his innocence. In the end, the House decided to merely censure Conrad, who was so enraged by the entire affair that he resigned, then commenced a lawsuit against the Speaker of the House.

117

Thomas said that the session was not nearly as productive as he would have hoped. Among the bills he had to consider was one from the committee on Vice and Immorality to prevent canal boats and railroads from running on Sunday. There was also a request from John T. M. Bedell to change his name to Gregory T. Bedell.

On March 19, 1836, Thomas voted against incorporation of the Girard Bank of Philadelphia, but it passed. This was one of the rare occasions when he did not vote with the majority.

On March 21, 1836, he presented a petition from some inhabitants of Montgomery County requesting that the court proceedings in the German counties be transacted and published in German. This was the last time his name appeared in the House proceedings until May 30th, a period of more than two months.

The reason was simple. Thomas was ill. This was not an ordinary illness, for it signaled his first step to the grave. My Thomas had begun to die.

He forced himself back to the House on Monday, May 30th for a very special purpose. My mother, Elizabeth Sommer of Lancaster, the widow of a soldier of the Revolutionary War, was granted forty dollars, the first installment of an annuity in that amount to be paid twice a year for the rest of her life.

My father, Leonard Sommer, had died on February 18, 1836, leaving her without income. Ill though he was, Thomas attended the session to make certain that his mother-in-law was provided for the rest of her days. She could not have had a more opportune or caring representative in the House.

118

Thomas's final task in the House was the presentation on June 7, 1836 of a petition from some Crawford County residents wishing to be furnished with arms so that they might form a cavalry troop. One week later, Governor Ritner signed an act relating to lunatics and habitual drunkards. With that, the House was adjourned. So, too, was Thomas Atkinson's political career.

Thomas returned home to me and to his farm of more than fifty acres on Woodcock Creek knowing that his lingering illness was irreversible. The yellow fever, contracted in Harrisburg during his first venture in the Legislature had begun his decline. Had he known in advance that he would contract the very disease which killed his father, I am certain that he would not have wavered in his determination to serve the citizens of Pennsylvania, even though it was generally known that Harrisburg, a low, damp site, was inviting to the mosquitoes carrying the dreaded disease.

Thomas was guided by his belief in himself and in his God. He knew that God would direct him on the right path, and if that path led to his own end, then it was the will of God. Along the way, he hoped to influence others, to help them realize their God-given rights, and to show through his own example the proper behavior and duties of a good citizen.

I was privileged to know that Thomas aspired to much higher offices. In freeing himself from his Messenger responsibilities, he planned to work toward the loftiest positions in our state and – God willing! – in our wonderful nation.

The slow, painful sickness which came over him could not be halted. Dr. Yates warned me that Thomas would not last for more than a year. If he told Thomas, I

119

never knew, but by the end of the summer of 1836, Thomas accepted his fate. On September 18th, he drew up a will in which he remarked that "death is near" and "a long state of indisposition admonishes me that life is retained by a slender thread."

He and I drew even closer in those last days, if that is possible, content in the knowledge that most of our children had married happily. To us, their happiness was a reflection of our own perfect love and a life spent trying to improve ourselves and – as Thomas would have jested – everyone we met.

On March 11, 1837, one year after his illness first called him away from the legislative session Thomas Atkinson died. I vividly remember the cold, crisp, blustery day when his body was returned to earth at the old Meadville Burying Grounds. At the solemn rite reached a climax and his coffin was lowered into the ground I could scarcely see it before me. Perhaps it was the heavy veiling. Perhaps it was my tears. It mattered not that I could no longer see my beloved husband, for I felt his presence beside me, even stronger than in life.

At the reading of the will, I learned that Thomas left everything to me, provided that I never remarry. For the first time since his death I smiled. He knew that no other man could take his place. Ours had been a perfect union, sweet, hopeful, exciting, and filled with contentment. Living with a man such as Thomas Atkinson is an honor. I thank God for so honoring me. The beautiful memories amassed during our life together are sufficient to sustain me until we meet again.

"She has labored and toiled hard for what little we shall have left," he wrote, "and has consequently the first and best right to enjoy whatever comfort it may impart to her is passing down the inclined plane of life."

Thomas's will was more than generous. He left me with far more than the creature comforts I needed. For a time, I stayed on at our comfortable Woodcock home and there welcomed visits from our children and close friends. The death of our precious Salome soon after her marriage to John McFarland came hard on the loss of my dear husband, but – as Thomas always philosophized – joy grows out of every tragedy.

John was so fond of the Atkinson daughters that he married two of them. In 1843, he and Lydia Augusta were happily united. Our Henrietta, too, overcame the tragedy of the death of her husband, Mr. Baldwin, by later marrying the fine gentleman, Mr. McCullough.

Adelaide and Eliza had less happy wedded lives. Adelaide had a difficult time with her first husband, George McElroy. He treated her so shabbily that she separated from him and came home to Woodcock for a while. Through friends, however, she met and married the distinguished Judge Hamon Conger of Janesville, Wisconsin. Today they live in a lovely town between the state capital at Madison and Chicago. I have not undertaken the long journey to visit her there, but she and her husband travel here frequently and tell me that Janesville is not unlike our own fair Meadville.

Eliza was the most unfortunate of our girls. In 1833, she eloped with Major John Clark, very much against Thomas's wishes. It was a sad time for us all. During her brief marriage, Eliza contracted an illness which never left her. Thomas provided for her in his will because of her sickly constitution. Today she rests by his side.

William never married, but our other sons were very fortunate in their choice of brides. Thomas our oldest, married the charming Miss Pfieffer of

Saegertown not far from Meadville, and Monroe married Miss Jane Sophia Pinks of Woodstock, Vermont. Their two children, Hale and Adelaide, brought me immense joy, always begging for stories of when I was a little girl and how I came over the Allegheny Mountains to the frontier. They and their equally adorable cousins were the sparks of my life which kept the fires of my fond memories ever kindled.

In time, I found life at Woodcock too demanding, and after their repeated pleadings, I moved back to Meadville to life with my sweet Sally Ann, her most gracious husband Edward Stebbins, and their remarkable children.

I have watched our lovely town progress from a tiny frontier village to one filled with stately homes, tall trees, and lovely gardens. As the center of the town expanded, there were bound to be changes. In 1855, the old Meadville Burying Grounds fell in the way of development and we had Thomas's body moved on December 6th to a more pleasant setting in Greendale Cemetery, where I will one day join him.

What memories I nourish! I have been blessed indeed by our Heavenly Creator. But no blessing has been so wondrous as that of knowing and loving Thomas Atkinson.

EPILOGUE

Sally Sommers Atkinson lived nearly forty years beyond her husband, Thomas Atkinson. She died on April 1, 1875 and was buried next to him in Greendale Cemetery. His original tombstone is so worn that the 'T' and 'A' are almost obliterated, but the site is well marked by a large monument on the lot which contains the graves of those two pioneers and three of their children, Henrietta, Eliza, and Thomas. Sally's obituary summed up her remarkable courage and character.

"Since Mr. Atkinson's death in 1837, Mrs. Atkinson had lived in great retirement, scarcely known outside of the circles and friends and the relatives. By them she will be remembered as a pure and noble woman of the olden type. She retained her faculties in remarkable vigor up to the last moments of her life, waiting calmly and patiently the time of her departure. She lived to see Meadville increase from a small settlement of a few log houses to a thriving city, and to witness three generations of her descendants rise up and call her blessed."

Sally was equally as remarkable as the man whom she cheerfully followed into the Pennsylvania wilderness. The home, the businesses, and the community endeavors which Thomas Atkinson headed were a joint venture, and if Sally politely hovered in the background during Atkinson's accomplishments, it was not because she was unessential to his success, but because her constant presence and encouragement were

123

so vital to her husband's life that to speak of him is to acknowledge her influence.

In years to come, historians may best remember Thomas Atkinson as a man who recorded a myriad of events of his time in a newspaper destined to be preserved for posterity. As Sally knew so wisely, readers perusing its pages years hence can share the sadness of death and misfortune on the frontier, vicariously sleigh-ride on the snow-filled lanes of Crawford County, view the election campaigns of America's political giants through the black, snappy eyes of an opinionated pioneer editor and evaluate the literature preferred by the common man of that period.

Omniscient and domineering as Thomas Atkinson may have appeared to some whose lives he touched, he believed that God had entrusted him with a duty to spread truth, honesty, and high moral character throughout the community. Above all, he left a detailed record of a unique era in American history. The success of his efforts may be measured by the constant demand for microfilms of the Crawford Messenger at the Meadville Public Library, the Pennsylvania State Archives in Harrisburg, and the Library of Congress in Washington, D. C.

Without Thomas and Sally Atkinson, Meadville would have thrived, Allegheny College would have been established, and the Meadville Chamber of Commerce may have been chartered early enough to retain its honor as the third oldest in the nation. Nevertheless, the town of Meadville, Allegheny College, the Chamber of Commerce, the Pennsylvania State Legislature, and all of Atkinson's other public endeavors would have been a bit poorer for the lack of his enthusiasm.

Sally Atkinson regretted, for her husband's sake, that Thomas never attained the fame of his idol, Benjamin Franklin, but she frequently pointed out that he founded the Crawford Messenger under more adverse conditions than even Franklin could have dreamed. And if Atkinson is remembered for nothing else, his vigor, honesty, and vision combined to create a genuine good citizen. What greater epitaph could a man, or his wife, wish?

Thomas Atkinson, Jr., Editor, The Crawford Messenger

THIS PORTRAIT OF THOMAS ATKINSON HANGS
AT ALLEGHENY COLLEGE

SALOME WEIDNER ATKINSON,

MOTHER OF THOMAS ATKINSON, JR.

During her lifetime, Salome Weidner Atkinson played many roles, among them daughter, wife, mother, teacher, temptress, and progenitor of famous Americans. Her story begins at Ephrata Cloister on Cocalico Creek in Lancaster County, Pennsylvania, where a gene pool mix sired a line of brilliant achievers, extraordinarily beautiful women, and movers and shakers of early Pennsylvania society.

Ephrata Cloister was founded in 1732 by Johann Conrad Beissel, a German religious eccentric and strict disciplinarian. Despite his promotion of celibacy as the true way to salvation, several followers strayed from that rule. The resulting mix precipitated a medical breakthrough five generations later.

Early in the 18th century, Pennsylvania already was becoming a melting pot of religious thinkers. Fervent beliefs propelled at least half of its early colonists to cross the ocean. William Penn ferried Quakers from England, Welsh Baptists fled the King's men to the Welsh Colony outside Philadelphia, and German and Swiss immigrants sought freedom to worship freely as Lutherans, Moravians, and Mennonites. Smaller sects like Beissel's began cropping up west of Philadelphia as early as 1711 when the Pietists settled in the Berks County village of Oley.

They were joined there in 1718 by the zealous New Borns (Die Neugeborne) founded by Matthias Bauman, a laborer from the Lower Palatinate. His religious conversion was in response to the vision he saw while in a trance that lasted several weeks. Many Germans and Swiss settled in Germantown just outside Philadelphia. Like the Quakers, they gradually made their way into the wilderness, drawn by men like Beissel who advocated close communities centered around their beliefs.

Several families destined to unite in later generations were already in place when Beissel established his settlement. About 1700, Thomas Atkinson arrived in Philadelphia with his infant son, Stephen, and other English Quakers sailing under the auspices of William Penn. By 1730, Stephen had purchased a farm on the Conestoga River in Lancaster County. In typical Quaker fashion, he raised eight well educated children, all trained in useful professions. His fourth son, Thomas, born in 1751, studied architecture and masonry, trades that would prove profitable in the growing communities.

Before the autumn of 1724, Johannes Heinrich Schneider, a cordwainer (maker of fine shoes), emigrated from Germany with his son Frederick, daughter Catherine, her husband Peter Weidner, and their children. After the death on August 18, 1725 of Johannes (identified as Henry Snider in Will Book E:8 of Philadelphia County, Pennsylvania), Peter and Catherine Weidner moved to the Oley Valley.

John Gorgas had emigrated to Philadelphia from Holland in 1708. A clockmaker, he anticipated great need for his craft by the newcomers and quickly established a business that would be regarded as the finest in the country for the next four generations. Not long after landing, he married Sytje (Psyche) Rittenhouse, whose parents had arrived from Holland prior to her birth in 1693. They settled in Germantown and soon began a family. Their fifth son, Jacob, born August 9, 1728, married Christina Mack, granddaughter of Brethren Church founder Alexander Mack. By 1763, Jacob Gorgas had settled in the town of Ephrata. There he passed along the skills learned from his father, teaching his son and grandson to construct grandfather clocks that remain valuable to this day.

Bernhard and Elisabetha Lorentz Gitter, emigrants from the Palatinate, first settled in Somerset County, New Jersey as members of the Amwell religious community. Their daughter, Susanna, was baptized on February 7, 1725 at the Sommerville Reformed Church.

Fate was about to unite these families. We will never know if they were drawn to the Ephrata Cloister by divine revelations, by the preaching of Johann Conrad Beissel, or by a personal yearning for perfection. Perhaps it was their common language still spoken by the Pennsylvania Amish. We do know that Peter and Catherine Weidner/Widener and their son, Peter, Jr. became part of the community in 1736. Two years later, the Gitter family left the Amwell group in New Jersey and moved to Ephrata Cloister.

The Ephrata Cloister was by 1740 a large complex consisting of a meeting house, printing office, bake house, various small buildings, and separate dormitories with individual cells for the single brethren and sisters. All men wore the habit of the Capuchins, or White Friars. It consisted of a shirt, trousers, and vest, with a long white gown and cowl made of woolen for the winter months and linen in summer. Except for petticoats instead of trousers, women dressed the same. All were given monastic names.

Beissel's Sabbatarian brotherhood required considerable discipline and personal restraints from the thirty-six brethren and thirty-five sisters living together. Each day, he read aloud confessions from the members detailing their sins. Strict celibacy, the ideal, was not mandatory for married couples. Young love, however, was frowned upon.

Contrary to the rules, Peter Weidner, Jr. and Susanna Gitter succumbed to human nature and fell in love. Their attraction became so strong that they rejected the celibacy clause in late 1747 or early 1748 and asked Conrad Beissel for permission to marry. According to the group's official history, the wedding ceremony proceeded uneventfully until Beissel and his brother "took leave of the bridegroom with a kiss…and thus weakened the conjugal love between (the bride and groom), …so much that they could not embrace each other for eight days… Much agonizing transpired, during which Peter Weidner requested and received from both Beissel and Susanna an annulment; she, however, had a change of heart and successfully petitioned the courts to enforce her marriage."

Susanna realized that the only hope for the couple to save their marriage was to leave Ephrata Cloister and Beissel's influence immediately. Once they made that break, their situation improved. They settled in Cumru Township, Berks County where, over the years, they obtained considerable property and had three daughters, Sophia, Salome, and Mary. Salome was born January 7, 1755, four years before her father's sudden death.

What might have been a tragedy for another widow proved fortuitous for the uncommonly attractive Susanna Widener. From a large and promising field of suitors, she chose attorney James Whitehead, a strong proponent of formal education for women. His loving tutelage opened unexpected doors for her daughters. Whitehead and his new family were baptized at St. Gabriel's Church (then Lutheran) in Amity Township in 1764, James on April 15, and Sophia, Salome, and Mary on June 10. Susanna and James Whitehead then had two children of their own, Penelope and Elizabeth.

For better or worse, all five of Susanna's daughters inherited her stunning beauty and quickly became known by those far and near for their good looks and intelligence. Sophia, the oldest, was the first to become embroiled in romance. She was only fourteen when John Boone, a cousin of Daniel, became enamored with her. In 1765, their first child was born out of wedlock.

Headstrong like her mother, Sophia defied tradition and local gossips and waited two years before agreeing to marry Boone. Soon after the birth of their third child, Boone died accidentally while working as a tanner. Barely a month passed after his death in March 1773 before the beauteous Sophia caught the fancy of John Biddle, the Surveyor General of Pennsylvania. They were married that October.

Despite his esteemed background and connections, Biddle proved to be a scoundrel. Accused of adulterating the flour used by the troops at the Battle of Brandywine, he fled to Nova Scotia under General Mifflin's threat to hang him from the nearest oak tree.

Meanwhile, Mary Widener married David Clymer, a son of George Clymer, a signer of the

Declaration of Independence. Clymer, a lawyer, is described in a letter written by family members as "a man of bad character, but of high standing and great wealth."

Salome determined to do better. Her marriage to Thomas Atkinson fulfilled all her dreams until his untimely passing. Despite the challenges she faced, she met them all. Once her sons' printing careers were under way, she focused on Elizabeth and Sophia who were enjoying a social whirl. The most attractive young ladies for miles around, they quickly caught the attention of two respectable bachelors. By 1792, Elizabeth had married the accomplished Jacob Hibschman, who was destined to lead his state and nation as a judge, a Major General, an insurance company president, and a member of the U.S. House of Representatives, defeating James Buchanan for the seat. On June 2, 1794, Sophia married Joseph Gorgas, son of the clockmaker and householder at the Ephrata community.

As time passed, the widow Salome grew closer to her friends and relatives in Ephrata. She frequently visited the printing shop to learn how her sons were doing and soon became ensnared by the influence wielded by the Cloister. Relieved of the burden of marrying off her older daughters and pleased that her sons had secured their future, Salome retreated into the Cloister, leaving her younger daughters, Sarah, Penelope, and Susan, with her aunt.

The Brethren soon discovered that Salome, like her amorous parents, had no intention of abiding by the Cloister regulations. She was not the celibate type. Neither was Benjamin Mayer the printer. Lonely, uncommonly beautiful, and tempestuous by all accounts,

Salome fell into a liaison with the printer, who was at least ten years her junior.

The affair threw the Cloister into a turmoil and prompted brother John Frederick to fling a full chamber pot through her open window. Salome and Mayer, their tryst exposed, ran after and attacked the retreating brother until they were apprehended and dragged before the justice of the peace on assault and battery charges.

The sordid affair sealed Salome's expulsion. A manuscript preserved at the Cloister State Historic Site reads: "at a Conference held...the 11th Day of February 1787 by the Elders and members of the German Religious Society called Seven-day Baptists at Ephrata...it appeared to said conference that Salome Atkinson, one of the Sisters of the said society, has for a length of time past created great disorder and Confusion in the said society and lives in open Violation of their Civil and religious principles...We the Elders and Members of the said society...so declare the said Salome Atkinson be henceforth suspended and Disbarred from all Rights and Privileges of the Society Whatsoever."

Salome tossed her nose and skirts at the Cloister by marrying Mayer and moving to Harrisburg. There Mayer began publishing the Harrisburger Morgenrithe newspaper in 1799. Despite an intellectual bent suggested by the large and varied library detailed in his will, Mayer's character and devotion to Salome, then in her mid-forties, are suspect.

In a letter to Jacob Hibschman, he cites the melancholy death of Salome's grandchild in a kettle of boiling water, and remarks, "...the old woman has a mind to go to Virginia." Although he made no effort to send Salome to her grieving daughter, he lost no time

133

remarrying on August 1, 1809, following Salome's death in March of the same year.

Perhaps Mayer's true character is best described by Mathew Atkinson in a letter he sent to Jacob Hibschman in August 1809. Besides lamenting his personal and financial woes, he says, "…as to old Mayer, I have but little regard or ever had, or ever shall have because his treatment to me has been base and malicious, and for all that ever he did for me, which was little or nothing, I thank him not…I wish him a heartfelt repentance of the many crimes which I believe him to have been guilty of, that he may go again to Ephrata and seclude himself in the brother house, a fit place for his repentance and amendment, a fit companion for the bats and midnight screech owl which no doubt infest that place."

DESCENDANTS OF STEPHEN ATKINSON I

Generation No. 1

I. Stephen Atkinson I was born in England and died in Lancaster County, Pennsylvania. In early manhood he came to this country as an emigrant with William Penn. He married (1) **Unknown**. He married (2) **Margaret Thornbury** March 02, 1735/36. The daughter of a Quaker, she was born in New Jersey and died in Lancaster County, Pennsylvania. At the New Garden Monthly Meeting August 19, 1737, Margaret Thornbury was "complained of marriage out of meeting" (dismissed from the right to attend Quaker meeting because of her marriage to a member of the Church of England). In the History of the Family of Stephen Atkinson by his grandson, General Josiah Gorgas, Gilbert Cope, the Quaker genealogist, claims that he came as an infant with his father, who was named Thomas.

Child of **Stephen Atkinson** and **Unknown** is:
  i.   **Stephen Atkinson II.**

Children of **Stephen Atkinson** and **Margaret Thornbury** are:
  ii.   **Matthew Atkinson.** He moved to Washington County, Pennsylvania.
  iii.   **Wilton Atkinson**, b. Abt. 1745

135

iv. **Thomas Atkinson, Sr.,** b. 1751,
Lancaster County, Pennsylvania; d. 1794
Loudoun County, Virginia

v. **Robert Atkinson,** b. Aft. 1751; d.
Baltimore.

vi. **Nancy Atkinson.**

vii. **Hannah Atkinson.**

viii. **Margaret Atkinson.**

Generation No. 2

2. Stephen Atkinson II (Stephen 1) married **Unknown.**
According to Fragments of History of the Family
Stephen Atkinson, by his granddaughter, Sophia
Atkinson Gorgas, on the demise of his father, Stephen
came into possession of the bulk of the estate, but he
died early, leaving an only son, an infant. Through the
misconduct of the administrator, the infant son Stephen
was disinherited and the property passed into the hands
of the Ross family. His wife was a Holliday of the
family that founded Hollidaysburg, Pennsylvania.

3.Wilton Atkinson (Stephen 1) married **Unknown.** He
had several sons, one of whom, an eminent jeweler,
lived in Baltimore. He was married to a French woman
and had two daughters who married two brothers by the
name of **Styger** of Baltimore.

4. Thomas Atkinson, Sr. (Stephen 1) was born 1751 in
Lancaster County, Pennsylvania and died 1794 in
Loudoun County, Virginia. He married **Salome**

Weidner October 18, 1771 in St. Gabriel's Episcopal
Church of Reading, Amity Township, Berks County,
Pennsylvania, daughter of **Peter Weidner** and
Susannah Gitter. She was born January 07, 1755 in
Reading, Berks County, Pennsylvania, and died March
25, 1809 in Lancaster County, Pennsylvania. After
Thomas's death, she married **Benjamin Mayer** (spelled
Moyer in court records) in Lancaster County. Upon her
death Salome was buried by Rev. Philip Gloninger of
Salem Reformed Church in the church cemetery.
Persons buried in Salem's cemetery were later moved to
the Harrisburg Cemetery, but no record of the existence
or location of Salome's tombstone has been found.

Children of **Thomas Atkinson** and **Salome Weidner**
are:

    i.   **Elizabeth Atkinson,** b. September 09,
           1772, Berks County, Pennsylvania. d.
           May 04, 1811, Ephrata, Pennsylvania.

    ii.   **Sophia Atkinson**, b. May 08, 1777,
           Berks County, Pennsylvania; d.
           November 23, 1849, Rochester, Ohio

    iii. **Thomas Atkinson, Jr.,** b. July 11, 1781,
           Carlisle, Lancaster County,
           Pennsylvania; d. March 11, 1837,
           Woodcock, Crawford County,
           Pennsylvania.

    iv.   **Mathew Atkinson**, b. Aft. 1781,
           Cumberland, now Perry County,
           Pennsylvania; d. December 07, 1860,
           Harrisburg, Pennsylvania.

v.   **Sarah Atkinson,** b. Abt. 1778, Cumberland County, Pennsylvania; d. 1842, Cambridge, Ohio

vi.   **Penelope Atkinson**, b. Aug. 10, 1787, Alexandria, Virginia; d. Aft. 1860, Harrisburg, Pennsylvania.

vii.   **Susan Atkinson**, b. Oct. 15, 1789, Virginia.

5. Robert Atkinson (Stephen 1) was born Aft. 1751 and died in Baltimore. He married (?) **Hughes.**

According to Sophia Atkinson's "Fragments of History," Robert, the youngest son, married a lady of Pittsburgh by the name of Hughes. He removed to Baltimore, where he lived until his decease. He left a widow with two children. Nancy, the eldest, married a Mr. Davis of Lancaster County. They had two sons, both of whom died in the Indian War at St. Clair's defeat. One of them, the younger, Mathew, was captured and tortured by the Indians.

Child of **Robert Atkinson** and (?) **Hughes** is

i.   **Nancy Atkinson.**

6. Hannah Atkinson (Stephen I). She married **James Brown.**

According to Sophia Atkinson's "Fragments of History," Hannah was married to a Mr. James Brown of Lancaster, Pa., who left her a widow with several children. She supported herself and her family by teaching school. One of her sons, David, became a printer. After a time, the family moved to Philadelphia where David by his vocation supported his mother and younger sister Margaret, who lived with her elder sister.

Generation No. 3

7. **Elizabeth Atkinson** (Thomas 2, Stephen 1) was born September 09, 1772 in Berks County, Pennsylvania and died May 04, 1811 in Ephrata, Pennsylvania. She married **Jacob Hibschman** Abt. 1792 in Ephrata. He was born 1771 in Ephrata, Pennsylvania and died 1852 in Lancaster County, Pennsylvania.

Notes for Elizabeth Atkinson:
Known also as Betsy, she was the oldest daughter of Thomas and Salome Atkinson. She was baptized on December 26, 1772 in St. Gabriel's Church, Berks County, Pennsylvania with both parents in attendance.

She had six or seven children between 1793 and 1807, but became deathly ill when the youngest child, John, was not yet four years old. Dr. Daniel Fehnestock, a physician associated with the Cloister/Seventh Day Baptist community, visited her on April 03, 1811, prescribing a preparation of digitalis. He dispensed medications on April 13, and again on April 15 and 23, but she died on May 04 at the age of 38. She was buried in the Hibschman family cemetery.

Notes for Jacob Hibschman:
He resided on North Church Street on a 50-acre farm willed to Wendel Hibschman by Wendel's father-

in-law, Johannes Heffley. Jacob was very talented and multi-faceted. He was a justice of the peace, a deputy surveyor of York, Lancaster, and Dauphin Counties, an associate Lancaster County judge (1810-1819) chairman of the board of canal appraisers, a Major General of the Pennsylvania Militia, and the organizer and first president of the Northern Mutual Insurance Company of Lancaster County. He also served a term (1819-1821) in the U.S. House of Representatives in the Sixteenth Congress, defeating James Buchanan for the sea and being in turn defeated by him when running for re-election. When General Lafayette visited the U.S. in 1824, Jacob Hibschman was named chairman of the committee appointed to welcome him to Lancaster County and was accorded the honor of introducing the General to the surviving veterans of the Revolution gathered to pay tribute to him. The Hibschman papers are housed in Pattee Library, Pennsylvania State University, State College, Pennsylvania.

Children of **Elizabeth Atkinson** and **Jacob Hibschman** are:

    i.   **Mary Polly Hibschman,** b. April 04, 1793; d. March 27, 1823, Reamstown, Pennsylvania; m. **Curtis Ream.** Buried Ream-Reddig cemetery, Reamstown.

    ii.   **Lydia Hibschman,** b. January 30, 1797; d. January 01, 1869.

    iii.   **Edward Hibschman** b. January 16, 1799; m. **Mary Sweitzer** buried Hibschman Cemetery.

    iv.   **Liza Hibschman**, b. January 1802; d. August 13, 1886.

140

v.	**Jacob Hibschman**, b. January 03, 1803, Ephrata, Pennsylvania; d. January 08, 1802.
vi.	**Amelia Hibschman**, b. May 17, 1804, Ephrata, Pennsylvania; d. October 06, 1851; m. **Samuel Bauman/Bowman;** buried Bowman's cemetery, Ephrata.
vii.	**John Hibschman**, b. March 07, 1807, Ephrata, Pennsylvania; d. October 15, 1871, Ephrata, Pennsylvania.

8. Sophia Atkinson (Thomas 2, Stephen 1) was born May 08, 1777 in Berks County, Pennsylvania and died November 23, 1849 in Rochester, Ohio. She married **Joseph Gorgas** June 02, 1794 in Ephrata, Lancaster County, Pennsylvania, son of **Jacob Gorgas** and **Christina Mack**. He was born April 17, 1770 in Ephrata, Lancaster County, Pennsylvania, and died May 27, 1841 in Louisville, Ohio.

Sophia Atkinson was baptized April 02, 1778 at St. Gabriel's Church of Reading, Berks County, Pennsylvania with her parents both in attendance.

Notes for Sophia Atkinson:

The financial struggles of Sophia and Joseph Gorgas were partially detailed by their affectionate son, Solomon Atkinson Gorgas, and copied by his descendants. They lived first at Ephrata, where they operated a sawmill, "but were obliged to work very hard and practice the extreme of frugality in order to live at all. In 1798, the family moved to Running Pumps, two miles west of Elizabethtown, where they operated a cotton processing mill; they prospered, but lost their money through a friend's economic downfall. In 1818, they traveled to the Valley of Fishing Creek, 5 miles north of Harrisburg, "experienced great hardship and disappointment," and moved to the opposite side of the Susquehanna in 1820. In 1830, they lived in Jackson Township, Lebanon County, near Myerstown. Ultimately, they settled in Louisville, Ohio.

Notes for Joseph Gorgas:

Taught by his father, Joseph Gorgas could make from crude materials an eight-day wall clock with all its parts finely polished and finished, including the wooden case. He could go into the wood shop or the blacksmith shop and build a four-or ten-house road wagon complete, or a "Dearborn" or a pleasure carriage, a wheel-barrow, a flour barrel, a wash tub, a plow, an organ or a piano, doing all the work required. He was passionately fond of music and could easily arrange a piece into different parts and for different instruments.

He performed on the organ and piano and was for years the organist for sacred music. He was unusually strong and robust: broad-shouldered, full chested, with large muscles. He was about 5 feet 9 inches tall, slow in speech, of ardent quick temperament, affable, and kind and courageous. He had dark hair and features and dark brown eyes. He spoke good English but was fond of using German with his acquaintances. In his childhood and youth, he attended the schools of "Eineamen" at Ephrata where the teaching was mainly in German of a pure, high order. He was 25 when he married Sophia Atkinson and she was 17. They removed to the sawmill belonging to his father, some three or four miles up the Cocalico from Ephrata. Four years later, they sold the sawmill house and moved to "Running Pumps" two miles west of Elizabethtown on the Lancaster Pike, purchasing their house June 12, 1806.

A constant stream of travel and merchandise passed to and from the west, so they opened a hotel with barn and outbuildings. He engaged in various enterprises: farming, a cotton factory, keeping of the Running Pumps Hotel, which was often overflowing. Sophia and her corps of helpers managed and cred for it. They were prosperous for a number of years until he became surety for a dear friend, Ulrich Shartle, for $5,000.00, he had to pay the greater part of this to extricate himself. In addition, he had to sell the hotel property on March 09, 1813. The buyers, Christina and Isaac Ober, paid him $2,480. He then turned his attention to the cotton factory, farming, and clock making. Jacob and Thomas helped him, while William, Charles, Sarah and Mary helped spin and weaver the cotton. It was a hard life, so they moved in 1818 to the Valley of Fishing Creek where they had even more hardships and disappointments, including sickness.

When all were stricken with fever, hardly anyone was left to hand the others a drink of water. After two years, William left home to learn the trade of carpenter and joiner. The family moved in the fall of 1820 to the opposite side of the Susquehanna River to a lovely tract of land, all cleared and under good cultivation, a commodious brick dwelling, a large barn, numerous out-buildings, and two or three slave chattels.

Children of **Sophia Atkinson** and **Joseph Gorgas** are:

i. **Jacob Gorgas**, b. August 16, 1795, Ephrata, Lancaster County, Pennsylvania; d. March 23, 1874.

ii. **William Gorgas.** b. November 08, 1797, Ephrata; d. December 25, 1853.

iii. **Thomas Gorgas,** b. January 09, Running Pumps, Pennsylvania; m. **Hannah Cline**. He was buried at Greentown, Ohio.

iv. **Sarah Gorgas** b. February 06, 1802, Running Pumps, Lancaster County, Pennsylvania; d. March 22, 1869.

v. **Charles Rittenhouse Gorgas,** b. April 08, 1804, Running Pumps, Lancaster County, Pennsylvania; d. January 08, 1892; m. (1) **Mary Snavely (Shively)**; m. (2) **Sarah Graeffe**.

Notes for Charles Rittenhouse Gorgas:

He was a physician. He was buried in Wooster Cemetery, Wooster, Ohio, lot 973 Section 4.

vi. **Mary Salome Gorgas**, b. August 10, 1806, Running Pumps, Lancaster County, Pennsylvania; d. October 29, 1869.

vii. **Elizabeth Gorgas**, b. March 12, 1809, Running Pumps, Lancaster; m. **Daniel Chapman**; buried Lyons, Wayne County, New York,

viii. **Christina Gorgas**, b. February 12, 1812, Running Pumps, Lancaster County, Pennsylvania; d. July 07, 1900.

ix. **Solomon Atkinson Gorgas**, b. July 11, 1815, Ephrata, Pennsylvania; d. January 18, 1898, Shelbyville, Indiana.

x. **Josiah Gorgas,** b. Fishing Creek, Pennsylvania; d. May 15, 1833, Tuscaloosa, Alabama.

9. **Thomas Atkinson, Jr.** (Thomas 2, Stephen 1) was born July 1, 1781 in Carlisle, Lancaster County, Pennsylvania and died March 11, 1837 in Woodcock, Crawford County, Pennsylvania. He married **Sarah Sommers** March 24, 1804 in Harrisburg, Pennsylvania, daughter of **Leonard Sommers** and **Elizabeth Philippe**. She was born November 28, 1787 in Germantown, Pennsylvania and died April 01, 1875 in Meadville, Crawford County, Pennsylvania.

Notes for Thomas Atkinson, Jr.:

Thomas Atkinson's legacy is found in his words and opinions published during the years he was Editor and Publisher of the Crawford Messenger, Meadville, Pennsylvania.

After marrying Sarah Sommers, he removed to Meadville, Crawford County, Pennsylvania in the fall of 1804. On January 02, 1805, he issued the first number of the Crawford Weekly Messenger, which he published until March 1833, when he retired from business.

The Crawford County Historical Society holds a copy of The Tribune Republican, Meadville, Pennsylvania, dated September 23, 1953, in which one editorial states: Pioneer Good Citizen – One of the privileges of living in a community such as ours, with its rich historical background is to be able to study the careers of Crawford County's good citizens. Thomas Atkinson, who founded the weekly Crawford Messenger in 1805, was one of those good citizens...only one man among many whose vision and labor for the French Creek Valley settlement had profound influence on the history of this area...

He came here as a young man of 23 with his bride of 17 in the late fall of 1804. Save for a few household goods and a printing press, his worldly goods were few. Within a few weeks, he had set up his home and a print shop in a log house on Center Street and Water Street. In this shop, on the historic morning of January 02, 1805, he struck off the No 1 issue of the messenger, the first newspaper published in the Northwestern Pennsylvania territory and only the fourth in the country west of Pittsburgh.

The youthful editor persevered in what he himself termed "an arduous and expensive task" in the face of many hazards: Frequent non-delivery of paper stock which had to be carried by pack horse along wilderness trails for 130 miles, raids on his shops by drunk-crazed marauding Indians, problems in getting and keeping partners and employees and in collecting bills from subscribers and other customers. He made of his little weekly news sheet a stout vehicle for news and community service and, incidentally, a precious source book for the lore of Northwestern Pennsylvania in the 1805-1835 period.

Yet even more impressive than his career as editor-printer was the record of T. Atkinson's vastly versatile activities on behalf of the community in many other fields. He was our first Chamber of Commerce secretary holding that office in the Meadville Society for

Encouragement of Domestic Manufactures and Useful Arts, founded in 1807 with Major Roger Alden as president. He served as first burgess of the Borough of Meadville, as County Commissioner 1810-1813, County Treasurer 1820-1822, and as Crawford County Representative to the Pennsylvania State Legislature 1826-27 and 1833-1836. He was one of the founders and charged trustee of Allegheny College, helped organize the Protestant Episcopal Church, and in 1814 was a co-founded with John Alden of the first Sunday School in Meadville, the Crawford County Sabbath School Union. He died March 11, 1837 after a long illness, leaving his wife and nine children"

Notes for Sarah Sommers:

Sarah (Sally) Sommers was the daughter of Leonard Sommers and Elizabeth Philippe of Germantown, PA. Leonard was born April 18, 1759 in Switzerland where his father, Leonhard Somers, was persecuted for his religious beliefs. Leonard served in the Revolutionary War. He and Elizabeth were married in Germantown on Mary 12, 1778. After the war, they moved to Lancaster County, where Elizabeth died in 1841.

Egle's Notes and Queries XXVII p. 182 cites a notice in a Dauphin County newspaper: Atkinson-Sommers. On Saturday, March 14, 1804, by the Rev. Mr. Peterson, Thomas Atkinson, printer, to the agreeable Miss Sally Sommers, all of this borough.

Children of **Thomas Atkinson** and **Sarah Sommers** are:

i. **Henrietta Atkinson**, b. Abt. 1805, Meadville, Crawford County, Pennsylvania; d. 1881, Meadville, Crawford County, Pennsylvania; m. **Thomas Harman.**

ii. **Salome Atkinson**, b. Abt. 1807, Meadville, Crawford County, Pennsylvania; d. September 18, 1842.

iii. **Eliza Atkinson**, b. Abt. 1810, Meadville, Pennsylvania. Never married.

iv. **Sarah Ann Atkinson,** b. January 04, 1812, Meadville, Crawford County, Pennsylvania; d. April 01, 1875.

v. **Thomas Sommer Atkinson,** b. Bef. 1814, Meadville, Pennsylvania.

vi. **Sophia Atkinson,** b. Abt. 1816.

vii. **Lydia Augusta Atkinson** b. Abt. 1820, Meadville, Pennsylvania; d. Meadville, Crawford County, Pennsylvania.

viii. **Mary Adelaide Atkinson**, b. Abt. 1822, Meadville, Pennsylvania; d. Janesville, Wisconsin; m. (1) **George W. McElroy**; m. (2) **Harman S. Conger,** a judge in Janesville.

ix. **Monroe Atkinson**, b. February 19, 1825, Meadville, Pennsylvania.

x. **Francis Atkinson,** b. Abt. 1827, Meadville, Crawford County, d. in childhood in Meadville.

xi. **Lehman Atkinson**, b 1828, Meadville, Crawford County, Pennsylvania

Notes for Lehman Atkinson:

The Crawford Messenger dated September 4, 1828, has this notice: Departed this life on Monday last, Lehman, infant son of the editor of this paper. "Of such is the kingdom of Heaven." Since the paper usually was issued on Wednesday, it is assumed that he died on Monday, September 2. He may have died shortly after birth.

10. **Mathew Atkinson** (Thomas 2, Stephen 1) was born Aft. 1781 in Cumberland, now Perry County, and died December 07, 1860 in Harrisburg, Pennsylvania. He married **Caroline Reubendorf/Rabenthal** August 03, 1804 in Northumberland, Pennsylvania. She died bef. 1860.

Notes for Mathew Atkinson:

Like his brother, Thomas Atkinson, Jr., Mathew was a printer. He and his wife, Caroline Rabenthal, or Reubendorf, lived in Lancaster, Pennsylvania. They must have been members of the Moravian Church, as two of their children, Thomas and Mathew, were baptized there.

According to the third installment of the Atkinson-Mayer Hibschman Family, by Cynthia Marquet, Library of the Historical Society of Cocalico Valley, Ephrata, Pennsylvania, information from a descendant indicates that Mathew Atkinson and his wife, Caroline Rabenthal, had a total of twelve children, but only one, a son named Reuben, lived as long, or nearly as long as his father. This has not been documented.

We know that three of the couple's sons died at Lancaster when the family lived there. In addition to Thomas and Mathew, Frederick, named for his uncle Frederick Albright, died suddenly in Lancaster "in his 18th year" in March of 1826. A letter from Mathew to Jacob Hibschman from Staunton, Augusta County, Virginia dated August 06, 1809 details the family's travels from Harrisburg to Hagerstown, Maryland and from there to Staunton. He asked Hibschman to send his employer, General Brown, Judge of the Chancery Court, a distiller to manage some of General Brown's operations. Mathew said that he was a plantation overseer for the General "with whom I intend staying one year, more than three months of which are elapsed...he gives me 120 dollars a year, 5000 weight of meat, food for two cows, besides house rent free, and my bread...I have become accustomed to all manner of hard work, such as cradling, mowing, ploughing, chopping...I have good Negroes to manage, who strictly obey my orders...The place I work contains better than one thousand acres, one half of which is cleaned, situated in the vicinity of Staunton...We have had four children, the youngest 11 days old, two boys we have buried, one in Hagerstown and one in Staunton...of the two that are living, one is a girl and the other a boy...the girl is named Sally, and the youngest has not yet received a name. We leave it to Betsy, your wife, and Sophia (Atkinson Gorgas) to give it a name, and whichever of the two names we like best we shall adopt." It is possible that the unnamed baby boy was the son Frederick who died in Lancaster early in 1826 in his 18th year. Letters and other records indicate that there were at least ten children.

By 1813, Mathew Atkinson was in Lancaster. For a time, he boarded Hibschman's daughter Eliza, whose mother had died. In October of 1813, he wrote to her father to ask for her board, and he mentions another child on the way. His four surviving letters to Jacob Hibschman indicate that he was well-educated, expressive with language, financially hopeful but without apparent reserve, somewhat restless like his father, and warmly opinionated. A letter to Hibschman on August 1809 says: I have encountered many painful vicissitudes of fortune,…at several times I have been on the confines of the yawning grave…dangers seen and unseen have encompassed me…it is with a considerable degree of pleasure that I can inform you that I have experienced a reformation in my life, for I do not pretend to deny that some years back my conduct was such as very poorly corresponded with the character of a Christian; I was a good deal given to the vices which are prevalent in this degenerate and perverse generation. But I bless God that I have seen the folly of all these vanities, and that I felt no desire to return to the practices of the same again. I received an account of the death of my mother a short time after it happened. I have continually felt a grief because of her sudden exit from us, as I had fondly expected to have seen her before she bid us an eternal farewell."

Mathew's letters and public records confirm that he worked as an overseer on a Virginia plantation, as a printer in Lancaster, and in 1821 he rented the Sign of the Plough Tavern on West King Street from George Ackerman. He left Lancaster County probably before 1839 and in the 1850s, approaching the end of his life, he arrived at the Harrisburg home of Widener Boyer, his nephew and son of his sister, Penelope Fremole. He died in December 1860 and is buried in Harrisburg in the same plot where Penelope was later buried. According to Howard Widener, whose book on the Widener family was published in 1904, Mathew died at the home of another niece, Penelope's sister Mary Fremole Olewine, and was buried from the Harrisburg home of his nephew, Weidner Boyer. The source of this story, in which Mathew arrives at the Olewine home broken in health and in the company of his sole surviving child, Reuben, is unknown, but there is no reason to doubt it. The 1860 census, taken in August of that year, does not include Mathew or Reuben in the Olewine's Susquehanna Township home or in Weidner Boyer's household, or at any other Pennsylvania location. He must have arrived at Olewine's in the autumn and died within three months. Benjamin and Mary Olewine and their son, daughter-in-law, and granddaughter were later buried, in turn, next to him and Penelope Fremole.

Caroline Reubendorf, whose life as a parent was every bit as hard as that of her husband, predeceased him, but her date of death is unknown. Even though Mathew was ungrateful to Benjamin Mayer for instructing him in the printing trade, he followed it for decades.

Children of **Mathew Atkinson** and **Caroline Reubendorf/Rabenthal** are:

     i.   **Sally Atkinson.**
     ii.   **Frederick Atkinson,** b. 1808; d. 1826.
     iii   **Thomas Atkinson,** b. October 01, 1815.

Notes for Thomas Atkinson:

He was baptized October 06, 1815, five days after he was born and designated "sick in the Lancaster Moravian Church. In 1850, then 35 years old, he lived in the Lancaster County Hospital, or Poorhouse, and was classed by the census-taker as an "idiot." This was a broad categorization used for all manner of mental disability and illness, but since Thomas was recognized as being ill at birth, is might be assumed that his condition was lifelong, perhaps something like cerebral palsy.

iv.   **Mathew Atkinson,** b. April 02, 1819, Lancaster, Pennsylvania; d. April 01, 1819.

v.   **Caroline Atkinson**, b. 1813; d. February 1849, Lancaster County, Pennsylvania.

vi.   **Charles Atkinson**, b; October 10, 1822; d. December 04, 1847, Lancaster, Pennsylvania, at the home of his father.

vii.   **Reuben Atkinson.**

Notes for Reuben Atkinson:

He was possibly the male child born July 25 or 26, 1809 in Staunton, Virginia, or the child expected "in one of two weeks," October 26, 1813. He is mentioned by genealogist Howard Widener, and also by Jay Widener as Mathew's only child who survived him, and the only child known to either Widener by name. Was his name derived from his mother's maiden name?

11. **Sarah Atkinson** (Thomas 2, Stephen 1) was born Abt. 1778 in Cumberland County, Pennsylvania, and

died 1842 in Cambridge, Ohio. She married **Frederick Albright** December 09, 1802 in Harrisburg, Pennsylvania. He was born in Germany, and died 1841 in Cambridge, Ohio.

Notes for Sarah Atkinson:

Sarah Atkinson married Dr. Frederick Albright, a Prussian immigrant. The couple moved as frequently as Joseph and Sophia Gorgas did. They are known to have been at Martinsburg, (West) Virginia in 1806, at Carlisle in 1811 and at least until 1816. They were in Bedford County between 1820 and 1824, and then in Allegheny County. They finally settled in Cambridge, Ohio at the home of their son, B. A. Albright, in 1832 and remained at Cambridge until their deaths in 1841 and 1842. The couple's property was compromised by physical disability; Dr. Albright gradually lost his eyesight during the period that the family lived in Bedford County and is said to have been completely blind for the last 18 years of his life.

Notes for Frederick Albright:

Frederick Albright was a German doctor. He and Sarah later moved to Cambridge, Ohio where he became Senator Albright. Egle's Notes and Queries XXVII p. 182 announces the marriage in Harrisburg, PA of Frederick Albright and Sarah (Sally) Atkinson and notes, "my dear Doctor Frederick Albright, late from Germany, via Lancaster and Hummelstown, but now of this town, to Miss Sally Atkinson, daughter of the late Mrs. Atkinson, now ycleped the consort of Mr. Benjamin Mayer, printer, of this borough."

Children of **Sarah Atkinson** and **Frederick Albright** are:

> i.   **Anna Nancy Albright**, b. Abt. 1805; d. September 03, 1806, Martinsburg, Virginia.

Notes for Anna Nancy Albright:

A letter written by Benjamin Mayer from Harrisburg to Jacob Hibschman was dated between 1805 and September of 1807: Sir, I have to inform you of a melancholy catastrophe, vic. Nancy Albright lost her Life by a Fall backwards into a Kettle with boiling Water, her mother being present, and took her out immediately. She lived 24 hours after it, and then she expired.

> ii.   **Eliza Albright,** b. Abt. 1811; d. Bef. 1841. Eliza Albright was mentioned by her mother as "a very fine baby: in a letter written from Carlisle, January 1811.
>
> iii. **Frederick Albright.** He lived in Cambridge, Guernsey County, Ohio in 1841.
>
> iv.   **B. A. Albright**.

Notes for B.A. Albright:

A letter written by B. A. Albright to his cousin, Edward Hibschman, Jacob's son, said that the whole family was settled in Cambridge, Ohio and Sarah and Frederick had eight grandchildren. B. A. Albright was living in Cambridge, Ohio in 1841.

v.   **Sarah Albright**.

vi.   **Charles Albright,** b. May 09, 1816; d. October 21, 1855, Cambridge, Ohio; m. **Nancy Birchard**. Charles Albright was a member of the 34th Ohio State Congress and held a great many political posts and appointments. He also published the Guernsey Times between 1848 and 1855.

vii.   **Unknown Daughter Albright.**

Notes for Unknown Daughter

According to Cynthia Marquet, there were seven children in the Albright family. This child apparently died before reaching maturity. Nancy was termed the "oldest daughter" upon her death in 1806. This implies that there was another girl in the household at time, and Eliza would not have been born yet though is it possible that Sarah was.

12. **Penelope Atkinson** (Thomas 2, Stephen 2, Stephen 1) was born August 10, 1787 in Alexandria, Virginia, and died aft. 1860 in Harrisburg, Pennsylvania. She married **William W. Boyer** Abt. 1810.

Notes for Penelope Atkinson:

She is listed in the 1830 Dauphin County census under her maiden name, as a head of household in Harrisburg in 1850, still recorded at Penelope Atkinson and living in the home of her son. She died at Harrisburg on December 06, 1864 and is buried in the Harrisburg

Cemetery under the name Penelope Boyer.

Child of **Penelope Atkinson** and **Willliam Boyer** is:

i.   **Widener William Boyer**, b. January 06, 1811, Lancaster, Pennsylvania; d. September 23, 1892.

Notes for Widener William Boyer:

Widener Boyer, a coachmaker, lived on Chestnut Street in Harrisburg all his adult life. His dwelling was described in 1888 by his first cousin Solomon Atkinson Gorgas as "a pattern of neatness, cleanliness, and comfort, a pleasant home, the reward...of a long life of patient toil and careful frugal living...: Dr. Byron James Reemsnyder of Hinkletown honeymooned in Harrisburg in 1871 and took care to visit Weidner Boyer while there; Dr. Reemsnyder's grandmother, Eliza Hibschman Gray, was Boyer's first cousin.

13. **Susan Atkinson** (Thomas 2, Stephen 1) was born October 15, 1789 in Alexandria, Virginia. She married **William Fremole** September 17, 1807 in Harrisburg, Pennsylvania. She was listed as a Harrisburg head of household in the 1830 Dauphin County census. Therefore, her husband may have died earlier. The place and date of her death are unknown.

Children of **Susan Atkinson** and **William Fremole** are:

i.   **Penelope Fremole**, b. January 07, 1808; d. January 16, 1812. Buried in Harrisburg Cemetery, Harrisburg, Pennsylvania

ii.	**Johann Fremole**, b, April 17, 1810; m. Catherine (?)
iii.	**Mary Elizabeth Fremole**, b. 1812; d. December 09, 1891; buried Harrisburg Cemetery; m. **Benjamin Olewine**, December 06, 1832, Harrisburg, Pennsylvania.; buried Harrisburg Cemetery
iv.	**Salome Fremole** m. (?) **Young**. The places and dates of birth and death of Salome Fremole are unknown. She is said to have married a Mr. Young and moved "west."

14. Nancy Atkinson (Robert 2, Stephen1). She married (?) **Davis**

Children of **Nancy Atkinson** and (?) **Davis** are:

i.	**Unknown Davis.**
ii.	**Mathew Davis.**

Generation No. 4

15. Eliza Hibschman (Elizabeth 3 Atkinson, Thomas 2, Stephen 1) was born January 1802 and died August 13, 1886. She married **Henry Gray.** She is buried in Bethany (Cocalico) Cemetery, Ephrata, Pennsylvania. Henry Gray was a physician

Children of **Eliza Hibschman** and **Henry Gray** are:

i.	**James Gray.**

ii.   **Charles Gray.**

iii.   **Mary Gray**, m. (?) **Reemsnyder**

16. **John Hibschman** (Elizabeth 3 Atkinson, Thomas 2, Stephen 1) was born March 07, 1807 in Ephrata, Pennsylvania and died October 15, 1871 in Ephrata, Pennsylvania. He married **Magdalena Shirk.**

Notes for John Hibschman:

    According to Cynthia Marquet citing earlier sources, John Hibschman traveled to Ohio in his youth (in Stark County he found the inhabitants "generally speaking not so wild" and "more saving with their money" than those in Lancaster County) but returned to his birthplace and inherited the 50-acre family homestead after Jacob Hibschman's death. He was buried in Hibschman family cemetery.

Child of **John Hibschman** and **Magdalena Shirk** is:

    i.   **Amelia Hibschman**; m. **Jacob Craig.** He was a teacher in Chester, Pennsylvania.

17. **Jacob Gorgas** (Sophia 3 Atkinson, Thomas 2, Stephen 1) was born August 16,1795 in Ephrata, Lancaster County, Pennsylvania, and died March 23,1874. He married **Catherine Ober** 1818. An aunt of Jacob Gorgas, Susan Atkinson Fremole, was a witness to his wedding ceremony. He was buried Graceland, Chicago, Illinois.

Child of **Jacob Gorgas** and **Catherine Ober** is:

    i.   **Daughter Gorgas**, m. **Dr. Webb**.

18. **William Gorgas** (Sophia 3 Atkinson, Thomas 2, Stephen 1) was born November 08, 1797 in Ephrata, Lancaster County, Pennsylvania, and died December 25, 1853. He married **Hannah Bossler**. She died August 29, 1876 in Pine Grove, Pennsylvania. William Gorgas was buried in Dixon, Illinois.

Child of **William Gorgas** and **Hannah Bossler** is:

    i.   **Sarah Gorgas.**

19. **Sarah Gorgas** (Sophia 3 Atkinson, Thomas 2, Stephen1) was born February 06, 1802 in Running Pumps, Lancaster County, Pennsylvania, and died March 22, 1869. She married **Philip Dorsheimer**. He died April 1868 in Buffalo, New York. Both were buried in Buffalo, New York.

Notes for Sarah Gorgas:

    In his Journals, Josiah Gorgas said on April 13, 1868: Rec'd a letter tonight from Buffalo saying that Mr. Philip Dorsheimer, husband of Sarah, was on his death-bed, and sent kind messages to me, but there is no doubt bitter feeling against all "rebels," and I do not look for good feeling from northern friends or relatives…

Children of **Sarah Gorgas** and **Philip Dorsheimer** are:

i.   **Elizabeth Dorsheimer**, m. **Harry Clifton,** b. England.

ii.   **William Edward Dorsheimer**. b. Feb. 05, 1832, Lyons, New York; d. March 26, 1888, Savannah, Georgia.

Notes for William Dorsheimer:

He was a lawyer and lieutenant governor of New York. On October 02, 1876, Solomon Gorgas noted that he stopped at Brainard's Hall to hear his nephew, Gov. William Dorsheimer, speak. "So were led up into the Gallery near the close. He is a handsome man and made a very enthusiastic and good democratic address. He did not see us or know about our presence."

William Dorsheimer was educated at Andover Academy and Harvard College. He was admitted to the bar in 1854 and practiced law in Buffalo, New York. During the Civil War, he served on the staff of John C. Fremont in the summer of 18651 before returning to Buffalo to practice law. In 1867, President Johnson appointed him federal district attorney for southern New York a post that he held until he resigned in 1871 to support the presidential efforts of Horace Greeley. He attended the Liberal Republican convention in 1872 and was elected lieutenant governor of New York in 1874 and 1876. In 1882, he was elected to the U. S. House of Representatives where he served on the judiciary committee. An active supporter of Grover Cleveland, Dorsheimer was appointed again as federal district attorney for southern New York in 1885. He soon resigned to operate the New York Star, an unsuccessful newspaper venture. In ill health in 1887, he moved to Savannah, Georgia, where he died on March 26, 1888.

SILHOUETTES OF JOSEPH GORGAS AND SOPHIA ATKINSON

Courtesy of Michelle Gorham Clifton

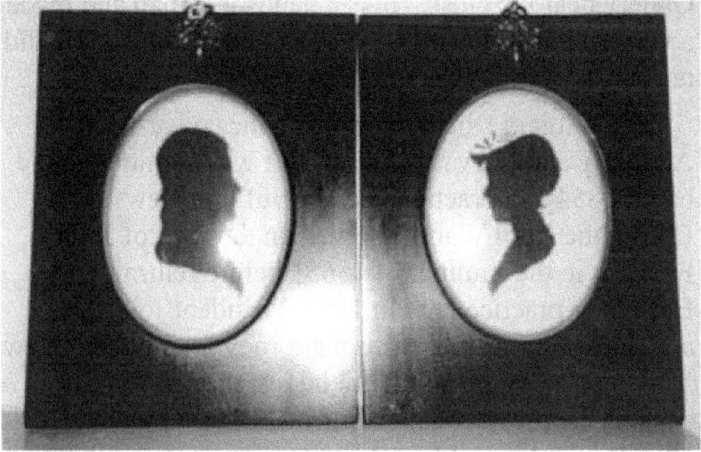

Philip Miller Dorsheimer
Owner of the Mansion House
in Buffalo, NY
Finest Hotel in Buffalo at the time
Apr 13 1797 in Darmstadt, Germany-
Apr 11 1868 in Buffalo, NY

Married Aug 23 1821
in Harrisburg, PA

Sarah Gorgas
Feb 3 1802-Mar 22 1869
Daughter of Joseph Gorgas
and
Sophia Atkinson

20. **Mary Salome Gorgas** (Sophia 3 Atkinson, Thomas 2, Stephen 1) was born August 10, 1806 in Running Pumps, Lancaster County, Pennsylvania, and died

October 29, 1869. She married **George Schlosser** Abt.
1834 in Ohio, son of **John Schlosser** and **Barbara
Minck**. He was born February 06, 1813 in Gettysburg,
Pennsylvania, and died July 03, 1902 in Paxton, Illinois.

Notes for Mary Salome Gorgas:

According to Frances E. Taft, Mary Gorgas
Schlosser died from cancer of the breast. She was buried
in Paxton, Illinois. George Schlosser was a minister,
Rev. George Schlosser. He was one of a family of 13
children, all boys but one, a sister Barbara who died in
childbirth, He was born on what is now the Gettysburg
Battlefield.

Child of **Mary Gorgas** and **George Schlosser** is:

    i.   **Frances E. Schlosser,** m. (?) **Taft**.

Notes for Frances Schlosser Taft:

She compiled the Gorgas family history,
unpublished.

21. **Christina Gorgas** (Sophia 3 Atkinson, Thomas 2,
Stephen 1) was born February 12, 1812 in Running
Pumps, Lancaster County, Pennsylvania, and died July
07, 1900. She married **Jonathan Zerbe**. She was buried
in Massillon Cemetery, Massillon, Ohio, Section 16, Lot
19.

Notes for Christina Gorgas:

In his Journals, Josiah Gorgas wrote on Sunday,
July 14, 1867; I had a letter a few days ago from my

sister Christina (Gorgas Zerbe) whom I have not heard from for 8 or 9 years. I do not know that it gives me much pleasure to revive communication with kindred who live among and sympathize with those who have so much oppressed us, but I used to be strongly attached to this sister who is the youngest of my sisters and is only five years my senior.

Children of **Christina Gorgas** and **Jonathan Zerbe** are:

    i.   **Ella Zerbe.**

    ii.   **Ida Zerbe,** d. Germantown, Pennsylvania

    iii.   **Rome Zerbe.**

22. **Solomon Atkinson Gorgas** (Sophia 3 Atkinson, Thomas 2, Stephen 1) was born July 11, 1815 in Ephrata, Pennsylvania and died January 18, 1898 in Shelbyville, Indiana. He married **Marie Frances Vier**.

Notes for Solomon Atkinson Gorgas:

According to Cynthia Marquet, Solomon Atkinson Gorgas was a successful hardware merchant at Shelbyville, and was also of a poetic turn. When he visited his Lancaster County birthplace at Running Pumps, two miles west of Elizabethtown, he wrote, "The Running Pumps." Here for the first time in my life I am gratified in my longings and dreams of a lifetime by the sight of and visit to that locality where I was born. Where my dear father and mother lived when they were young...It is now noon and the loveliest of bright summer days and here as I stand in the roadway is a picture which memory has treasured since childhood like a dream, now verified by its actual appearance before me just as I had retained it in my memory and just as I have often recalled it to my mind since a child about three years old. The gratification is indescribable – never before have I more enjoyed an event in my life."

Solomon Gorgas, his daughter Nellie, and his sister Sarah Gorgas Dorsheimer visited Josiah and Amelia Gorgas in Maine, according to Gorgas's entry in his Journals on September 20, 1857. No information is given about Nellie and/or her date of birth.

In his Journals, Josiah Gorgas remarked on November 05, 1869: My losses in running the furnace are about two thousand dollars; if pt. Alvis cannot pay me for the stock turned over to him, my losses will be fully four thousand dollars. In fact, all I had. The iron property is now offered for sale on the 13th of December, and if the money loaned to the Company is also lost, as I fear it will be, we shall be literally penniless. To increase the trouble, my brother Solomon declines to pay me the balance due me by him, which is about $1,500.

Children of **Solomon Atkinson Gorgas** and **Marie Vier** are:

    i.   **Nellie Gorgas**.

    ii.   **William Rittenhouse Gorgas**, b. May 08, 1806.

23. **Josiah Gorgas** (Sophia 3 Atkinson, Thomas 2, Stephen 1) was born July 01, Fishing Creek, Pennsylvania, and died May 15, 1883 in Tuscaloosa, Alabama. He married **Amelia Ross Gayle**, December

29, 1853 near Mount Vernon Arsenal, north of Mobile, Alabama, daughter of **John Gayle** and **Sarah Haynsworth**. She was born June 01, 1826 in Greensboro, Alabama, and died January 03, 1913 in Tuscaloosa, Alabama.

Notes for Josiah Gorgas:

General Josiah Gorgas was a West Point graduate. He served in the Mexican War and married Amelia Ross Gayle, daughter of an ex-governor of Virginia. He was a member of the nation's Ordnance Board at the outbreak of the Civil War, but he resigned his post to become Chief of Ordnance for the Confederate States of America. In 1877, he was elected President of the University of Alabama. He is mentioned in the memoirs of Jefferson Davis as follows: "remarkable for his scientific attainments, of the highest administrative capacity and mental purity, all crowned by zeal and fidelity to his trusts, in which he achieved results greatly disproportionate to the means at his command."

In his compilation of the Atkinson Family history, Josiah Gorgas notes that he lived in Lyons, Wayne County, NY between 1830 and 1835 and frequently visited with his sisters and their aunt, Elizabeth Taylor, on Lake Seneca near Geneva. He is buried in the Gorgas plot, Evergreen Cemetery, Tuscaloosa, Alabama.

Notes for Amelia Ross Gayle:

She lived with Mrs. Alva Woods for two years after her mother died. After her father remarried, she attended Columbia Female Institute in Columbia,

167

Tennessee. She accompanied her father to Washington when he was elected to the U.S. House of Representatives in 1847 and they lived in the same boarding house as John C. Calhoun of South Carolina and his family. Calhoun treated Amelia like a daughter.

Amelia became librarian of the University of Alabama after her husband suffered a stroke and was appointed librarian, a ghost position. Amelia and her older daughters carried out the work. In March 1886, she became university postmistress and in 1905, she was presented with a silver loving cup. She retired in 1907 at the age of 80 but continued to live in the Gorgas home on the campus of the University of Alabama until her death. She is buried in the Gorgas plot, Evergreen Cemetery, Tuscaloosa, Alabama.

Children of **Josiah Gorgas** and **Amelia Gayle** are:

i. **William Crawford Gorgas,** b. October 03,1854, Toumlinville, near Mobile, Alabama; d. July 04, 1920, Queen Alexandria Military Hospital, Millbank, England.

ii.. **Jesse Gorgas**, b. March 17, 1856, Mount Vernon, Alabama; d. September 13, 1925, Tuscaloosa, Alabama.

iii. **Mary Gayle "Mamie" Gorgas**, b. October 18, 1857, Augusta, Maine; d. December 27, 1944, Tuscaloosa, Alabama. She never married. She was Assistant librarian at the University of Alabama and lived in the Gorgas home until her death.

iv.   **Christina Amelia "Minnie" Gorgas**, b. June 04, 1859, Charleston, South Carolina; d. February 03, 1953, Tuscaloosa, Alabama.

v.   **Maria Bayne "Ria" Gorgas**, b. August 04, 1861, Charleston, South Carolina; d. June 11, 1953.

Notes for Maria Bayne "Ria" Gorgas:

She taught at Fairmount Female College Monteagle, Tennessee until 1880 when she moved to New York and entered nursing school. She remained there and became nurse-companion to a semi-invalid, traveling to Europe until 1904. She helped to plan a program of study for the care of the mentally ill for the nurses at Bryce Hospital, Alabama Insane Hospital, in Tuscaloosa. She never married, and by 1906 retired to live in the Gorgas home in Tuscaloosa. She is buried in the Gorgas plot, Evergreen Cemetery, Tuscaloosa, Alabama.

vi.   **Richard Haynsworth Gorgas**, b. November 03, 1864 Richmond, Virginia; d. September 29, 1935, Birmingham, Alabama.

Notes for Richard Haynsworth Gorgas:

He first studied medicine, then law, receiving an LL. B degree in 1890 from the University of Alabama, then practiced law in Florence, Alabama. In WWI, he was a captain in the Sanitary Corps stationed at Camp McClellan near Anniston, Alabama. He worked in

Washington as assistant attorney with the Veterans
Bureau and continued in government service until he
retired in 1931 to live in Tuscaloosa with his sisters
Mary and Maria Gorgas. He never married, and one
family member recalled that he was deeply in love with
his cousin Minna Bayne, one of the daughters of Maria
and T.L. Bayne. After a lengthy illness, he entered a
Birmingham hospital for a major operation and died the
next day. He was buried in the Gorgas plot, Evergreen
Cemetery, Tuscaloosa, Alabama.

24. Salome Atkinson (Thomas 3, Thomas 2, Stephen 1)
was born Abt. 1807 in Meadville, Crawford County,
Pennsylvania, and died September 18, 1842. She
married **John McFarland**, August 1825 in Meadville,
Crawford County, Pennsylvania, son of **John
McFarland** and **Margaret Forster**. He was born
February 13, 1800, probably in Lycoming County,
Pennsylvania, and died September 02, 1881 in
Meadville, Crawford County, Pennsylvania.

Notes for Salome Atkinson:

The Crawford Messenger dated September 01,
1825 has the following notice: Married on Thursday last
by the Rev. Mr. Alden, Mr. John McFarland to Miss
Saloma (sic) Atkinson, both of Meadville.

Notes for John McFarland:

John McFarland was a president of Allegheny
College, Meadville. He was the oldest son of Margaret
Forster Stuart by her first husband. He married two
Atkinson sisters, Salome first, then Augusta after her

170

death, saying that he found the Atkinson girls so charming he had to marry two of them.

Children of **Salome Atkinson** and **John McFarland** are:

    i.   **Thomas McFarland**.

    ii.   **John McFarland**.

    iii. **Archibald McFarland**.

    iv. **William McFarland**.

    v.   **Margaret McFarland**.

    vi. **George McFarland**.

    vii. **Georgina McFarland**.

25. **Sarah Ann Atkinson** (Thomas 3, Thomas 2, Stephen1) was born January 04, 1812 in Meadville, Crawford County, Pennsylvania, and died April 01, 1875 in Meadville, Crawford County, Pennsylvania. She married (1) **Edward Stebbins** December 03, 1829 in Meadville, Crawford County, Pennsylvania, son of **Edward Stebbins** and **Anna Taylor**. He was born October 26, 1793 in Springfield, Hampden County, Massachusetts, and died November 06, 1846 in Meadville, Crawford County, Pennsylvania. She married (2) **Joseph Douglas** Aft. 1847 in Meadville, Crawford County, Pennsylvania.

Notes for Sarah Ann Atkinson:

The Crawford Messenger dated December 03, 1839 has the following notice: Married yesterday evening by the Rev. Mr. James, Mr. Edward Stebbins to Miss Sally Ann Atkinson, all of this city.

An email from Dan Cahill August 06, 2001, contained a letter in his mother's possession from one of Joseph Douglas' children to her older sister. He said that his mother had several letters ranging from 1851 to 1853 and believes that Sally Ann and Joseph were married sometime in that time span. Joseph had several children from his first marriage to Harriet Williams.

A letter to Harriett Douglas McCandless from her 14-year-old sister, Agnes M. Douglas, the daughter of Joseph Douglas written from Meadville, March 24, 1852 includes mention of Sarah Atkinson Stebbins who was being courted at the time by her father: "Mrs. Stebbins has got two more of her angels here, Lizzie and Henry, my dear. I have expected it all along I guess. Father do not like it too well, but I do not care two snaps of your finger. They don't trouble me nor I them. I feel very independent."

The 1860 census for Meadville Borough, Crawford County, Pennsylvania lists on page 572 Joseph Douglas, age 61, head of household, Farmer, $9000 real estate and $2000 personal. Others In that household are Sarah age 48 (Sally Atkinson Stebbins), Wilson Douglas age 19 (idiotic), Adda Stebbins, age 16 (in the same column a sub-note indicates that she was married within the year.)

In the Sixth Concluding Installment of the Atkins-Mayer family papers by Cynthia Marquet, HSCV Librarian, the June 1997 Quarterly Issue of Cocalico Valley Footprints, published by the Historical Society of the Cocalico Valley, Ephrata, Pennsylvania, it is noted that Sarah Ann Atkinson later married Joseph Douglas. This would have been after the death of her first husband, Edward Stebbins. He died November 01, 1846 in Meadville, prior to the birth of their youngest daughter, Henrietta Atkinson Stebbins, who lived less than a year after her birth on February 10, 1847 in Meadville. Sally Ann died April 01, 1875. Therefore, she would have been 63 at the time of her death.

Notes for Edward Stebbins:

The August 01, 1823 issue of the Crawford Messenger has the following death notice: Mrs. Delilah Stebbins, died July 17, 1823. This was just one month after the marriage of Edward Stebbins and Miss Delilah Ellis was performed on June 24, 1823 by Rev. T. Alden. Therefore, Stebbins was a widower when he married Sarah Atkinson. He was an officer in the Episcopal church with her father, Thomas Atkinson, editor of the newspaper. He was buried in Meadville. (See Stebbins Family History.)

Children of **Sarah Atkinson** and **Edward Stebbins** are:

 i. **Edward E. Stebbins**, b. November 13, 1830, d. 1919, Mount Dora, Lake County, Florida.

 ii. **Thomas Atkinson Stebbins**, b. October 25, 1832, Meadville, Crawford County, Pennsylvania; d. January 26, 1921, Meadville, Crawford County, Pennsylvania.

 iii. **Elizabeth Ann Stebbins**, b. December 11, 1834, Meadville, PA; d. March 1897, Meadville, Pennsylvania.

 iv. **James Henry Stebbins** b. March 05, 1837; d. July 16, 1895, Meadville, PA.

Notes for James Henry Stebbins:

The obituary of James Henry Stebbins reads: "Well-Known Meadville Printer Dies Suddenly. James Henry Stebbins, as well-known printer of this city, was found lying in front of the boiler in the press room of the Tribune-Republican this morning, and upon examination it was found that life was extinct. The janitor in the office, Mr. S. C. Hitchcock, came about 5:30 and found Mr. Stebbins lying on his back in the hall. He assisted him to his feet and sat him down on a table and at Mr. Stebbins' request got him a drink of water, then went in search of assistance. When he got back, Stebbins was lying in front of the boiler as above stated. Mr. Stebbins was about 57 years of age and unmarried. He was a member of Meadville Typographical Union 181 and was one of the oldest printers in the city. The body was taken to the rooms of Undertaker Byrum and friends were wired of his death. The funeral will take place from the residence of his sister, Mrs. Steward, No. 838 North Water Street, Thursday at 3 o'clock p.m.''

v. **Delila Ellis Stebbins**, b. October 24, 1839, Meadville, Crawford County, Pennsylvania; d. Bet. 1897-1910, Meadville, Crawford County, Pennsylvania.

vi. **Frederick Wallace Stebbins**, b. May 08, 1842, Meadville, Crawford County Pennsylvania; d. Cleveland, Ohio.

vii. **Mary Jane Adelaide Stebbins** b. October 24, 1844, Meadville, Crawford County, Pennsylvania; d. June 30, 1910,

Rochester, Pennsylvania; m. **Henry Laycock,** April 07, 1872.

viii. **Henrietta Atkinson Stebbins**, b. February 10, 847, Meadville, Crawford County, Pennsylvania; d. September 16, 1848, Meadville, Crawford County, Pennsylvania.

26. **Thomas Sommer Atkinson** (Thomas 3, Thomas 2, Stephen 1) was born Abt. 1814 in Meadville, Pennsylvania. He married **Eliza Graff**, December 17, 1835 in Woodcock Township, Crawford County, Pennsylvania. She was born 1813 in North Whitehall Township, Lehigh County, Pennsylvania, and died 1882 in Concordia, Cloud County, Kansas.

Note for Thomas Sommer Atkinson:

The Meadville Courier dated December 22, 1835 has the following entry: Married on the17th inst. By the Rev. Mr. Rathburn, Mr. Thomas S. Atkinson to Miss Eliza Graff, both of Woodcock township. With the foregoing notice we received a very large slice of the wedding cake, and in return we wish the new married couple abundant prosperity and a long life. May they experience joy as boundless as their present to us was and happiness as pure as it was sweet. Since the groom is himself a Printer, we will lay aside a little of our selfishness and give him the key to happiness in the married life. It may be found in the following lines: "What mortal man can have the power or skill to stem the torrent of a woman's will for if she will, she WILL, you may depend on it, and if she won't she WON'T, so there's an end to it."

N.B. as our paper is now in press, truth compels us to state that the above article was penned in anticipation. The parties were married, as stated, but we received NO CAKE! We most confidently expected that the groom, being a member of the craft, would conform to a law prescribed by custom. What prevented this compliance we cannot tell: probably EXCESSIVE JOY! At all event, we wish it had been done, so that we might not occupy the ridiculous position we do at present.

Notes for Eliza Graff:

The Crawford Journal of June 23, 1882, p. 81, Column 3, contains the following obituary: Mrs. Eliza Atkinson died recently at the resident of her son, George B. Atkinson, near Concordia, Cloud County, Kansas, in the 69th year of her age. She was born in North Whitehall Township, Lehigh County, Pennsylvania in 1813 and came to this county (Crawford) in 1827. Her maiden name was Graff. She resided in Woodcock Township in this county until 1878 when she removed with her son to Kansas. She was the daughter-in-law of Thomas Atkinson, the first editor in Northwestern Pennsylvania. In Woodcock Township of this county where she was well known, she was beloved and respected by all. Throughout her life she was a consistent member of the German Reformed Church. "None knew her but to love her; None named her but to praise."

Children of **Thomas Atkinson** and **Eliza Graff** are:

    i.   **George B. Atkinson**, b. 1838, Woodcock Township, Crawford County,

Pennsylvania; d. August 02, 1899,
Concordia, Cloud County, Kansas.

    ii.   **Henry Clay Atkinson**, b. December 08,
1836, Woodcock Township, Crawford
County, PA; d. May 12, 1881, Bradford,
Pennsylvania.

27. Sophia Atkinson (Thomas 3, Thomas 2, Stephen 1)
was born Abt. 1816. She married **John Clark**. He was
born February 20l 1808, and died April 29, 1876 in
Crawford County, Pennsylvania.

Notes for John Clark:

       John Clark was a Major. This information came
from Gloria Clark in Corpus Christi, Texas who is
descended from Sarah E. Clark, daughter of Sophia
Atkinson and Major Clark.

       Egle's Notes and Queries Third series, Volume
III, pp. 263-264: John Clark, born February 20, 1807,
lived most of his life in Crawford County; was a major
in the State militia, and engaged in the tanning business.
He died April 19, 1876. He married Sophia Atkinson.

Children of **Sophia Atkinson** and **John Clark** are:

    i.   **Sarah E. Clark**, b. June 22, 1834,
Meadville, Pennsylvania; d. Bef. 1909,
Meadville, Pennsylvania.

    ii.   **Anna Clark**, m. **H. Shippardson.**

    iii.   **William Clark.**

    iv.   **Thomas Clark.**

    v.   **James Clark.**

vi.   **Henry Clay Clark.**

28. Augusta Atkinson (Thomas 3, Thomas 2, Stephen 1) was born Abt. 1820 in Meadville, Pennsylvania, and died in Meadville, Crawford County, Pennsylvania. She married **John McFarland,** May 17, 1843 in Meadville, Crawford County, Pennsylvania, son of **John McFarland** and **Margaret Forster**. He was born February 13, 1800 in (probably) Lycoming County, Pennsylvania, and died September 02, 1881 in Meadville, Crawford County, Pennsylvania.

Notes for Augusta Atkinson:

      She was sometimes listed as Lydia Augusta. She was the second wife of John McFarland. His first wife was her sister Salome.

Notes for John McFarland:

      John McFarland was a president of Allegheny College, Meadville. He was the oldest son of Margaret Forster Stuart by her first husband. He married two Atkinson sisters, Salome first, then Augusta after her death, saying that he found the Atkinson girls so charming he had to marry two of them.

Children of **Augusta Atkinson** and **John McFarland** are:

      i.   **Salome McFarland.**
      ii.   **Malcolm McFarland.**
      iii.   **Sarah Atkinson McFarland.**
      iv.   **Frank Monroe McFarland.**

29. **Monroe Atkinson** (Thomas 3, Thomas 2, Stephen 1) was born February 19, 1825 in Meadville, Pennsylvania. He married **Jane Sophia Pinks**. She was born in Woodstock, Vermont.

Notes for Monroe Atkinson:

Monroe Atkinson was a surgeon in the Mexican War and is said to have acquired a great knowledge of frontier life and American Indian culture becoming conversant in several Indian languages. He married Jane Sophia Pinks, daughter of **John Pinks** and **Mary Sartwell.**. She was from Vermont. Monroe died in Los Angeles.

Children of **Monroe Atkinson** and **Jane Pinks** are:

    i.   **Hale Atkinson.**

    ii.   **Mary Adelaide Atkinson**, b. Pennsylvania; d. Meridian, Connecticut; m. **Walter Lyman Cheyney**. She entered the DAR on the Thomas Atkinson Sr. line.

30. **Johann Fremole** (Susan 3 Atkinson, Thomas 2, Stephen 1) was born April 17, 1810; He married **Catherine (?)**.

Notes for Johann Fremole:

In 1850, John Fremole lived in Woodcock Township, Crawford County, not far from Meadville, with his wife Catherine and eight children ranging in age from 4 to 20, The eldest child was named Susan, for her grandmother; the second child was "Soloma"; the youngest was Matthew.

Children of **Johann Fremole** and **Catherine** (?) are:

i	**Susan Fremole.**
ii.	**Soloma Fremole.**
iii.	**Child Fremole.**
iv.	**Child Fremole.**
v.	**Child Fremole.**
vi.	**Child Fremole.**
vii.	**Child Freemole.**
viii.	**Matthew Fremole.**

Generation No. 5

31. **Sarah Gorgas** (William 4, Sophia 3 Atkinson, Thomas 2, Stephen1) married **Daniel Kitzmiller**, a school-fellow of Solomon Gorgas at Myerstown.

Child of **Sarah Gorgas** and **Daniel Kitzmiller** is:

i.   **Augusta Kitzmiller**.In his memoirs, Solomon Gorgas remarked that Augusta "shows great artistic talent and gives promise of a future…"

32. **William Crawford Gorgas** (Josiah 4, Sophia 3 Atkinson, Thomas 2, Stephen 1) was born October 03, 1854 in Toumlinville, near Mobile, Alabama, and died

July 04, 1920 in Queen Alexandria Military Hospital, Millbank, England. He married **Marie Doughty** September 1885 in Cincinnati, Ohio. She was born 1864 in Cincinnati and died 1929.

Notes for William Crawford Gorgas:

William Gorgas became sanitarian and surgeon general of the US. Army, 1904. While in Panama, he rid the Canal Zone of yellow fever and made the cities of Colon and Panama into models of good health. In 1913, he traveled to South Africa to advise on the control of pneumonia among black miners. In 1914, he was appointed surgeon general and promoted to major general. During W.W. I, he headed the medical service of the Army until the armistice, then returned to public health work. In 1920, he investigated yellow fever on the west coast of Africa before going to London and the International Hygiene Congress in Brussels, where he had a severe stroke on May 30. King George came to the hospital to present him the insignia of the Order of St. Michael and St. George. He died on July 04, 1920 and an elaborate funeral was held in St. Paul's Cathedral in London. The body was then returned to the United States for a funeral at the Church of the Epiphany in Washington, DC on August 06, 1920. He is buried in Arlington National Cemetery.

Child of **William Gorgas** and **Marie Doughty** is:

    i.   **Aileen Lyster Gorgas**.

Notes for Aileen Lyster Gorgas:

She may have been the one responsible for defacing pages of the Journal. The journal of Josiah's mother-in-law, Sarah Haynsworth Gayle, located in the Hoole Special Collections Library has been defaced in the same fashion as have the Gorgas journals with words and lines cut from it. The original of the Gayle journal was at one time with the Gorgas manuscript in the Gorgas home in Tuscaloosa. Maria Gorgas, wife of William Crawford Gorgas, copied by hand portions of the Gayle journal in 1901 while she and her husband were stationed in Ecuador. The same defacing appears in this copy in the same style with the same ink as mars the Gorgas journals. That copy appears to have been in the hands of only William Crawford and Marie Gorgas; the latter permitted the University of North Carolina Library to microfilm that copy, which has since disappeared.

The Hoole Special Collections Librarian suggests one other person who may have been responsible for defacing the Gorgas journals. After the Gorgas papers were donated to the university library, one of Josiah's descendants came regularly to the library and read through the Gayle and Gorgas journals. She was seen applying scotch tape to mend them and otherwise "fussing" with both journals. The librarian always has presumed that this lady defaced both journals.

33. **Christine Amelia "Minnie" Gorgas** (Josiah 4, Sophia 3 Atkinson, Thomas 2, Stephen 1) was born June 04, 1859 in Charleston, South Carolina, and died February 03, 1953 in Tuscaloosa, Alabama. She married **George Declouet Palfrey** September 19, 1881. He was born 1858 in St. Mary's Parish, Louisiana, and died

1930. In 1947, Minnie Gorgas Palfrey returned to Tuscaloosa to live with her sister, Ria, in the Gorgas home.

Frank E. Vandiver, Gorgas researcher, lists the living Josiah Gorgas descendants in his forward of the Gorgas Journals in 1958, the date when the manuscripts were given to the University of Alabama. They are: Aileen Gorgas Wrightson, daughter of William Crawford Gorgas; Minna Palfrey Tait and Jessie Palfrey Leake, daughters of Josiah's daughter Minnie; and Gene Palfrey Ellis and William Gorgas Palfrey, grandchildren of Minnie Gorgas Palfrey. It is not clear if Gene Palfrey Ellis is the child of a second (or first) marriage of either Minnie Palfrey Tait or Jessie Palfrey Leake. Both Christine Amelia "Minnie" Gorgas and George DeClouet Palfrey are buried in the Gorgas plot, Evergreen Cemetery, Tuscaloosa, Alabama.

Children of **Christine Gorgas** and **George Palfrey** are:

    i.   **Jessie Gorgas Palfrey**, b. 1883; d. 1971, m. **(?) Leake**. Since it is not known who was responsible for defacing the Gorgas papers, two possibilities are Jessie Gorgas Palfrey Leake and her sister, Amelia Gayle Minnie Palfrey Tait, who both lived until 1970. The other strong possibility is Aileen Gorgas Wrightson daughter of William Crawford.

    ii.   **William Taylor Palfrey**, b. 1885; d., 1957.

    iii.   **Amelia Gayle "Minnie" Palfrey**, b. 1888; d. 1971.

34. **Edward E. Stebbins** (Sarah Ann 4 Atkinson, Thomas 3, Thomas 2, Stephen 1) was born November 13, 1830 in Meadville, Crawford County, Pennsylvania, and died 1919 in Mount Dora, Lake County, Florida. He married **Elizabeth Linegar** December 25, 1852 in Cleveland, Ohio, daughter of (**?**) **Linegar** and **Mary Walters**. She was born June 28, 1837 in Weisentine, Switzerland, and died Abt. 1900 in Mount Dora, Florida or Rochester, Pennsylvania.

Notes for Edward E. Stebbins:.

Edward E. Stebbins was a very colorful gentleman. He began his career as a teacher in Fredonia, New York where he wrote his "Rules for Students" which have been published in several periodicals, among them the Alpha Delta Kappan in November 1981. He joined the Seventh Regiment Ohio Volunteer Infantry on June 20, 1861 and served for three years as a musician. He was sent to an Army hospital from Fredericksburg, Virginia and mustered out with his company on July 06, 1864. During a lull in the battle at Fredericksburg, he reported that he was visited by a vision and told that he would be wounded, but his life would be spared if he promised to return to the South at the end of the war and help to build it back up again, He gladly promised this and – as the vision prophesied – he was wounded, but not severely. From that moment on, he collected every newspaper account of psychic phenomena that he could find and left a sizable notebook of these accounts which he amassed over the years. At the close of the Civil War, he indeed headed South. He went first to Sorrento, Florida, where he was one of the first orange growers in the state. He became so prosperous that he maintained two homes, a winter

184

one in nearby Mount Dora, and another in Rochester, Pennsylvania near the Laycock family. An account of his adventures in Florida, "The Colonel Comes South," appeared in FloridAgriculture, November 1977. His burial in 1919 may have been in either Mount Dora, Florida or Rochester, Pennsylvania.

Notes for Elizabeth Linegar:
The Stebbins Family Tree #2887 in Broderbund Family Archives Volume 14 states that Anne Elizabeth was born in Weisentine, Switzerland. This may be true; however, she was living in Cleveland, Ohio when she was married to Edward E. Stebbins.

Child of **Edward Stebbins** and **Elizabeth Linegar** is:
    i.   **William Stebbins**, b. 1856; d. 1857, Cleveland, Ohio.

35. **Thomas Atkinson Stebbins** (Sarah Ann 4 Atkinson, Thomas 3, Thomas 2, Stephen 1) was born October 25, 1832 in Meadville, Crawford County, Pennsylvania, and died January 26, 1921 in Meadville, Crawford County, Pennsylvania, He was buried in Meadville, and his title was Colonel Thomas Stebbins. He married **Caroline A. Coburn** November 06, 1858 in Meadville, Crawford County, Pennsylvania. She was born December 11, 1836 and died August 11,1891 in Meadville, Crawford County, Pennsylvania. She also was buried in Meadville.

Children of **Thomas Stebbins** and **Caroline Coburn** are:

i.   **Edward Ellsworth Stebbins,** b. April 01, 1861. Meadville, Crawford County, Pennsylvania; b. November 21, 1941, Meadville, Crawford County, Pennsylvania.

ii.   **Henrietta Stebbins**, b. October 15, 1864, Meadville, Crawford County, Pennsylvania; m. **Edward Eiler**.

iii.   **Gertrude Stebbins**, b. Nov. 06, 1867, Meadville, Crawford County, Pennsylvania; d. November 23, 1869, Meadville, Crawford County, Pennsylvania. She was buried in Meadville.

iv.   **Thomas Burton Stebbins**, b. April 20, 1872, Meadville, Crawford County, Pennsylvania; d. 1951, Meadville, Crawford County, Pennsylvania.

36. **Elizabeth Ann Stebbins** (Sarah Ann 4 Atkinson, Thomas 3, Thomas 2, Stephen 1) was born December 11, 1834 in Meadville, Pennsylvania and died March 1897 in Meadville, Pennsylvania. She married **James Edward Stuart** May 06, 1858 in Meadville, Pennsylvania, son of **Thomas Stuart** and **Margaret Forster.** He was born December 26, 1811 in Erie, Pennsylvania and died 1881 in Meadville, Pennsylvania.

Notes for Elizabeth Ann Stebbins:

Her obituary in the Meadville Tribune was found in the notebook of Edward E. Stebbins: Mrs. Elizabeth Stuart died at her home on North Water Street about 10 o'clock Sunday morning, after an illness of several weeks. Mrs. Stuart was a daughter of Edward Stebbins, and a granddaughter of Thomas Atkinson, who established and edited the Crawford Messenger, the first newspaper published west of Pittsburgh. She was born in this city December 11, 1834 and was married to James Stuart in this city on May 06, 1858, by Rev. Maltby, and has always lived in Meadville. Her husband, who died 16 years ago, was for many years one of the leading undertakers in this section. Of her own family, Mrs. Stuart is survived by the following children: Otto K., William F., Albert Edward, Harry S. and James Henry Stuart, all of Meadville; Mrs. Maggie Delo of Chicago Junction, Ohio, and Mrs. Andrew Mulrainey, of this city, with the latter of whom Mrs. Stuart resided. Mrs. Stuart was a true Christian woman, of exceptionally beautiful character. She was a helpful and encouraging wife, and nobly sustained the duties which devolved on her with the death of her husband. Her Christianity was practical, and was manifested in all her relations in life, and particularly in her final illness, through all the trying weeks of which she made not one complaint, remaining prayerfully patient and trusting to the last. Announcement of the funeral will be made later.

Children of **Elizabeth Stebbins** and **James Stuart** are:

i.   **Otto K. Stuart**, b. 1858, Meadville, Crawford County, Pennsylvania.

ii. **Margaret E. Stuart**, b. 1862, Meadville, Crawford County, Pennsylvania

iii. **William Stuart**, b. 1864, Meadville, Crawford County, Pennsylvania.

iv. **Sarah Stuart,** b. 1865, Meadville, Crawford County, Pennsylvania; m. **Andrew Mulrainey**, Meadville, PA, b. December 1865.

Notes for Sarah Stuart:

Sarah Stuart is not listed in my mother's records, but she appears in the 1870 Census from Woodcock Twp., Crawford County, Pennsylvania. at which time she was five years old. She is the only daughter who qualifies as the wife of Andrew Mulrainey listed in her mother's obituary.

Notes for Andrew W. Mulrainey:

The 1900 Census for Meadville lists Andy W. Mulrainey, b. December 1865, as divorced and living with his father widowed sister, and nephew. There is no mention of a Sarah Mulrainey, suggesting that she remarried or moved out of the area.

v. **Albert Edward Stuart**, b. March 14, 1867, Meadville, Pennsylvania; d. January 16, 1929, Grafton, West Virginia.

vi. **Harry S. Stuart**, b. 1869, Meadville, Pennsylvania

vii.   **James Henry Stuart**, b. Aft. 1870, Meadville, Crawford County, Pennsylvania.

37. Delila Ellis Stebbins (Sarah Ann 4 Atkinson, Thomas 3, Thomas 2, Stephen 1) was born October 24, 1839 in Meadville, Crawford County, Pennsylvania, and died Bet. 1897-1910 in Meadville, Crawford County, Pennsylvania. She married (1) **William Frey,** January 06, 1858 in Meadville, PA. He was born in Weisbaden, Germany, and died (?) 1864 in Meadville, Crawford County. She married (2) **Dewitt Clinton Herrington** December 29, 1868 in Meadville, PA, son of **Edward Herrington** and **Nancy Burchfield**. He was born April 1847 in Pennsylvania and died July 31, 1910 in Meadville, Crawford County, Pennsylvania.

Notes for Delila Ellis Stebbins:

There is a discrepancy about Charles William Frey, first husband of Delila Stebbins Frey Herrington. Her obituary states that he died in 1864. However, a Herrington researcher, William Moore (wbmoore@gremlan.org), found their divorce record in Crawford County Common Pleas Court, No. 94, April Term, 1868, dated December 21, 1868, which means that he could not have died in 1864 as indicated in her obituary.

The obituary of Delila Stebbins Frey Herrington from the Meadville Tribune was found in the notebook of her brother, Edward E. Stebbins (no month or year cited):

"Mrs. Dewitt C. Herrington died on Sunday, the 24th inst. At the home of her daughter, Mrs. W. H. Andrew, East Main street, at 9:50 p.m. The immediate cause of death was asthma, but she had been in failing health and much suffering from that and other causes for five years past. The deceased was born at Meadville, Pennsylvania October 27, 1838 to Edward and Sarah Atkinson Stebbins, and her whole life was spent in this vicinity. Her maternal grandfather, Hon. Thomas Atkinson, came to Meadville from Germantown, PA in 1804. (Note: This is not accurate – his wife, Sarah Sommers, was from Germantown, but he was born in Lancaster County.) He published the Crawford Messenger, the first newspaper in this region, and he also represented the county in the state legislature. Her father, Edward Stebbins, came to Meadville from West Springfield, Massachusetts, and took up land in that vicinity. On January 06, 1858, she was married to Charles William Frey, born in Weisbaden, Germany, who came to this country early in life, by whom she had two children, Maggie Louise and Mary Adelaide, of whom the latter (now Mrs. Andrews) survives her. Mr. Frey died in 1864 (disproved), and in 1868 she was married to Dewitt C. Herrington, by whom she had one son, Edward Augustus, who also survives her. Mrs. Herrington has been a faithful member of Christ Church, Meadville, from which she will be buried tomorrow.

"Three brothers and one sister survive her: Edward Stebbins of Mt. Dora, Florida; Colonel Thomas Stebbins of Meadville; Frederick Stebbins of Cleveland, Ohio, and Mrs. Henry C. Laycock of Rochester, PA.

"A service will be held at the home of Mrs. Andrews on Tuesday at 5 p.m. Conducted by the Rev. Mr. Lewis of St. James Memorial Church. Funeral services will also be held in Christ Church, Meadville, on Wednesday at 11 a.m. in charge of Rev. Mr. Edwards of that church."

Delila was named by her father, Edward Stebbins, for his first wife, who died two months after their marriage. He later married Sally Ann Atkinson, Delila's mother. Her marriage to DeWitt Clinton Herrington is cited in the Crawford Democrat January 09, 1869.

Children of **Delila Stebbins** and **William Frey** are:

    i.   **Maggie Louise Frey**, b. Aft. 1858, Meadville, Crawford County, Pennsylvania. Because the obituary for Delila Stebbins Frey Herrington states that she is survived by her daughter Mary Adelaide, this indicates that Maggie died before that time.

    ii.   **Mary Adelaide Frey**, b. Bef. 1864, Meadville, Crawford County, Pennsylvania; d. Aft. January 1919.

Child of **Delila Stebbins** and **Dewitt Herrington** is:

    iii.   **Edward Augustus Herrington**, b. Aft. 1869, Meadville, Crawford County, Pennsylvania.

38. **Frederick Wallace Stebbins** (Sarah Ann 4 Atkinson, Thomas 3, Thomas 2, Stephen 1) was born May 08, 1842, Meadville, Crawford County,

Pennsylvania, and died in Cleveland, Ohio. He married **Martha Catchall** Abt. 1867.

Children of **Frederick Stebbins** and **Martha Catchall** are:

    i.   **Harry Stebbins,** b. 1857.

    ii.   **Maud Stebbins**, b. Aft. 1867.

39. George B. Atkinson (Thomas Sommer 4, Thomas 3, Thomas 2, Stephen 1) was born 1838 in Woodcock Township, Crawford County, Pennsylvania, and died August 02, 1899 in Concordia, Cloud County, Kansas. He married (1) **Sarah Lasher** in 1861. She died 1863. He married (2) **Judith C. Pfeiffer**, November 12, 1868 in Kern's Hotel, Saegertown, Crawford County, Pennsylvania. She was born in Saegertown, and died in Concordia, Cloud County, Kansas.

Notes for George B. Atkinson:

    The Crawford Journal dated December 09, 1868, p. 1, column 5, has the following notice: "Marriages: On the 12th ult. at Kern's Hotel, Saegertown, by Rev. D. B. Ernst, Mr. George Atkinson, of Scrubgrass, and Miss Judith Pfeiffer of Franklin, Pennsylvania."

    The Evening Republican dated August 11, 1899, p. 3, column 3, has the following obituary: "Death of George B. Atkinson, formerly a resident of this county, died at his home in Concordia, Cloud County, Kansas, on the 2nd inst, in his 61st year. He had been a sufferer for the last two years from kidney disease and was confined to his bed for one day preceding his death the immediate cause of which was paralysis.

Mr. Atkinson was born in 1838 near Saegertown in the Pfeiffer settlement and lived there until grown to manhood. His many friends and relatives in that vicinity will be deeply grieved to hear of his death. In the spring of 1861 he was married to Miss Susan Lasher of Venango, who died childless two years later. His second wife, whom he married in1870 (this is incorrect compared with the marriage entry in the Crawford Journal) was Judith C. Pfeiffer, daughter of Israel Pfeiffer of Saegertown. To this marriage were born four sons and four daughters, who with their mother live to mourn his loss.

Mr. Atkinson served honorably in the Civil War, enlisting in Co. #111 Pennsylvania Infantry, in November 1861 and re-enlisting in the same organization in December 1863, serving until the close of the war. After his return from the Army, he worked for some years in the oil region in the vicinity of Franklin, PA. In 1871, he moved with his father-in-law's family to Kansas, where until a few years ago he was engaged in farming, which occupation he was obliged to relinquish because of ill health. He was a grandson of Thomas Atkinson, who in 1805 published the first newspaper in Crawford County and the first one in the state west of the Allegheny mountains and north of Pittsburgh."

A shorter obituary also appears in the Crawford Journal of August 17, 1899, p. 8, column 5: "In Concordia Kansas, August 2, George P. Atkinson, formerly of Crawford County, in the 61st year of his age. Deceased was born near Saegertown in 1838 and removed to Kansas in 1871. He was twice married, his first wife being Miss Susan Lasher of Venango, and his second wife, who, with four sons and four daughters, survives him, Judith C. Pfeiffer of Saegertown. She also was buried in Concordia, Cloud County, Kansas. Deceased was a veteran of the Civil War. He was the grandson of Thomas Atkinson who, in 1805, published the first newspaper in Crawford County."

Children of **George Atkinson** and **Judith Pfeiffer** are:

i.	**Child Atkinson.**
ii.	**Child Atkinson.**
iii.	**Child Atkinson.**
iv.	**Child Atkinson.**
v.	**Thomas Atkinson.**
vi.	**Child Atkinson.**
vii.	**Child Atkinson.**
viii.	**Child Atkinson.**

40. **Henry Clay Atkinson** (Thomas Sommer 4, Thomas 3, Thomas 2, Stephen 1) was born December 08, 1836 in Woodcock Township, Crawford County, Pennsylvania, and died May 12, 1881 in Bradford, Pennsylvania. He was buried May 13, 1881 in Oakland Township, Venango County, Pennsylvania. He married **Elizabeth McElwee** November 18, 1861 in Franklin, Venango County, Pennsylvania. she was born June 20, 1838 in Ireland, and died October 11, 1916 in Oakland Township, Venango County, Pennsylvania.

Notes for Henry Clay Atkinson:

Henry Atkinson's widow made a Widow's Claim for Pension on August 14, 1883 in Venango

County, Pennsylvania. At that time, Elizabeth McElwee
Atkinson was a resident of Kane City in Venango
County, aged 43. She swore that she was the widow of
Henry Clay Atkinson who was in Company A
commanded by Capt. Hundekofer (?) in the 211
Regiment of Pennsylvania Volunteers in the War of
1861, that her maiden name was Elizabeth McElwee and
that she was married to Henry C. Atkinson the 18th day
of November at Franklin, Venango County,
Pennsylvania, by J. Bunts. She said that her husband
died at Bradford, Pa. on May 12, 1881 of inflammatory
rheumatism contracted in the Army and she has been a
widow ever since. Her attorney was S. W. Fitzgerald of
Washington, DC. The attached general affidavit quotes
from the Family Bible which was printed in 1835 and
contained dates of marriage and births written in her
own hand. She swore that she was born June 20, 1838.

Children of **Henry Atkinson** and **Elizabeth McElwee**
are:

> i. **John S. Atkinson**, b. September 05,
>   1863; d. 1845, Oakland Township,
>   Venango County, Pennsylvania; m.
>   **Clara Mullen**, April 10, 1901, Oil City,
>   Venango County, Pennsylvania; d. 1945,
>   Oil City, Venango County, Pennsylvania.
>   He was buried in Oakland Seceders
>   Cemetery, Venango County,
>   Pennsylvania.
>
> ii. **Catherine A. Atkinson**, b. March 23,
>   1865; d. November 05, 1866; buried in
>   Oakland Seceders Cemetery, Venango
>   County, Pennsylvania. Pennsylvania.

iii.   **Mary Jane Atkinson**, b. July 17, 1867,
         Oakland Township, Venango County,
         Pennsylvania; d. February 17, 1967,
         Oaklane Township, Venango County.

iv.   **Eliza Groff Atkinson**, b. July 07, 1869;
         d. December 23, 1941, Brush Run,
         Clarion County, Pennsylvania; m.
         Harlan Abner Gross, December 04,
         1895; Kaneville, Venango County,
         Pennsylvania. Eliza was buried
         December 26, 1941, New Rehobeth
         Church Cemetery, Clarion Township,
         Clarion County, Pennsylvania.

v.   **Sarah M. Atkinson,** b. January 25, 1872,
         Oakland Township, Venango County PA;
         d. January 31, 1969, Lakeland, Florida;
         m. **John Cooper,** July 07, 1896,
         Franklin, Venango County, Pennsylvania.
         She was buried February 03, 1969,
         Lakeland, Florida.

vi.   **Charles Henry Atkinson**, b. June 08,
         1874, Oakland Township, Venango
         County, PA; m. **Katherine Elizabeth
         Masterson**, October 11, 1898, Franklin,
         Venango County, Pennsylvania.

Notes for Charles Henry Atkinson:

   According to Sherry Shepherd of Northfield,
Ohio, the granddaughter of Eliza Groff Atkinson and
Harlan Abner Groff, John, Mary, Sarah and Charles
Atkinson all stayed in the Oakland Township, Venango
County, Pennsylvania area. Samuel and Charles moved
west, possibly Texas and/or California.

vii. **Samuel G. Atkinson**, b. September 24, 1876, Oakland Township, Venango County, Pennsylvania.

viii. **Thomas D. Atkinson**, b. March 12, 879, Oakland Township, Venango County, Pennsylvania.

41. Sarah E. Clark (Sophia 4 Atkinson, Thomas 3, Thomas 2, Stephen 1) was born June 22, 1834 in Meadville, Pennsylvania, and died Bef. 1909 in Meadville, Pennsylvania. She married **Fitz-Henry Bemis** November 1852 in Meadville, Pennsylvania, son of **Samuel Bemis** and **Betsy Bigelow**. He was born November 09, 1823 in Sturbridge, Massachusetts.

Children of **Sarah Clark** and **Fitz-Henry Bemis** are:

i   **Frank Laroy Bemis,** b. January 26, 1855.

ii   **John C. Bemis.**

iii. **Harry C. Bemis.**

iv. **Ella Sophia Bemis.**

v.   **Herman H. Bemis.**

vi. **Cora Bemis.**

vii. **Annie Bemis.**

viii. **George Herbert Bemis.**

Generation No. 6

42. **William Taylor Palfrey** (Christine Amelia "Minnie" 5, Josiah 4, Sophia 3 Atkinson, Thomas 2, Stephen 1) was born 1885 and died 1957.

Child of **William Taylor Palfrey** is:

    i.   **William Gorgas Palfrey**

43. **Amelia Gayle "Minnie Palfrey** (Christine Amelia "Minnie" 5 Gorgas, Josiah 4, Sophia 3 Atkinson, Thomas 2, Stephen 1) was born 1888 and died 1971. She married **(?) Taft**.

Child of **Amelia Palfrey** and (?) **Taft** is:

    i.   **George Taft.**

44. **Edward Ellsworth Stebbins** (Thomas 5 Atkinson, Sarah Ann 4, Thomas 3, Thomas 2, Stephen 1) was born April 01, 1861 in Meadville, Crawford County. Pennsylvania, and died November 21, 1941 in Meadville, Crawford County, Pennsylvania. He married **Mary Elizabeth Stafford** October 27, 1885. She was born June 23, 1864 and died November 01, 1949.

Children of **Edward Stebbins** and **Mary Stafford** are:

    i.   **Edward E. Stebbins**, b. August 26, 1886, Meadville, Crawford County, Pennsylvania, d. September 06, 1886, Meadville, Pennsylvania.

    ii.   **Thomas Atkinson Stebbins**, b. September 01, 1890; d. February 01, 1891.

iii. **Carrie Elizabeth Stebbins**, b. December 13, 1891, Meadville, Crawford County, Pennsylvania; d. May 31, 1963; m. **Parke Grismore.**

iv. **Edna Henrietta Stebbins,** b. July 12, 1894, Meadville, Crawford County, Pennsylvania; d. April 01, 1968, Pittsburgh, Allegheny County, Pennsylvania.

v. **Charles Stafford Stebbins**, b. March 02, 1896. Meadville, Crawford County, Pennsylvania; d. June 01, 1976, Akron, Summit County, Ohio.

vi. **Frank Marvin Stebbins,** b. August 21, 1897, Meadville, Crawford County, Pennsylvania; d. May 29, 1907 Meadville, Crawford County, Pennsylvania.

vii. **Robert Lewis Stebbins,** b. February 20, 1903, Meadville, Crawford County, Pennsylvania; d. March 15, 1903, Meadville, Crawford County, Pennsylvania.

viii. **Thomas Atkinson Stebbins, Sr.,** b. March 07, 1904, Meadville, Crawford County, Pennsylvania; d. July 01, 1985.

ix. **Harold Burton Stebbins,** b. May 31, 1907, Meadville, Crawford County, Pennsylvania; d. September 09, 1976, Wadsworth, Summit County, Ohio.

x. **Edward Ellsworth Stebbins,** b. July 04, 1909, Meadville, Crawford County,

Pennsylvania; d. October 10, 1969; m.
(1) **Catherine (?).** m. (2) **Ethel (?)**

45. **Margaret E. Stuart** (Elizabeth Ann 5 Stebbins,
Sarah Ann 4 Atkinson, Thomas 3, Thomas 2, Stephen 1)
was born 1862 in Meadville, Crawford County,
Pennsylvania. She married **William B. Delo,** Bef. 1888,
son of **Samuel Delo** and **Rebecca Otto**. He was born
1861 in Pennsylvania.

Notes for Margaret E. Stuart:
    In 1897, Margaret Stuart Delo lived in Chicago
Junction, Huron County, Ohio. A communication from
the Ohio Historical Society's Research Services
Department Archives/Library Division dated August 15,
2001 says that Chicago Junction was a post office from
1910-1918. Prior to that, the town was called Chicago.
After the post office was dissolved in 1918, mail was
forwarded to Willard, Ohio, also in Huron County.
    The 1910 Ohio census Miracode Index notes that
William B. Delo, age 49, born in Pennsylvania, was the
head of household in Chicago Junction, Huron County.
Other residents were his wife Margaret E. age 48, born
in Pennsylvania, daughter Bernice A., age 21, born in
Pennsylvania, and his mother Rebecca Delo, age 74,
born in Pennsylvania.

Child of **Margaret Stuart** and **William Delo** is:
    i.   **Bernice A. Delo,** b. 1889, Pennsylvania.

46. **Albert Edward Stuart** (Elizabeth Ann 5 Stebbins,
Sarah Ann 4 Atkinson, Thomas 3, Thomas 2, Stephen 1)

was born March 14, 1867 in Meadville, Pennsylvania, and died January 26, in Grafton, Taylor County, West Virginia. He married **Uda Dietta Bell**, December 13, 1886 in Meadville, PA, daughter of **Samuel Whitaker Bell** and **Mary Agnes Caldwell**. She was born August 03, 1868 in Burgettstown, Washington County, Pennsylvania, and died January 13, 1951 in Swarthmore, Delaware County, Pennsylvania.

Notes for Albert Edward Stuart:

He was an original stockholder of Labor Journal, a paper established July 04, 1901 as a weekly newspaper, but which appeared January 13, 1902 as an evening daily. The daily was the outgrowth of a disagreement between employers and printers on the other daily newspapers of Marietta, Ohio. In December 1902, the printers declared a strike to be on, and according to agreement ceased work. The establishment is popularly financed in small holdings owned by members of the trades and labor organizations of Marietta. It has been a success from the start, finding general favor among the people who are friendly toward organized labor; and its columns are well filled with advertisements of the substantial concerns of the city.

The original stockholders forming the incorporation were D. E. Blair, Louis Sharp, M.L Purkey, Joseph Jones, Harry Hill, A.E. Stewart (sic) and Frank Ackerman. The company took charge of affairs March 17, 1901. Since starting the company has become much scattered, but it is owned entirely by men who are members of labor societies.

Marietta City Directory, p. 209: Stuart, Albert E., plumber, 129 Putnam, H.E. Greene, and Plum, Norwood.

Washington County and Williamstown, WV Directory, p. 194: Stuart, A.E. plumber, 728 ½ Fifth, owner of Stuart Plumbing Company in Washington, Pennsylvania, Marietta, Ohio, and Clarksburg, West Virginia.

He died of pneumonia while working on an industrial heating system project in Grafton, Taylor County, West Virginia. He was buried January 19, 1920 in the Masonic Cemetery, Clarksburg, West Virginia. His wife, Uda Dietta Bell, was also buried in the Masonic Cemetery, Clarksburg, West Virginia on January 16, 1951.

Children of **Albert Stuart** and **Uda Bell** are:

    i.   **Virginia Stuart**, b. July 10, 1893, Marietta, Washington County, Ohio; d. July 17, 1982, Chicago, Illinois.

    ii.   **Adelaide Elizabeth Stuart**, b. March 20, 1900, Marietta, Washington County, Ohio; d. May 1969, Springfield, Delaware County, Pennsylvania.

    iii.   **Harold Albert Stuart**, b. 1902, Marietta, Washington County, Ohio; d. September 23, 1937, Pittsburgh, Allegheny County, Pennsylvania; m. **(?) Betty (?).**

Notes for Harold Albert Stuart:

His death certificate says that he was employed by Standard Oil Company and died in Pittsburgh's

Naval Hospital of tuberculosis. He was buried in the Masonic Cemetery, Clarksburg, West Virginia.

Notes for Betty (?):

Betty's surname is unknown. About 1933, Harold and Betty arrived in Pittsburgh to visit Adelaide Stuart Pritchard. At that time, Uda Bell Stuart, his mother, gave Betty the family china which she had intended for Adelaide Goode. Shortly afterward, Betty and Harold separated or divorced. Betty never returned the china and her whereabouts were unknown at the time of Harold's death.

47. **Mary Adelaide Frey** (Delila Ellis 5 Stebbins, Sarah Ann 4 Atkinson, Thomas 3, Thomas 2, Stephen 1) was born 1864 in Meadville, Crawford County, Pennsylvania, and died Aft. January 1919. She married **William Henry Andrews.** He was born January 14, 1846 in Youngsville, Warren County, Pennsylvania, and died January 16l 1919, in Carlsbad, Eddy County, New Mexico.

Notes for Mary Adelaide Frey:

On the back of a photo taken of Mary Adelaide wearing an outfit chosen for the Presidential inauguration, there is a note stating that she was known as a great beauty. Her hat cost $50.00, a great deal of money for that time. She was known as Maggie.

Notes for William Henry Andrews:

The U.S .Congress Bioguide (http://bioguide.congress.gov/scripts/biodisplay.pl?index

A000252) information about William Henry Andrews (1846-1919) is as follows:

ANDREWS, William Henry, a Delegate from the Territory of New Mexico; born in Youngsville, Warren County, Pennsylvania January 14, 1846; attended the public schools; engaged in mercantile pursuits at Cincinnati, Ohio and at Meadville and Titusville, Pennsylvania 1880-1890; was also a builder of railroads; president of the Santa Fe Central Railway Co.; chairman of the Republican State committee of Pennsylvania 1889-1891; member of the State House of Representatives 1889-1893. served in the State senate in 1895, moved to the territory of New Mexico in 1900 and engaged in the mining business in Sierra County; was a member of the Territorial council in 1903 and 1904, elected as a Republican to the Fifty-ninth, Sixtieth, Sixty-first, and Sixty-second Congresses and served from March 4, 1905 to January 7, 1912, when pursuant to law, his term expired, the Territory of New Mexico having been admitted as a state into the Union and the Representative-elect having qualified; became engaged in the development of oil in the southern part of new Mexico in 1912, died in Carlsbad, Eddy County, New Mexico, January 16, 1919; interment in Woodlawn Cemetery, Titusville, Crawford County, Pennsylvania.

Verna Reed (verna@carlsbadnm.com) sent me his obituary and noted that two other papers reported the same cause of death, effects from influenza. The Carlsbad Argus also had a photograph of him.

Carlsbad Argus, January 17, 1919:

"Thursday morning, between 2 and 3 o'clock, Hon. William H. Andrews died in his rooms in the Crawford Hotel, after an illness of nearly two months. During the epidemic of Spanish influenza, Mr. Andrews was among those attacked, and owing to his advanced age was unable to withstand its weakening effect. He lingered until Thursday morning when he passed peacefully to the Great Beyond.

"Mr. Andrews came to Carlsbad some three months ago, after a long siege of sickness at his home in Titusville, Pennsylvania, his restless nature calling on him for business activity, and he at once took up his former business venture of sinking an oil well on property east of town, the work being done by a company known as Andrews Oil and Gas Company, which has a hole in the ground said to be over two thousand feet deep, and from which encouraging indications were had of the presence of oil if the well was sunk below sea level, and this was the belief of Mr. Andrews, who declared he would never be satisfied until this had been done.

"Owing to his delicate health, Senator Andrews did not do much work after arriving in Carlsbad, but up to the time of his last sickness was busy preparing to do so.

"His wife was telegraphed the news of his death yesterday morning and wired to have the body prepared for shipment to the old home at Titusville near Philadelphia (the writer of the article did not know the geography of Pennsylvania). Besides the wife, the deceased leaves a brother a son and daughter, the latter said to live at Erie, Pennsylvania.

"The autobiography and life work of Senator Andrews must be undertaken by someone better acquainted with the facts than the editor of the Argus, but this much the writer will say: New Mexico was never represented in congress than it was during the two terms served by Wm. H. Andrew as a delegate.

Essentially a politician, he brought to his duties an experience ripe with years of association with politicians of an age now passed, but he "did things," big things which may have not been considered as legitimate, but essential things, and that was what county in those days. May be rest in peace." He was buried in Woodlawn Cemetery, Titusville, Crawford County, Pennsylvania."

Children of **Mary Frey** and **William Andrews** are:

    i.   **Son Andrews.**

    ii.   **Daughter Andrews.**

48. **Thomas Atkinson** (George B. 5, Thomas Sommer 4, Thomas 3, Thomas 2, Stephen 1) married (1) **Unknown**; He married (2) **Harriet Scrivins,** 1897. She was born 1861 in North Hadley, Pennsylvania, and died March 12, 1895 in Sandy Lake, Pennsylvania.

Notes on Harriet Scrivins:

      Obituary dated March 14, 1895, p. 263, Sandy Lake: Atkinson, Harriet, 34, wife of Thomas, died at her home on Laycock Street, Sandy Lake on March 12, of consumption. She was formerly Miss Scrivins, born near Hadley, where her father and step-mother still reside. Married eight years ago, she was the second wife of Thomas. Four children were born to them. She is also survived by five sisters and two brothers. Funeral March 14, 1895.

Children of **Thomas Atkinson** and **Harriet Scrivins**
are:

    i.   **Child Atkinson.**

    ii.   **Child Atkinson.**

    iii.   **Child Atkinson.**

    iv.   **Child Atkinson.**

49. **Mary Jane Atkinson** (Henry Clay 5, Thomas
Sommer 4, Thomas 3, Thomas 2, Stephen 1) was born
July 17, 1867 in Oakland Township, Venango County,
Pennsylvania, and died February 17, 1967 in Oakland
Township, Venango County, Pennsylvania. She married
Thomas G. Carter December 24, 1889. He died August
12, 1941 in Franklin, Venango County, Pennsylvania

Notes for Mary Jane Atkinson:

    An obituary from Franklin, Pennsylvania reads:
Mrs. Mary J. Carter, widow of Thomas G. Carter of
Franklin RD3, died suddenly in her home at 12:30 p.m.
Friday, February 17. 1867. Mrs. Carter had been in
failing health for the past three months. Born in Oakland
Twp., July 17, 1867, she was the daughter of Henry C.
and Elizabeth McElwee Atkinson. She spent her entire
life in the area.

    Mr. Carter preceded her in death on August 12,
1941. She was also preceded in death by one daughter,
Lydia, and a son, Ira. Surviving are five sons, Arthur of
Beaumont, Calif., Jess of Oil City, Boyd of Franklin,
Floyd of Youngstown, Ohio, Howard of Hydetown, and
a daughter Miss Elizabeth Carter of Franklin RD3. Also
surviving are 27 grandchildren and numerous great-
grandchildren.

Children of **Mary Atkinson** and **Thomas Carter** are:

    i.   **Lydia Carter**, d. Bef. 1967.

    ii.   **Ira Carter**, b. Venango County, Pennsylvania; d. Bef 1967.

    iii.   **Arthur Carter,** b. Venango County, Pennsylvania. Living in Beaumont. California in 1967.

    iv.   **Jess Carter**, b. Venango County, Pennsylvania. Living in Oil City, Pennsylvania in 1967.

    v.   **Boyd Carter**, b. Venango County, Pennsylvania. Living in Franklin, Pennsylvania in 1967.

    vi.   **Floyd Carter**, b. Venango County, Pennsylvania. Living in Youngstown, Ohio in 1967.

    vii.   **Howard Carter**, b. Venango County, Pennsylvania; Living in Hydetown, Pennsylvania in 1967.

    viii.   **Elizabeth Carter**. Living in Franklin, Pennsylvania in 1967.

50. **Frank Laroy Bemis** (Sarah E. 5 Clark, Sophia 4 Atkinson, Thomas 3, Thomas 2, Stephen 1) was born January 26, 1855. He married **Sarah Ellen Thompson** November 19, 1881.

Child of **Frank Bemis** and **Sarah Thompson** is:

> i.   **Frank Brooks Bemis**, b. December 15, 1897, Meadville, Pennsylvania; d. January 12, 1994.

Generation No. 7

51. Edna Henrietta Stebbins (Edward Ellsworth 6, Thomas Atkinson 5, Sarah Ann 4, Thomas 3, Thomas 2, Stephen 1) was born July 12, 1894 in Meadville, Crawford County, Pennsylvania, and died. April 01, 1968 in Pittsburgh, Allegheny County, Pennsylvania. She married **Lear Markel**, 1922.

Child of **Edna Stebbins** and **Lear Markel** is:

> i.   **Gordon Allen Markel,** b. March 09, 1924.

52. Charles Stafford Stebbins (Edward Ellsworth 6, Thomas Atkinson 5, Sarah Ann 4, Thomas 3, Thomas 2, Stephen1) was born March 02, 1896 in Meadville, Crawford County Pennsylvania, and died July 01, 1976 in Akron, Summit County, Ohio. He married **Matilda (?)** in 1923.

Child of **Charles Stebbins** and **Matilda** (?) is:

> i.   **Lois Stebbins** b. Aft. 1923; m. **Robert Augstadt**. In 1984, Lois Stebbins Augstadt was living at 500 S. Kensington, Le Grange, Illinois.

53. **Thomas Atkinson Stebbins, Sr.** (Edward Ellsworth
6, Thomas Atkinson 5, Sarah Ann 4, Thomas 3, Thomas
2, Stephen 1) was born March 07, 1904 in Meadville,
Crawford County, Pennsylvania, and died July 02, 1935.
He married **Inez Brand** 1929. She was born December
28, 1907 and died March 02, 1987.

Children of **Thomas Stebbins, Sr.** and **Inez Brand** are:
- i.   **Thomas Atkinson, Jr.,** b. June 01, 1932.
- ii.   **Shirley Watson Stebbins.**
- iii.   **Dolores Stebbins**, b. October 02, 1937.
- iv.   **William Edward Stebbins, Sr.,** b. June 30, 1942.

54. **Harold Burton Stebbins** (Edward Ellsworth 6,
Thomas Atkinson 5, Sarah Ann 4, Thomas 3, Thomas 2,
Stephen 1) was born May 31, 1907 in Meadville,
Crawford County, Pennsylvania, and died September
09, 1976 in Summit County, Ohio. He married **Muriel
Alice Sharrock,** July 03, 1932 in Akron, Ohio. She was
born April 22, 1905 in Galion, Crawford County, Ohio.

Children of **Harold Stebbins** and **Muriel Alice
Sharrock** are:
- i.   **Carol Ann Stebbins**, b. November 24, 1933, Akron, Summit County, Ohio.
- ii.   **Kathleen Stebbins**, b. May 11, 1944, Wooster, Wayne County, Ohio.

55. **Virginia Stuart** (Albert Edward 6, Elizabeth Ann 5,
Sarah Ann 4 Atkinson, Thomas 3, Thomas 2, Stephen 1)

was born July 10, 1893 in Marietta, Ohio, and died July 17, 1982 in Chicago, Illinois. She married **Joseph Goode** July 01, 1916 in Martinsburg, Berkeley County, West Virginia. She was 24 and well over the age requiring parental approval, but she gave her father's name as Charles, perhaps to avoid being found out by her family who did not approve of her choice. He was the son of **Alonzo Goode** and **Columbia Smith**. He was born July 25, 1882 in Ritchie County West Virginia, and died June 07, 1952 in Auburn, Ritchie County, West Virginia. Both Virginia and Joe are buried in Auburn Cemetery, Auburn, West Virginia.

Children of **Virginia Stuart** and **Joseph Goode** are:

 i   **Joseph Stuart Goode,** b. 1920, \Aubuen, Ritchie County, West Virginia; d. December 26, 2001, Richmond, Virginia.

 ii.   **Adelaide Goode**, b. 1920, Auburn, Ritchie County, West Virginia; d. June 13, 2002, Western Springs, Illinois.

56. **Adelaide Elizabeth Stuart** (Albert Edward 6, Elizabeth Ann 5 Stebbins, Sarah Ann 4 Atkinson, Thomas 3, Thomas 3, Stephen 1) was born March 20,.1900 in Marietta, Ohio, and died May 1969 in Springfield, Delaware County, Pennsylvania. She married **Ernest Markwood Pritchard** June 01, 1927 in Clarksburg, Harrison County, West Virginia son of **Rev. Millard Fillmore Pritchard** and **Rosa Bell Nestor.** He was born September 12, 1892 in Coleta, Whiteside County, Illinois, and died February 03, 1979 in Hackettstown, Warren County, New Jersey. Both are

buried in Elk View Masonic Cemetery, Clarksburg, West Virginia.

Child of **Adelaide Stuart** and **Ernest Pritchard** is:

    i.   **Emily Marshall Pritchard**, b. September 06, 1931, Pittsburgh, Allegheny County, Pennsylvania.

Generation No. 8

57. **Gordon Allen Markel** (Edna Henrietta 7 Stebbins, Edward Ellsworth 6, Thomas Atkinson 5, Sarah Ann 4, Thomas 3, Thomas 2, Stephen 1) was born March 09, 1924,

Children of **Gordon Allen Markel** are:

    i.   **Steve Markel.**

    ii.   **Judy Markel.**

58. **Dolores Stebbins** (Thomas Atkinson 7, Edward Ellsworth 6, Thomas Atkinson 5, Sarah Ann 4, Thomas 3, Thomas 2, Stephen 1) was born October 02, 1937. She married **Fred D. Long**, 1958.

Children of **Dolores Stebbins** and **Fred Long** are:

    i.   **Larry Leland Long.**

    ii.   **Paul A. Long.**

59. William Edward Stebbins, Sr. (Thomas Atkinson 7, Edward Ellsworth 6, Thomas Atkinson 5, Sarah Ann Atkinson 4, Thomas 3, Thomas 2, Stephen 1) was born June 30, 1942. He married **Rena L. Tippens** 1966. She was born May 1949.

Children of **William Stebbins** and **Rena Tippens** are:

    i.   **William E. Stebbins, Jr.**

    ii.   **Amy L. Stebbins.**

    iii.   **Carrie E. Stebbins.**

60. Carol Ann Stebbins (Harold Burton 7, Edward Ellsworth 6, Thomas Atkinson 5. Sarah Ann 4 Atkinson, Thomas 3, Thomas 2, Stephen 1) was born November 24, 1933 in Akron, Summit County, Ohio. She married **John Harold Moss** September 13, 1958 in Medina, Medina County, Ohio. He was born February 18, 1934 in Chloe, Braxton County, West Virginia.

Children of **Carol Stebbins** and **John Moss** are:

    i.   **Jean Elizabeth Moss,** b. November 23, 1959.

    ii.   **Lois Kay Moss,** b. January 17, 1961, Wooster, Wayne County, Ohio; m. (1) **Scott Cowan,** m. (2) **William Charles Nixon**, May 30, 1981; b. August 17, 1959.

    iii.   **James Harold Moss.** b. November 17, 1962.

    iv.   **David Scott Moss**, b. November 17, 1962.

61. **Kathleen Stebbins** (Harold Burton 7, Edward Ellsworth 6. Thomas Atkinson 5, Sarah Ann 4 Atkinson, Thomas 3, Thomas 2, Stephen 1) was born May 11, 1944 in Wooster, Wayne County, Ohio. She married **James Charles Thompson** September 02,1967 in Wadsworth, Summit County, Ohio. He was born November 01, 1942 in Akron, Summit County, Ohio.

Children of **Kathleen Stebbins** and **James Thompson** are:

    i.   **Christine Louise Thompson,** b. September 17, 1969, Wooster, Wayne County, Ohio.

    ii.   **Paul Andrew Thompson**, b. June 20, 1973, Wooster, Wayne County, Ohio.

62. **Joseph Stuart Goode** (Virginia 7 Stuart, Albert Edward 6, Elizabeth Ann 5 Stebbins, Sarah Ann 4 Atkinson, Thomas 3, Thomas 2, Stephen 1) was born 1920 in Auburn, Ritchie County, West Virginia, and died December 26, 2001 in the Veterans Hospital, Richmond, Virginia. He married **Kay Bolt** Jan. 01, 1946 in the 1st Baptist Church, Charleston, South Carolina. She was born Oct. 29, 1917 in Anderson, South Carolina.

Child of **Joseph Stuart Goode** and **Kay Bolt** is:

    i.   **Deborah Goode** (adopted). She married **Douglas Wilson Bailey**.

Children of **Deborah Goode** and **Douglas Wilson Bailey** are:

     i.   **Allyson Kay Bailey.**
     ii.   **Angela Marie Bailey.**

63. **Adelaide Goode** (Virginia 7 Stuart, Albert Edward 6, Elizabeth Ann 5 Stebbins 5, Sarah Ann 4 Atkinson, Thomas 3, Thomas 2l Stephen 1) was born 1923 in Auburn, Ritchie County, West Virginia, and died June 13, 2001 in Western Springs, Illinois. She married **Earl Jennings Grimm** 1943 in West Virginia. He was born 1922 in Pennsboro, Ritchie County, West Virginia and died October 04, 2001 in Western Springs, Illinois. Both Adelaide and Jennings were buried 2003 in Arlington National Cemetery, Arlington, Virginia.

Children of **Adelaide Goode** and **Jennings Grimm** are:

     i.   **Diana Lee Grimm,** b. 1944, Auburn, Ritchie County, West Virginia.
     ii.   **Linda Grimm.**

64. **Emily Marshall Pritchard** (Adelaide Elizabeth Stuart 7, Albert Edward 6, Elizabeth Ann 5 Stebbins, Sarah Ann 4 Atkinson, Thomas 3, Thomas 2, Stephen 1) was born September 06, 1931 in Pittsburgh, Allegheny County, Pennsylvania. She married **Boyd Balford Cary, Jr.** September 28, 1953 at the Presbyterian Church, Rutledge, Delaware County, Pennsylvania, son of **Boyd B. Cary, Sr.,** and **Margaret Grace McLaughlin.**

Children of **Emily Pritchard** and **Boyd Cary** are:

i.   **Matthew Roger Cary**, b. September 09, 1954 in Philadelphia, Pennsylvania.

ii.   **Roland Mylles Cary**, b. September 05, 1958 in Philadelphia, Pennsylvania.

Generation No. 9

65. Jean Elizabeth Moss (Carol Ann 8 Stebbins, Harold Burton 7, Edward Ellsworth 6, Thomas Atkinson 5, Sarah Ann 4 Atkinson, Thomas 3, Thomas 2, Stephen 1) was born November 23, 1959. She married **Brian Lundquist** September 12, 1982 in Medina, Medina County, Ohio. He was born August 28, 1960.

Children of **Jean Moss** and **Brian Lundquist** are:

i   **Megan Jean Lundquist**, b. September 28, 1989.

ii.   **Briana Jean Lundquist**, b. March 03, 1993.

66. Christine Louise Thompson (Kathleen 8 Stebbins, Harold Burton 7, Edward Ellsworth 6, Thomas Atkinson 5, Sarah Ann 4 Atkinson, Thomas 3, Thomas 2, Stephen 1) was born September 17, 1969 in Wooster, Wayne County, Ohio. She married **John David O'Hara** April 09, 1994 in Barberton, Summit County, Ohio. He was born October 19, 1969 in Highland County, Ohio.

Child of **Christine Thompson** and **John O'Hara** is:

i.   **Elizabeth Kathleen O'Hara**, b. October 08, 1996, Akron, Ohio.

216

67. **Diana Lee Grimm** (Adelaide 8 Goode, Virginia 7 Stuart, Albert Edward 6. Elizabeth Ann 5 Stebbins, Sarah Ann 4 Atkinson, Thomas 3, Thomas 2, Stephen 1) was born May 06, 1944 in Auburn, Ritchie County, West Virginia. She married **Stephen Wright**. He was born March 20,1942 in Arkansas. They met while both were attending Hendricks College in Arkansas. Stephen Wright became a doctor. They have lived in Salt Lake City, Utah, and currently live in Amarillo, Texas.

Children of **Diana Grimm** and **Stephen Wright** are:

    i.   **Stuart Wright**, b. May 04, 1969. He is a pediatrician and began medical practice in Oneida, New York.

    ii.   **Stephanie Lee Wright,** b. 1944.

STUART/STEUART FAMILY HISTORY

The STUART/STEUART/STEWART clan goes back many generations in Scotland. Some of the line belonged to the royalty before spreading westward to Ireland where they settled in what is now Northern Ireland. There are several Stewart mansions there today. Archibald Steuart is thought to have belonged to the Stewart clan of Ballintoy, which claims several generations of men named Archibald. However, it is not known precisely where he was living in Northern Ireland before emigrating to the colonies. He lived in both New Jersey and Pennsylvania prior to the Revolutionary War.

Generation No. 1

1.**Archibald Steuart** was born Abt. 1737 in North Ireland and died Aft 1798 in Lycoming County, Pennsylvania. He married **Jane Kirkpatrick** February 20, 1759 in Old Swede's Church, Philadelphia, Pennsylvania. She was born Abt. 1740 in New Jersey and died Aft. 1780 in Northumberland (Lycoming) County, Pennsylvania.

Notes for Archibald Steuart:
The surname of Archibald Steuart and his descendants appear in various spellings in both legal

records and narrative accounts. It appears as Steuart, Stuart, and Stewart. Stuart is the preferred spelling of his direct descendants.

The Stewart Clan Magazine June 1913, Vol. VIII, No. 12, pp. 182-183 has the following information about the Stewarts of Northumberland County, Pennsylvania: Archibald Stewart (sic) was an early settler in Northumberland County, Pennsylvania before the Revolutionary war. At that time, Northumberland County comprised nearly the whole of northwestern Pennsylvania, a vast, thinly settled region inhabited by hostile Indians. Portions of it were in the state of Connecticut until the Pennsylvania and New York borders were confirmed. He was living in that section which was set off in 1795 as Lycoming County. He served as a ranger in the Northumberland County militia during the Indian troubles.

Children of **Archibald Steuart** and **Jane Kirkpatrick** are:

i. **Jane Stuart** was born 1762. She married **John Moffet/Maffet.** He died in 1801.

ii. **James Stuart**, b. 1764, Pennsylvania; d. 1813, Lycoming County, Pennsylvania.

iii. **Matthew Stuart**, b. 1768, Pennsylvania; d. Urbana, Ohio.

iv. **Archibald Stuart**, b. 1770, Pennsylvania; d. 1831, Centre County, Pennsylvania.

v. **Andrew Stuart**, b. 1774, Pennsylvania; d. February 15, 1850, Butler County, Pennsylvania

vi. **Thomas Stuart**, b. 1776 Lycoming County, Pennsylvania; d. March 06, 1839, Erie, Pennsylvania.

vii. **Eleanor Donaldson Stuart,** b. 1778, Northumberland, Lycoming County, Pennsylvania; d. May 16, 1842, Mill Creek, Erie County, Pennsylvania

viii. **Charles Stuart**, b. 1780, Pennsylvania; d. 1834, Florissant, Missouri.

Generation No. 2

2. **Jane Stuart** was born 1762. She was known to the family as "Aunt Maffitt." She married **John Moffet**. He died in 1801. Jane, his widow, petitioned the orphans' court of Lycoming Count, February 01, 1802 to appoint Charles and James Steuart as guardians of John (over 14 years), William, Samuel, and Robert Maffett (sic) (three under 14) orphan children of John, for purpose of binding them to useful trades and occupations.

Children of **Jane Stuart** and **John Moffet** are:
i. **John Moffet**, b. Abt. 1786.
ii. **William Moffet**, b. Aft. 1787
iii. **Samuel Moffet**, b. Aft. 1788.
iv. **Robert Moffet**, b. 1791, Pennsylvania; d. 1833.

3. **James Stuart** was born 1764. In Pennsylvania, and died 1813 in Lycoming County, Pennsylvania. He married **Mary Elizabeth Armstrong** Abt. 1794 in

Lycoming County, Pennsylvania, daughter of **Andrew Armstrong** and **Sophia** (?). She died February 24, 1807 in Lycoming County, Pennsylvania

Notes for James Stuart:

According to the application of Charles Steuart to the Pennsylvania Society Sons of the Revolution, James probably was a resident of Jersey Shore, Pennsylvania, or lived nearby, as he was listed on the tax rolls as a farmer. He was commissioned Justice of the Peace June 18, 1800. His wife's parents were Andrew and Sophia Armstrong, who took up land at the Big Spring near Linden, Lycoming County in 1775. Andrew was abducted by Indians in 1778 and presumably put to death by them.

Notes for Mary Armstrong Stuart:

Mary Armstrong Stuart died February 24, 1807, and James six years later. Both are listed in the Lycoming Presbyterian Church Cemetery records, Williamsport. James's will states: "my beloved wife Elizabeth is to receive in full all the property that she brought with her after our marriage." This seems proof of a prior marriage, as she has been referred to in previous records as Widow Knox. Their young children evidently made their home with their grandmother Sophia Armstrong. She was born in 1736 and died August 20, 1831, having been listed as over 90 years old in the family of A. A. Stuart. Both she and her husband were buried in Lycoming Presbyterian Cemetery, Williamsport, Pennsylvania.

Children of **James Stuart** and **Mary Armstrong** are:

i.   **Andrew Armstrong Stuart**, b. Jan. 04, 1795, Jersey Shore, Lycoming County, Pennsylvania; d. December 29, 1863.

ii.   **Archibald Stuart**, b. June 02, 1797, Jersey Shore, Lycoming County, Pennsylvania; d. Chartiers Township, Washington County, Pennsylvania.

iii. **Sophia Stuart**, b. August 22, 1799; m. **William McMeen.** His name may also have been spelled MacMahan or McMehan.

iv.   **Charles Stuart**, b. January 17, 1802, Jersey Shore, Lycoming County, Pennsylvania; m. **Hannah Saltzsman** February 25, 1830.

v.   **Thomas Donaldson Stuart**, b. September 16, 1804, Jersey Shore, Lycoming County, Pennsylvania; m. **Frances Ferguson Riddell**, December 03, 1829, Jersey Shore, Lycoming Count, Pennsylvania.

vi.   **James Stuart**, b, 1807, Jersey Shore, Lycoming County, Pennsylvania; d. March 2, 1857; m. **Sarah H. Hahn**, b. February 27, 1845.

4. **Matthew Stuart** was born 1768 in Pennsylvania and died in Urbana, Ohio. He married **Elizabeth (?)**. He has been listed as both Matthias and Matthew. Matthias is more likely correct. It is believed that his mother's father's given name was Matthias. He and Elizabeth first

lived in Lycoming County, Pa., according to Portrait and Biographical Record of Allen and Van Wert Counties, Ohio, 1896, p. 427, and had ten children. Among them were William, who removed to Allen County, Ohio in 1824, and Samuel who married (?) **Thomas**, Champaign County, Ohio. This information appears in Stewart Clan Magazine, June 1830, Vol. VIII, No. 12, p. 183.

Children of **Matthew Stuart** and **Elizabeth** (?) are

    i.   **William Stuart**. He lived in Allen County, Ohio, m the northwest part of the state near Lima.

    ii.   **Samuel Stuart** m. (?) **Thomas,** Champaign County, Ohio, near Urbana, north of Springfield. This information comes from the Stewart Clan Magazine, June 1930, Vol. VII, No. 12, p. 183.

5. **Archibald Stuart** was born 1770 in Pennsylvania, moved to Cherry Hill, Indiana County, and died 1831 in Centre County, Pennsylvania. He married **Eleanor Allison.**

Children of **Archibald Stuart** and **Eleanor Allison** are:

    i.   **Archibald Stuart** b. 1794; m. **Jane Cummins**.

    ii.   **John Stuart**, b. 1796.

    iii.   **Samuel Stuart** b. 1803; d. December 19, 1879, Center Township, Indiana County, Pennsylvania; m. **Susan Cummins**, Abt. 1822.

6. **Andrew Stuart** was born 1774 in Pennsylvania and died February 15, 1850 in Butler County, Pennsylvania. He married **Mary Russell**. She was born 1775, and died January 16, 1860 in Butler County, Pennsylvania.

Notes for Andrew Stuart:

Andrew brought his bride Mary, her parents, and their other two daughters to Cherry Township, Butler County, Pennsylvania in 1798. The Russell family settled north of there in Scrubgrass and Andrew settled on 400 acres in Cherry Township. Many of the Stuart descendants, including Andrew and Mary, are interred in the Mt. Varnum Cemetery close by.

Stewart Clan Magazine, Tome D., December 1941, Vol. XIX, No. 6, pp. 239-240: Andrew Steuart in the History of Butler County, PA., 1883, p. 425: During the year 1798, Andrew Stewart removed from Northumberland County, of which he was a native, to the farm in Cherry Township, Butler County, now owned by his son David. His wife was Mary Russell, whom he married prior to his settlement here. He was one of the pioneer school teachers of the county and served at Black Rock in the War of 1812. He and Mary reared a large family. His children, all born in Cherry Township, were: Margaret (married David Phipps of Venango County), James, William, Archibald, Andrew, Charles (married Martha Perry in May 1836), Perry, David, Ellen (married Patton Pollock) and Sarah (married James Hindman).

Children of **Andrew Stuart** and **Mary Russell** are:

i. **Margaret Stuart**, b. 1799 Cherry Twp., Butler County Pennsylvania.

ii. **James Stuart,** b. 1802 Cherry Twp., Butler County, Pennsylvania; d. November 04, 1866, North Washington, Butler County, Pennsylvania.

iii. **Archibald Stuart,** b. 1803, Cherry Twp., Butler County, Pennsylvania; d. 1850, Cherry Twp., Butler County, Pennsylvania.

iv. **William Stuart**, b. 1803, Cherry Twp., Butler County, Pennsylvania; d. 1850, Cherry Twp., Butler County, Pennsylvania.

v. **Andrew Stuart, Jr.**, b. 1807, Cherry Twp., Butler County, Pennsylvania; d. 1807, Cherry Twp., Butler County, Pennsylvania.

vi. **Charles Stuart**, b. 1809, Cherry Twp., Butler County, Pennsylvania; d. 1885, Cherry Twp., Butler County, Pennsylvania.

vii. **Ellen Stuart**, b. 1811, Cherry Twp., Butler County, Pennsylvania.

viii. **Sarah Stuart**, b. 1814, Cherry Twp., Butler County, Pennsylvania.

ix. **Perry Stuart**, b. 1816, Cherry Twp., Butler County, Pennsylvania.

x. **David Stuart**, b. July 18, 1818, Cherry Twp., Butler County, Pennsylvania.

7. **Thomas Stuart** was born 1776 in Lycoming County, Pennsylvania, and died March 06, 1838 in Erie, Pennsylvania. He married **Margaret Forster,** February 17, 1803 in Erie, Pennsylvania daughter of **John Forster** and **Catherine Dickey**. She was born Abt. 1780 in Lower Paxtang, Lancaster County, Pennsylvania, and died January 16, 1835 in Mill Creek, Erie County, Pennsylvania.

Notes for Thomas Stuart:

History of Erie County, Early Settlers of Erie County, Pennsylvania, p. 315: American Army Officers; The members of Captain Thomas Forster's company of Erie Light Infantry who spent the winter of 1812 at Buffalo were as follows, First Lieutenant Thomas Rees, Ensign Thomas Stewart (sic), etc.

The Stewart Clan Magazine, December 1931, p. 240 says that Thomas Steuart, son of Archibald, was born in 1776, probably on the West branch of the Susquehanna River in Northumberland (now Lycoming) County, PA. He was a tailor. He went with Thomas Forster to Erie County soon after that country was established in 1800 and became an ensign in the first militia company organized in the county. He married Feb. 17, 1803 Margaret Forster McFarland, daughter of John and Catherine (Dickey) Forster of Paxtang, Dauphin County, and widow of John McFarland. The marriage was performed at Erie by Thomas Rees, Esq. Margaret was a sister of Thomas Forster and had a little son, John McFarland, Jr.

Her sister Dorcas married William Bell, and Dorcas and Margaret helped make the "Don't Give Up the Ship" flag at the Steuart home in Erie which Capt.

226

Oliver Perry carried through the historic naval battle on Lake Erie, Sept. 10, 1813. Thomas Forster of Erie borough in his will dated May 31, 1836, and registered July 14, 1836, appointed Thomas Stewart Esq. of Erie one of the executers. Margaret Forster Steuart died January 16, 1835. Thomas Steuart died March 06, 1838, aged about 62 years, at the home of his step-son, John McFarland, at Meadville, Crawford County, and was buried at Erie, Erie County.

Notes for Margaret Forster:

Sanderson, Alfred, "The Making of the Flag," published in Egle's Notes and Queries Historical and Genealogical, pp. 157-16:

Margaret Forster Steuart made the "Don't Give Up the Ship Flag" for Captain Oliver Hazard Perry after the death of Captain Lawrence at the Battle of Lake Erie during the War of 1812. It hangs in Annapolis today. It is about nine feet square of close woven, coarse muslin or sheeting, dark blue, "now rather frequently patched." The letters are of white muslin, thirteen inches in length by nine inches wide. The dark blue of the material is now quite rusty, while the letters are yellowed with age.

It is preserved in a case in the library of the U.S. Naval Academy at Annapolis. It was made at the house of Thomas Steuart, then an officer of the Pennsylvania troops, by Margaret Forster Steuart, his wife, assisted by Dorcas Bell, wife of Captain William Bell, an officer of the Revolution, and her daughters Jane, afterward married to Samuel Hays, and Elizabeth, afterward married to James Tewksbury of the U.S. Navy, who was badly wounded in the Battle of Lake Erie. Joining them were their Forster cousins, Elizabeth Rachel, who married James E. Herron, an artillery officer of the US. Army and who was taken prisoner by the British; Mary Theodosia, afterward married to Colonel John Harris, U.S. Navy and subsequently commandant of the Marine Corps; and Catherine Ann, afterward wife of Richard T. Timberland, U.S. Navy, an officer of the fleet (daughters of Colonel Thomas Forster a personal friend of Lieutenant Perry, who on his return to Erie after the battle went at once to the house of Colonel Forster on French Street and was his guest during his stay in the village). In passing, the names of Hannah Wickersham and Margaret Wallace, also daughters of Colonel Forster should be noted. The one subsequently married to General E. V. Sumner of the U.S. Army, and the other to General George Wright, U.S. Army, who was lost with her husband in the wreck of the "Brother Jonathan" off Portland, Oregon, July 30, 1865. Mrs. Sumner and Mrs. Wright were children at the time, the first old enough perhaps to assist in the making of the flag, the second a little tot, but with sufficient intelligence to know that some great event was about to transpire. From a letter written by a granddaughter of Mrs. Steuart, comes the following extract: "Grandmother had a number of friends among the officers, and they asked her to make this flag for them. She further states that the making of it was kept a secret until it was ready for use."

Children of **Thomas Stuart** and **Margaret Forster** are:

    i.   **Eleanor Stuart**, b. Nov. 21, 1803; d. April 30, 1830, Meadville Crawford County, Pennsylvania, Meadville, Crawford County, Pennsylvania.

    ii.   **Eliza Stuart**, b. July 12, 1809, Erie, Pennsylvania; m. **Joseph Kelsey**, April

09, 1840, Meadville, Crawford County, Pennsylvania.

iii. **William Bell Stuart**, b. March 10, 1808; d. Abt. 1833, Erie, Erie County, Pennsylvania. The Stuart Clan Magazine December 1941, p. 240, says that William died at the age of 25 years.

iv. **James Edward Stuart**, b. December 26, 1811, Erie, Pennsylvania; d. 1881, Meadville, Pennsylvania.

v. **Charles Wallace Stuart, Sr.** b. Abt. 1812.

vi. **Thomas Heron Stuart**.

8. **Eleanor Donaldson Stuart** (Archibald 1) was born 1778 in Northumberland, Lycoming County, Pennsylvania, and died May 16, 1847 in Mill Creek, Erie County, Pennsylvania. She married **John Stewart**. He was born Abt. 1764 in Antrim, North Ireland, and died March 24, 1847 in Mill Creek, Erie County, Pennsylvania.

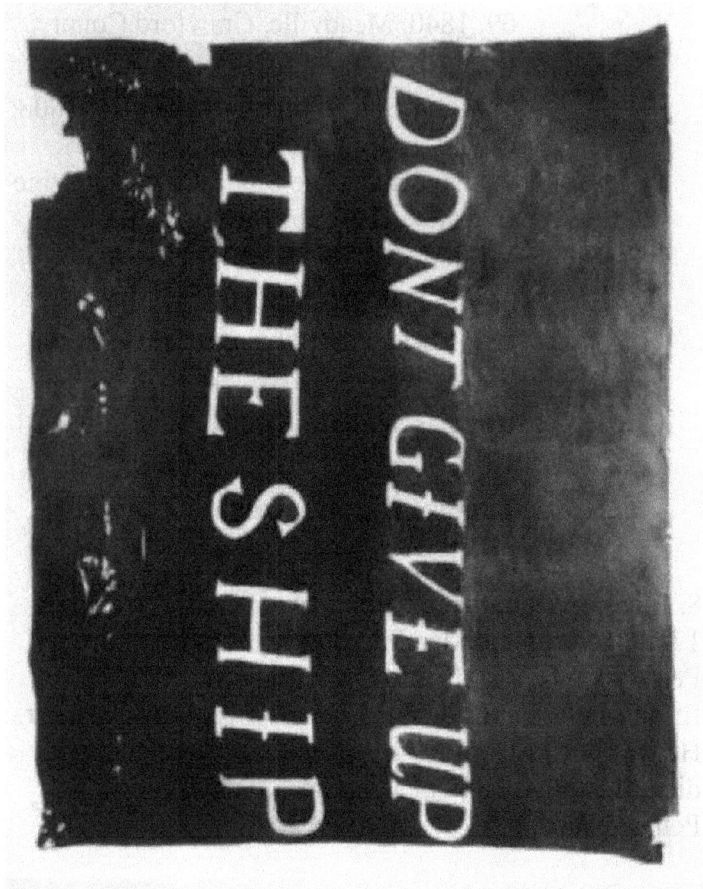

Notes for John Stewart:

     John Stewart, born in 1764, probably had a brother William. Born about 1766 (in Pennsylvania or Ireland) who was living by himself when the first census was taken for Northumberland County. He was engaged in the importation of pure-bred cattle from Ireland, making the trip to Donegal to buy the best animals. This suggests that there was a connection between John and William Stewart and Charles Stewart, who married

Elizabeth Hunter, said to have been a cousin of Archibald Stewart. William married Jane Quigley on October 18, 1792. His brother John joined him in the purchase November 12, 1794 of a 200-acre tract of land on the West Branch of the Susquehanna River, opposite the plantation of Charles Stewart.

This was in Lycoming County in 1995 and this part of Lycoming County became Mifflin Township. On December 09, 1799, James Duffy of Mifflin Township and Samuel Stewart Esq. of Nippenose Township (across the river) made an agreement with John Knox, millwright, to sell Knox a certain piece of land in Mifflin Township for a dam and a mill, the site being described as beginning at a corner on the bank of the Susquehanna between the lands of the said James Duffy and John Stewart, then along the said John Stewart's line to the great road from Larry's Creek to Pine Run (Lycoming County deeds D 7). On June 09, 1801, John Stewart and wife Eleanor of Crawford County, PA. deeded to John Knox, millwright of Mifflin Township, Lycoming County, for 300 pounds a moiety of 200 acres on the north side of the West Branch of the Susquehanna River in Mifflin Township, which the said John Stewart and William Stewart bought Nov. 12, 1794 of William Cook, then in Lycoming Township (deeds D 116).

When John sold his land to John Knox and moved to Crawford County, William retained his 100-acre part. At that time, the place was described as having a log house, a log barn, and a blacksmith shop. After Jane Quigley's death, William Stewart married Eleanor Knox "of Harrisburg," who may have been related to John Knox. William settled in Harrisville Township, Medina County. Ohio probably as early as 1827.

The Stewart Clan Magazine, Tome 8, Vol. 39, Number 8, February 1962, pp. 197-201, says while in Donegal County, Ireland on a cattle-buying mission, William contacted his Stewart cousins who were living on a farm called Carnamauga at Green Hill, said to have been grandchildren or great-grandchildren of one Alexander Stewart. It also states that in 1831 a Samuel Stewart descended from one Alexander Stewart in Donegal emigrated to the United States with his wife Elizabeth and grown children Alexander, David, Martha, and Elizabeth, and made his home with or close by the Stewarts in Medina and Wayne Counties. An identical story comes down from the John Stewart line: a family of Stewarts from Ireland, on their way to settle in Ohio about 1830, stopped a while at John Stewart's home in Erie County to visit. William died July 13, 1839 in Harrisville Township, Medina County, Ohio.

Children of **William Stewart** and **Jane Quigley** are:

    i.   **Alexander Stewart**, b. Oct. 26, 1793; m. **Eunice Ward**; d. June 04, 1872.

    ii.   **John Stewart,** b. Apr. 08, 1796; d. May 14, 1796.

    iii.   **William Quigley Stewart**, b.. Sept. 11, 1797; m. Jan. 17, 1829 **Phoebe Lawrence.**

    iv.   **Samuel Stewart**, b. Jan. 21,1800.

    v.   **Marie Stewart**, b. July 06, 1802; d. Jan.20, 1815.

    vi.   **Anna Stewart**, b. Aug. 25, 1805; m. **Bennett Scott Thrappe**; d. June 14, 1862.

vii. **James S. Stewart**, b. Aug. 12, 1809; m. Aug. 30, 1832 **Harriet Patience Mason**.

viii. **Melinda Stewart**, b. Nov. 08, 1812, m. **William Weed**; d. Jan. 01, 1860.

ix. **Sara Lucinda Stewart**, b. Aug. 06, 1815; m. **Daniel Ward**.

Children of **Eleanor Stuart** and **John Stewart** are:

i. **Mary Stewart,** b. June 08, 1802 m. **John Stewart**.

ii. **Charles Stewart**, b. May 03, 1804, d. Elgin, Indiana; m. **Margaret Kane.** One account says that Charles had three children.

iii. **Eleanor Donaldson Stewart**, b. August 21, 1806, North East, Erie County, Pennsylvania; d. August 11, 1888, Guy Mills, Crawford County, Pennsylvania.

iv. **Eliza H. Stewart**, b. August 03. 1808; m. **John McCreary.** Eliza died two years after her marriage to John McCreary.

v. **Jane Stewart** b. February 25, 1811; d. March 23, 1901; m. **William Roger Brawley**, January 12, 1832.

vi. **Archibald Stewart**, b. August 31, 1813; m. **Mary Sullivan**; b. Erie, Pennsylvania. One account says that Archibald had three children in Woodbury, Iowa.

vii. **Alexander John Stewart,** b. February 26, 1816, Erie County, Pennsylvania; m. (1) **Annie Mast** b. Champaign County, Ohio; m. (2) **Lili (?)** According to one account in Family Tree Maker, Alexander John Stewart had three children with Annie Mast and lost all. He served in the Civil War three years, three months.

viii. **Samuel Stewart**, b. May 2, 1819, Erie County, Pennsylvania; d. July 29, 1899, Bedford Township, Calhoun County, Michigan.

ix. **Margaret Stewart**, b. June 03, 1822; d. June 19, 1900; m. **William Sullivan**, November 13, 1851.

Generation No. 3

9. **Robert Moffet** (Jane 2 Stuart, Archibald 1 Steuart) was born 1791 in Pennsylvania and died 1833. He married **Unknown**, He was Commissioner of Lycoming County in 1830 and 1833.

Children of **Robert Moffet** and **Unknown** are:

i. **William Moffet**.

ii. **John Moffet**.

iii. **Samuel Moffet** m. **Hannah Tomb**, January 06, 1848.

iv. **Robert Grier Moffet**, b. 1823, d. 1894, m. **Matilda Tomb**, September 15, 1845.

v. **James Moffet**.

vi. **Stranges Moffet**.

vii. **Mary Ellen Moffet**.

234

viii.   **Sarah Ann Moffet**, m. **Joseph Cramer**, Lewisburg, Pennsylvania.

10. **Andrew Armstrong Stuart** (James 2, Archibald Steuart) was born January 04, 1795 in Jersey Shore, Lycoming County, Pennsylvania, and died December 19, 1863. He married (1) **Mary Richey** August 25, 1819 in Jersey Shore, Lycoming County, Pennsylvania. She was born December 18, 1796 and died September 14, 1847. He married (2) **Harriet Bowman** March 17. 1831. She died April 02, 1856.

Notes for Andrew Armstrong Stuart.

Andrew Armstrong Stuart was named after his maternal grandfather. Eventually he became owner of the Armstrong farm at the Big Springs. He was County Commissioner in 1835 and served a term as State Representative in 1844. His wife Mary is believed to have been the daughter of Robert and Rosana Richey, as a boy and girl were named for them; and he likely was the man who served as Lieutenant in Capt. Cookson Long's Company of Northumberland County Militia from May 16 to June 20, 1778 (Pennsylvania Archives, Vol. 8, p. 670). Andrew and both his wives are buried in Williamsport Cemetery.

Children of **Andrew Stuart** and **Mary Richey** are:

i.   **James Stuart,** b. June 27, 1820; d. August 04, 1869; m. **Caroline Thompson**, June 05, 1848.

ii.   **Rosanna Stuart**, b. March 14, 1822; d. March 23, 1822.

235

iii. **Eliza Stuart** b. July 12, 1823; d.
December 25, 1869; m. **P. M. Housel**,
October 25, 1852.

iv. **Robert Richey Stuart**, b. April 19,
1826; d. Denton, Doniphan County,
Kansas.

v. **Charles Stuart**, b. May 15, 1829; m.
Nancy (?).

vi. **Anna Mary Stuart**, b. July 30, 1831; m.
J. F. Walker, March 30, 1853.

11. **Archibald Stuart** (James 2, Archibald Steuart) was
born June 02, 1797 in Jersey Shore, Lycoming County,
Pennsylvania, and died in Chartiers Township,
Washington County, Pennsylvania. He married (1)
Martha Johnston. He married (2) **Wealthy Farr**.

Child of **Archibald Stuart** and **Martha Johnston** is:

i. **Jane Stuart**, b. 1821; d. August 21,
1881, Canonsburg, Washington County,
Pennsylvania.

12. **John Stuart** (Archibald 2, Archibald 1 Steuart) was
born in 1796. He married **Unknown** They lived in
Center Township, Indiana County, Pennsylvania.

Child of **John Stuart** and **Unknown** is:

i. **Levi Stuart**, b. March 18, 1823.

13. **James Stuart** (Andrew 2, Archibald 1 Steuart) was born 1802 in Cherry Twp., Butler County, Pennsylvania, and died November 04, 1866 in North Washington, Butler County, Pennsylvania. He married **Elizabeth Goe**.

Children of **James Stuart** and **Elizabeth Goe** are:

i.	**Andrew Stuart,** b. 1829.
ii.	**Thomas Stuart**, b. 1830.
iii.	**Mary Stuart**, b. 1831.
iv.	**Reed Russell Stuart**, b. November 07, 1833, Cherry Township, Butler County, Pennsylvania.
v.	**Eleanor E. Stuart**, b. 1835.
vi.	**Perry Stuart**, b. 1836.
vii.	**Joseph B. Stuart**, b. 1837.
viii.	**Charles C. Stuart**, b. 1841.
ix.	**Lily A. Stuart**, b. 1843.
x.	**Jane E. Stuart**, b. 1845.
xi.	**Margaret E. Stuart**, b. 1846.
xii.	**James Leonard Stuart**, b. November 07, 1848, Butler County, Pennsylvania; d. March 28, 1893, North Washington, Butler County, Pennsylvania.

14. **Archibald Forster Stuart** (Thomas 2, Archibald 1 Steuart) was born December 25, 1805 in Erie, Pennsylvania, and died August 27, 1867 in Meadville, Crawford County, Pennsylvania. He married **Rebecca Reynolds** November 03, 1842.

Children of **Archibald Stuart** and **Rebecca Reynolds** are:

    i.   **Edward Reynolds Stuart**, b. Meadville, Crawford County, Pennsylvania.

    ii.   **Margaret Forster Stuart**, b. Meadville, Crawford County, Pennsylvania.

    iii.   **Mary Catharine Stuart**, b. Meadville, Crawford County, Pennsylvania.

    iv.   **Marie Reynolds Stuart**, b. Meadville, Crawford County, Pennsylvania; d. probably Denver, Colorado.

    v.   **Archibald Forster Stuart**, b. Meadville, Crawford County, Pennsylvania,

    vi.   **George Runyon Stuart**, b. Meadville, Crawford County, Pennsylvania

    vii.   **Juliet Stuart**, b. Meadville, Crawford County, Pennsylvania.

15. **James Edward Stuart** (Thomas 2, Archibald 1 Steuart) was born December 26, 1811 in Erie, Pennsylvania, and died 1881 in Meadville, Crawford County, Pennsylvania. He married **Elizabeth Ann Stebbins** May 06, 1858 in Meadville, daughter of Edward Stebbins and Sarah Atkinson. She was born December 11, 1834 in Meadville, Pennsylvania, and died March 1897 in Meadville, Pennsylvania.

Children of **James Stuart** and **Elizabeth Stebbins** are:

    i.   **Otto K. Stuart**, b. 1858, Meadville, Crawford County, Pennsylvania.

ii.   **Margaret E. Stuart**, b. 1862 Meadville, Crawford County Pennsylvania.

iii.   **William F. Stuart**, b. 1864, Meadville, Crawford County, Pennsylvania.

iv.   **Sarah Stuart**, b. 1865, Meadville, Crawford County, Pennsylvania; m. **Andrew W. Mulrainey,** Meadville, 1865.

v.   **Albert Edward Stuart**, b. March 14, 1867, Meadville, Pennsylvania; d. January 26, 1920, Grafton, Taylor County, West Virginia.

vi.   **Harry S. Stuart**, b. 1869, Meadville, Crawford County, Pennsylvania.

vii.   **James Henry Stuart**, b. Aft. 1870, Meadville, Crawford County, Pennsylvania.

16. **Charles Wallace Stuart Sr.** (Thomas 2, Archibald 1 Steuart) was born Aft. 1812. He married **Juliet Bell Baird** June 22, 1817, daughter of Jonathan Baird and Lucinda (?).

Children of **Charles Stuart** and **Juliet Baird** are:

i.   **Thomas Baird Stuart,** b. May 25, 1838; d. April 22, 1841.

ii.   **Lucy Catharine Stuart**, b. April 30, 1840; d. August 04, 1885.

iii.   **Thomas Heron Barber Stuart**, b. February 25, 1842; d. October 06, 1860.

iv. **Edward Ellis Stuart**, b. June 28, 1845; d. March 03, 1872.

v. **Rebecca Reynolds Stuart**, b. November 14, 1847; d. April 17, 1867.

vi. **Eliza Bell Stuart**, b. October 02, 1849; d. November 20, 1879.

vii. **Georgiana Stuart**, b. February 05, 1852; d. August 31, 1853.

viii. **Charles Wallace Stuart, Jr.**, b. June 02, 1854; d. February 28, 1892.

ix. **Alfred Clark Stuart.** b. March 29, 1856; d. September 21. 1856.

x. **Joseph Kelsey Stuart**, b. September 07, 1857; lived at Warren Pennsylvania.

xi. **Carrie Benton Stuart**, b. January 08, 1860.

xii. **Jennie Forster Stuart**; b. February 14, 1865; d. July 19, 1865.

17. **Thomas Heron Stuart** (Thomas 2, Archibald 1 Steuart). He married **Susan Cody**. He was a surgeon in the Civil War, according to Stewart Clan Magazine, Vol, XIX, No. 6, December 1941, p. 240.

Children of **Thomas Stuart** and **Susan Cody** are:

i. **Frank Stuart**.

ii. **James Stuart**.

18. Eleanor Donaldson Stewart (Eleanor Donaldson 2 Stuart, Archibald 1 Steuart) was born August 21, 1806 in North East, Erie County, Pennsylvania, and died August 31, 1888 in Guy Mills, Crawford County, Pennsylvania. She married **Francis Roy Brawley** March 08, 1838 in North East, Erie County, Pennsylvania.

Children of **Eleanor Stewart** and **Francis Brawley** are:

    i.   **James Brawley**.

    ii.   **John Newton Brawley**.

    iii.   **Marin Francis Brawley**.

    iv.   **Sabine Eliza Brawley**.

    v.   **Ella Brawley**.

    vi.   **Charles Milton Brawley**, b. September 12, 1852. Meadville, Crawford County, Pennsylvania; d. November 11, 1930, Brea, Orange County, California.

    vii. **James Harvey Brawley**.

19. Samuel Stewart (Eleanor Donaldson 2 Stuart, Archibald 1 Steuart) was born May 27, 1819 in Erie County, Pennsylvania, and died July 29, 1899 in Bedford Twp., Calhoun County, Michigan. He married **Mary Barr** February 06. 1849 in Battle Creek, Michigan. She was born in Erie County, Pennsylvania and died November 06, 1905 in Battle Creek, Michigan. She founded Harmonia M. E. Church in Bedford Twp., Calhoun County, Michigan. Both Samuel Stewart and Mary Barr Stewart are buried in Oak Hill Cemetery.

Children of **Samuel Stewart** and **Mary Barr** are:

    i.   **Elizabeth Ann Stewart**, b. March 05, 1850; m. (?) **Lusk,** Battle Creek, Michigan. She was a teacher.

    ii.   **Clark Addison Stewart**, b. December 30, 1850; d. Aug. 09, 1893.

    iii.   **Florence Merilla Stewart**, b. Feb. 05, 1854; d. 1934; m. **Stanley Lothridge**.

    iv.   **Walter Scott Stewart**, b. March 30, 1856; d. September 13, 1895.

    v.   **Otto Barr Stewart**, b. May 07, 1861; d. August 09, 1894, Chicago, Illinois.

    vi.   **Charles Samuel Stewart**, b. September 19, 1862.

    vii.   **Cassius Kirk Stewart,** b. April 23, 1865, Bedford Twp., Calhoun County, Michigan; d. June 01, 1918, Chicago, Illinois.

    viii. **Chauncey Leeroy Stewart,** b. March 29, 1867, Bedford Twp., Michigan; d. March 07, 1895.

    ix.   **Herbert Harper Stewart**, b. July 02, 1868, Bedford Twp., Michigan; d. Flint, Michigan.

    x.   **Ralph Ray Stewart**, b. September 15, 1874.

Generation No. 4

20. Robert Richey Stuart (Andrew Armstrong 3, James 2, Archibald 1 Steuart) was born April 19, 1826, and died in Denton, Doniphan County, Kansas. He married **Sarah Catherine Kaufman** December 09, 1856 in Jersey Shore, Lycoming County, Pennsylvania. She was born in Buffalo Valley, Union County, Pennsylvania, and died in Denton Doniphan County, Kansas.

Notes for Robert Richey Stuart:

In consideration for his aid in farming the home place, Robert Richey Stuart was given a 2/5 share of his father's estate and was named one of the Executors. He removed his family to Sandusky County, Ohio in 1864. His wife was a daughter of John and Elizabeth Kaufman of Buffalo Valley, Union County, Pennsylvania, where she was born. Her grandfather, Johann Nagel, was born in Hettle Twp. In 1811. Sarah's family moved to Jersey Shore or vicinity where she taught school. Rev. Henry Wiegand performed the marriage of Robert and Sarah and christened the three eldest children. After a sojourn of eight years in Sandusky and Erie Counties, the family removed to Doniphan County, Kansas to a farm near Denton, where many of his descendants live.

Children of **Robert Stuart** and **Sarah Kaufman** are:

i.   **John Andres Stuart**, b. September 01, 1857; d. July 01, 1904, New Orleans, Louisiana.

ii.   **Anna Mary Stuart**, b. March 27, 1860; d, December 02, 1863.

iii.   **Carrie Elizabeth Stuart**, b. Abt. 1861.

iv.   **James H. Stuart**, b. Abt. 1862.

v.   **Luella M. Stuart**, b. Abt. 1863.

vi.   **William Watson Stuart**, b. October 18, 1865, Sandusky County, Ohio; m. **Sarah L. Schleigh**; b. August 05, 1869; d. June 14, 1936. William Watson Stuart was the first doctor in Cortland County, Kansas.

vii.   **Charles Stuart**, b. September 06, 1889.

21. **Jane Stuart** (Archibald 3, James 2, Archibald 1 Steuart) was born 1821 and died August 21, 1881 in Canonsburg, Washington County, Pennsylvania. She married **William Snodgrass White** March 31, 1839. He was born December 12, 1812 in Cecil Township, Washington County, Pennsylvania, and died Aft. 1893 in Canonsburg, Washington County, Pennsylvania.

Notes for William Snodgrass White.

From Beers History of Washington County, Pennsylvania, p. 760: William Snodgrass White, retired agriculturist, is one of the highly respected citizens of Washington County. His grandfather, William White, came at an early date to this county and was married here. He died in Canonsburg and his wife followed him in 1827. They had three children, one son, John, and two daughters.

John White, father of our subject, grew to manhood in Canonsburg, and after attending the elementary schools of his native town, he entered Jefferson College, where he graduated in 1804. He next began studying law at Steubenville, where he was admitted to the bar. Later he returned to Washington County, where he married Agnes Park, daughter of John Park, of Cecil Township. He took up residence in Washington and acted as prothonotary one year.

Abandoning the law about this time, he commenced the study of medicine at Thompsonville, Peters Township, under the tuition of Dr. Robert Thompson. He resided in Cecil Township and taught school while he studied medicine. After taking his diploma, he commenced the practice of his new profession, and in November 1815 located about one and one-half miles east of Hickory where he practiced. In the following April he moved to Hickory where he continued to follow his profession up to the time of his death, July 1853, he then being 67 years of age. His wife followed him to the grave August 19, 1866 in her 77th year. In religion they were Presbyterians, and in politics he was a Whig.

William Snodgrass White was born December12, 1812 in Cecil Township, Washington County, and was three years old when his parents moved to Hickory. He received his education in the common schools and an academy. From 1835 to 1841, he conducted a general store in Hickory, and then moved on a farm on which he remained until the spring of1872, at which time he came to Canonsburg. On March 31, 1838, he married Miss Jane, daughter of Archibald Stewart of Chartiers township, Mr. White was a member of the old Know-Noting party, but since the formation of the Republican party he enrolled under their banner. He has frequently declined to accept positions of honor and trust. For forty years he has been a consistent member of the Presbyterian Church. His farm, containing 300 acres, lies about a half mile north of Hickory, and in addition he has ninety acres on which there is a coal mine, located near Hickory. Mr. White has retired from active life and his home is cared for by his dutiful and affectionate daughters, Jenette and Matilda. Both his paternal and maternal ancestors were of Scotch-Presbyterian descent, from the North of Ireland.

Children of **Jane Stuart** and **William White** are:

i. **John Stewart White**; d. May 1888. He served in the Civil War.

ii. **Agnes Ann White**, m. **John M. Miller**; d. May 1888.

iii. **Margaret Jane White**; m. **R. H. Black.** They lived in Canonsburg, Pennsylvania.

iv. **William Vance White**.

v. **Rebecca Jane White**, d, 1845.

vi. **Archibald Park White**, b. 1847; d. April 19, 1859,

vii. **Jenette White.**

viii. **Howard White**. He moved to Ohio.

ix. **Matilda K. D. White.**

22. **James Leonard Stuart** (James 3, Andrew 2, Archibald 1 Steuart) was born November 07, 1848 in Butler County, Pennsylvania, and died March 28, 1893 in North Washington, Butler County, Pennsylvania. He married **Esther McClymonds**.

Children of **James Leonard Stuart** and **Esther McClymonds** are:

i. **James Dallas Stuart.** b. 22, 1871, North Washington, Butler County, Pennsylvania; d. 1926. North

Washington, Butler County, Pennsylvania.

ii.   **Hugh Elmer Stuart,** b. 1873. North Washington, Butler County, Pennsylvania, d. 1949, Bruin, Butler County, Pennsylvania.

iii.   **Aldo M. Stuart,** b. 1878, North Washington, Butler County, Pennsylvania; d. January 16, 1893, North Washington, Butler County, Pennsylvania.

iv.   **Herbert T. Stuart**, b. 1879, North Washington, Butler County, Pennsylvania; d. 1958, North Washington, Butler County, Pennsylvania.

23. Margaret Forster Stuart (Archibald Forster 3, Thomas 2, Archibald 1 Steuart) was born in Meadville, Crawford County, Pennsylvania. She married **John H. Derby,** the Honorable John H. Derby of Sandy Hill, Washington County, New York. Margaret Forster Stuart's DAR National number 26172 is listed in the DAR lineage Book #27, p. 62.

Children of **Margaret Stuart** and **John Derby** are;

i.   **Archibald Stuart Derby.**

ii.   **Anna Louise Derby.**

iii.   **John H. Derby.**

24. **Maria Reynolds Stuart** (Archibald Forster 3, Thomas 2, Archibald 1 Steuart) was born in Meadville, Crawford County, Pennsylvania, and probably died in Denver, Colorado. She married the **Honorable William B. Rundle** of Denver, Colorado.

Children of **Maria Stuart** and **William Rundle** are:
    i.   **William B. Rundle.**
    ii.   **Mary Stuart Rundle.**
    iii.   **Alice P. Rundle.**

25. **Archibald Forster Stuart** (Archibald Forster 3, Thomas 2, Archibald 1 Steuart) was born in Meadville, Crawford County, Pennsylvania. He married **Elizabeth Johnson** in Meadville.

Children of **Archibald Stuart** and **Elizabeth Johnson** are:
    i.   **Louise Stuart.**
    ii.   **Henry Stuart.**
    iii.   **Norman Stuart.**

26. **Margaret E. Stuart** (James Edward 2, Thomas 2, Archibald 1 Steuart) was born in Meadville, Crawford County, Pennsylvania. She married **William B. Delo** Bef. 1888, son of **Samuel Delo** and **Rebecca Otto.** He was born 1861 in Pennsylvania.

Notes for Margaret E. Stuart:
    In 1897, Margaret Stuart Delo lived in Chicago

248

Junction, Huron County, Ohio.

Child of **Margaret Stuart** and **William Delo** is:

    i.   **Bernice A. Delo,** b. 1889, Pennsylvania.

27. **Albert Edward Stuart** (See also pp. 200-203 #46.) Albert Edward Stuart was born March 14, 1867 in Meadville, Pennsylvania and died January 26, 1920 in Grafton, Taylor County, West Virginia. He married **Uda Dietta Bell**, December 13, 1886 in Meadville, Pennsylvania, daughter of **Samuel Whitaker Bell** and **Mary Agnes Caldwell**. She was born August 03, 1868 in Burgettstown, Washington County, Pennsylvania, and died January 13, 1951 in Swarthmore, Delaware County, Pennsylvania.

Children of **Albert Stuart** and **Uda Bell** are:

    i.   **Virginia Stuart**, b. July 10, 1893, Marietta, Ohio; d. July 17, 1982 Chicago, Illinois (See also pp. 210-211, #55.)

    ii.   **Adelaide Elizabeth Stuart**, b. March 20, 1900, Marietta, Washington County, Ohio; d. May 1969, Springfield, Delaware County, Pennsylvania. (See also page 211-212, #56.)

    iii.   **Harold Albert Stuart**, b. 1902, Marietta, Ohio; d. September 23, 1937, Pittsburgh, Pennsylvania.

28. **Lucy Catharine Stuart** (Charles Wallace 3, Thomas 2, Archibald 1 Steuart) was born April 30. 1840

and died August 04, 1885. She married **Robert Taylor Shank**.

Children of **Lucy Stuart** and **Robert Taylor Shank** are: are:

    i.   **Robert Taylor Shank, Jr.**

    ii.   **Charles Wallace Shank.**

29. **Charles Wallace Stuart, Jr.** (Charles Wallace 3 Sr., Thomas 2, Archibald 1 Steuart) was born June 02, 1854, and died February 28, 1892. He married **Mary Josephine Houser.**

Children of **Charles Stuart** and **Mary Houser** are:

    i.   **Marion West Stuart.**

    ii.   **Juliet Bell Stuart.**

    iii.   **Adelaide Lucy Stuart.**

    iv.   **George Wallace Stuart.**

30. **Carrie Benton Stuart** (Charles Wallace 3, Thomas 2, Archibald Steuart 1) was born January 08, 1860. She married **Dudley Bemis**, son of **George Bemis** and **Juliana Bemus**. He was born June 12, 1864 in Meadville, Crawford County, Pennsylvania, and died May 12, 1945 in Lincoln, Nebraska. He was buried in Meadville, Pennsylvania.

Children of **Carrie Stuart** and **Dudley Bemis** are:

    i.   **Stuart Hamlin Bemis**, b. 1890.

ii.   **Marvin Prendergast Bemis**, b. June 22, 1891, Meadville, Crawford County, Pennsylvania.

Notes for Marvin Prendergast Bemis:

Marvin P. Bemis lived at 107 Shiloh Street, Mount Washington, Pittsburgh, PA on November 29, 1917 when he wrote to Adelaide Stuart, addressing her as "My Dear Cousin." The letter was about their mutual ancestor, Margaret Forster Stuart, who made the "Don't Give Up the Ship" flag. He mentioned an article which he wrote about her feat for its 100th anniversary in 1913, and talked about Aunt Adelaide Laycock, their mutual aunt.

Information about the parentage of Marvin Bemis was received from D. Bemis on April 20, 2001 (CDBemis@charter.net) stating that Carrie Stuart's middle name was Benton and that Dudley Bemis was a direct line to the Bemis family from Bemis Point, New York.

31. **Charles Milton Brawley** (Eleanor Donaldson Stewart 3, Eleanor Donaldson Stuart 2, Archibald 1 Steuart) was born September 12, 1852 in Meadville, Crawford County, Pennsylvania; d. November 11, 1930 in Brea, Orange County, California. He married **Unknown** October 07, 1876 in Guy Mills, Crawford County, Pennsylvania.

Children of **Charles Brawley** and **Unknown** are:

i.   **Roy Francis Brawley**, b. August 29, Guy Mills, Crawford County,

Pennsylvania; d. March 26, 1943, Brea,
Orange County, California.

ii.   **Roma Mary Brawley.**

32. **Charles Samuel Stewart,** b. 1862. He married
Flossie (?). She died September 12, 1944 in Conneaut,
Ohio.

Child of **Charles Stewart** and **Flossie** (?) is:

i.   **Margaret Stewart,** m. **Malcolm
        MacFarland. S**he lived in New Smyrna
        Beach, Florida.

33. **Cassius Kirk Stewart** (Samuel 3, Eleanor
Donaldson Stuart 2, Archibald 1 Steuart) was born April
23, 1865 in Bedford Twp., Calhoun County, Michigan,
and died June 01, 1918 in Chicago, Illinois. He married
Della Acker. She was born 1867 in Bedford County,
Michigan, and died September 23, 1953 in Chicago,
Illinois.

Notes for Cassius Kirk Stewart:
        The individual who submitted the Descendants
of Eleanor Stewart line to Family Tree Maker does not
identify herself. In the notes about Cassius Stewart and
Della Acker, she states: My mother Lulu (she hated her
name and renamed herself Luella) married first Mr.
William L. Fowler about 1916 and they had my sister
Peggy, whose real name was Della Fowler, but my
father adopted her. Mother married Dad April 23, 1923.

Children of **Cassius Stewart** and **Della Acker** are:

    i.   **Hazel Kirk Stewart**, b. 1886, Bedford Twp., Calhoun County, Michigan; d. June 15, 1907, Chicago, Illinois

    ii.   **Anna Stewart**, b. Abt. 1887; d.1918, Influenza epidemic.

34. Chauncey Leeroy Stewart (Samuel 3, Eleanor Donaldson 2, Archibald 1 Steuart) was born March 29, 1867 in Bedford Twp., Michigan and died March 07, 1895, He married **Unknown**.

Child of **Chauncey Leeroy Stewart** and **Unknown** is:

    i.   **Russell Stewart.**

35. Herbert Harper Stewart (Samuel 3, Eleanor Donaldson 2, Archibald 1 Steuart) was born July 02, 1868 in Bedford Twp., Michigan, and died in Flint, Michigan. He married **Unknown**.

Child of **Herbert Harper Stewart** and Unknown is:

    i.   **Herberta Chearer Stewart.**

Generation No. 5

36. Charles Stuart (Robert Richey 4, Andrew Armstrong 3, James 2, Archibald 1 Steuart was born September 06, 1889. He married **Grace Koppe.**

Notes for Charles Stuart:

He graduated from Colorado College and Yale University He spent eight years in the U. S. Forest Service, then wholesale lumber in New York City.

Notes for Grace Koppe:

Grace is a graduate of Colorado State University.

Child of **Charles Stuart** and **Grace Koppe** is:

      i.   **Charles Robert Stuart**, b. February 17, 1931

37. **James Dallas Stuart** (James Leonard 4, James 3, Andrew 2, Archibald 1 Steuart) was born June 22, 1871 in North Washington, Butler County, Pennsylvania, and died 1926 in North Washington, Butler County, Pennsylvania. He married **Sara Melzina Redic**.

Children of **James Stuart** and **Sara Redic** are:

      i.   **Esther Ellen Stuart**, b. August 17, 1897, North Washington, Butler County, Pennsylvania; d. October 23, 1960, Butler County, Pennsylvania.

      ii.   **Hugh Kenneth Stuart**, b. July 08, 1903, North Washington, Butler County, Pennsylvania; d. 1958; m. **Clara Morris**.

38. **Virginia Stuart** (Albert Edward 4, James Edward 3, Thomas 2, Archibald 1 Steuart) was born July 10, 1893 in Marietta, Washington County, Ohio, and died July 17,

1982 in Chicago, Illinois. She married **Joseph Smith Goode**, July 01, 1916 in Martinsburg, Berkeley County, West Virginia. She was 24 and well over the age requiring parental approval, but she gave her father's name as Charles, perhaps to avoid being found out by her family who did not approve of her choice, He was the son of **Alonzo Goode** and **Columbia Smith**. He was born July 25, 1882 in Richie County, West Virginia, and died June 07, 1952 in Auburn, Ritchie County, West Virginia. Both Virginia and Joe are buried in Auburn Cemetery, Auburn, West Virginia. (See also pp 210-211, #55)

Children of **Virginia Stuart** and **Joseph Goode** are:

    i.   **Joseph Stuart Goode**, b. 1920, Auburn, Ritchie County, West Virginia, d. December 26, 2001.

    ii.   **Adelaide Goode**, b. 1923, Auburn, Ritchie County, West Virginia; d. June 13, 2002, Western Springs, Illinois.

39. **Adelaide Elizabeth Stuart** (Albert Edward 4, James Edward 3, Thomas 2, Archibald 1, Steuart was born March 20, 1900 in Marietta, Washington County, Ohio, and died May 1969 in Springfield, Delaware County, Pennsylvania. She married **Ernest Markwood Pritchard**, son of **Rev. Millard Fillmore Pritchard** and **Rosa Bell Nestor** on June 01, 1927 in Clarksburg, Harrison County, West Virginia. He was born September 12, 1893 in Coleta, Whiteside County, Illinois, and died February 03, 1979 in Hackettstown, Warren County, New Jersey. Both Adelaide and Ernest are buried in Elk View Masonic Cemetery Clarksburg.

(See also pp. 211-212, #56)

Child of **Adelaide Stuart** and **Ernest Pritchard** is:

i.   **Emily Marshall Pritchard**, b. September 06, 1931, Pittsburgh, Allegheny County, Pennsylvania.

40. **Roy Francis Brawley** (Charles Milton 4, Eleanor Donaldson 3 Stewart, Eleanor Donaldson 3 Stuart, Archibald 1 Steuart) was born August 29, 1878 in Guy Mills, Crawford County, Pennsylvania, and died March 26, 1943 in Brea, Orange County, Pennsylvania. He married **Mary Cena Chase** November 30, 1898 in Guy Mills, Crawford County, Pennsylvania.

Children of **Roy Brawley** and **Mary Chase** are:

i.   **Walza Vera Brawley.**

ii.   **Ralph A. Brawley.**

iii.   **Leda Irene Brawley.**

iv.   **Charles Milton Brawley.**

v.   **Ray Martin Brawley.**

vi.   **Lucinda Brawley.**

vii.   **Vesta Brawley, b.** August 24, 1915, Guy Mills, Crawford County, Pennsylvania; d. November 01, 1994, Coarsegold, Madera County, California.

41. **Lulu Stewart** (Cassius Kirk 4, Samuel 3, Eleanor Donaldson 2 Stuart, Archibald 1 Steuart). She married (1) **William J. Fowler** Abt. 1916. She married (2)

Unknown April 23, 1923. She did not like the name Lulu, so she changed it to Luella.

Child of **Lulu Stewart** and **William Fowler** is:

       i.   **Della Peggy Fowler**.

Notes for Della Peggy Fowler:

      According to a descendant, Della Peggy Fowler was adopted after her father died by her mother's second husband. No surname of the latter is indicated in the notes.

42. **Herberta Chearer Stewart** (Herbert Harper 4, Samuel 3, Eleanor Donaldson Stuart 2, Archibald 1 Steuart. She married (?) **Tibbets**.

Child of **Herberta Stewart** and (?) **Tibbets** is:

       i.   **William Tibbets.** He lived in Pasadena, California.

Generation No. 6

43. **Charles Robert Stuart** (Charles 5, Robert Richey 4, Andrew Armstrong 3, James 2, Archibald 1 Steuart) was born February 17, 1931. He married **Joan F. Connell** March 07, 1958. Charles worked for Sperry Rand. He lived in Roslyn Heights, New York.

Children of **Charles Stuart** and **Joan Connell** are:

i.   **Donald Edward Stuart**, b. December
        16, 1958.

ii.   **Doreen Linda Stuart**, b. April 1961.

44. Esther Ellen Stuart (James Dallas 5, James
Leonard 4, James 3, Andrew 2, Archibald 1 Steuart was
born August 17, 1897 in North Washington, Butler
County, Pennsylvania, and died October 23, 1960 in
Butler County, Pennsylvania. She married **Clarence
Calvin Kelly.**

Children of **Esther Stuart** and **Clarence Kelly** are:

i.   **Louise Stewart Kelly**, b. August 11,
        Bruin, Butler County, Pennsylvania; m.
        (?) **Brosius**.

ii.   **Kenneth Kelly**, b. May 20, 1926, Butler
        County, Pennsylvania; m. **Norma (?).**

45. Joseph Stuart Goode (Virginia 5, Stuart, Albert
Edward 4, James Edward 3 Thomas 2, Archibald 1
Steuart) was born 1920 in Auburn, Ritchie County, West
Virginia, and died December 26, 2001 at the Veterans
Hospital in Richmond, Virginia. He married **Kay Bolt**
Jan. 01, 1946 in the 1st Baptist Church, Charleston,
South Carolina. She was born Oct. 29, 1917 in
Anderson, South Carolina. (See p. 221).

Child of **Joseph Stuart Goode** and **Kay Bolt** is:

i.   **Deborah Goode**, m. **Douglas Wilson
        Bailey**.

Children of **Deborah Goode** and **Douglas Wilson Bailey** are:

     i.   **Allyson Kay Bailey.**
    ii.   **Angela Marie Bailey.**

46. Adelaide Goode (Virginia 5 Stuart, Albert Edward 4, James Edward 3, Thomas 2, Archibald 1 Steuart was born 1923 in Auburn, Ritchie County, West Virginia, and died June 13, 2001 in Western Springs, Illinois. She married **Earl Jennings Grimm** 1943 in West Virginia. He was born 1923 in Pennsboro, Ritchie County, West Virginia, and died October 04, 2001 in Western Springs, Illinois. After serving in the U.S. Navy during World War II, Jennings obtained a master's degree in business from West Virginia University and moved to Chicago where he spent his career with Swift and Company. Both Adelaide and Jennings are buried in Arlington National Cemetery, Arlington, Virginia. (See p. 215, #63.)

Children of **Adelaide Goode** and **Earl Jennings Grimm** are:

     i.   **Diana Lee Grimm**, b. May 06, 1944 in Auburn, Ritchie County, West Virginia. She married **Stephen Edgar Wright**, b. March 20, 1942.
    ii.   **Linda Grimm**, b. Abt. 1948.

47. Emily Marshall Pritchard (Adelaide Elizabeth 5 Stuart, Albert Edward 4, James Edward 3, Thomas 2, Archibald 1 Steuart) was born September 06, 1931 in Pittsburgh, Allegheny County Pennsylvania. She married **Boyd Balford Cary, Jr.** September 28, 1953 in Rutledge, Delaware County, Pennsylvania. He was born October 29, 1923 in Enid, Garfield County, Oklahoma, the son of **Boyd Balford Cary, Sr.** and **Margaret McLaughlin.** (See p. 215.)

Children of **Emily Pritchard** and **Boyd Cary** are:
    i.   **Matthew Roger Cary**, b. September 09, 1954.
    ii.   **Roland Mylles Cary**, b. September 05, 1958.

48. **Vesta Brawley** (Charles Milton 4, Eleanor Donaldson 3 Stewart, Eleanor Donaldson 2 Stuart, Archibald 1 Steuart) was born August 24, 1915 in Guy Mills, Crawford County, Pennsylvania. She married (?) **Deelstra**.

Children of **Vesta Brawley** and (?) **Deelstra** are:
    i.   **Janelle Deelstra.**
    ii.   **Sharon Deelstra.**
    iii.   **Christine Deelstra.**
    iv.   **Janet Deelstra.**

Generation No. 7

49. **Diana Lee Grimm** (Adelaide 6 Goode, Virginia 5 Stuart, Albert Edward 4,, James Edward 3, Thomas 2, Archibald 1 Steuart) was born May 06, 1944 in Auburn, Ritchie County, West Virginia. She married **Stephen**

Edgar Wright, b. March 20, 1942. They met at Hendricks College in Arkansas. He became a doctor. They have lived in Salt Lake City, Utah and currently (2018) live in Amarillo, Texas.

Children of **Diana Grimm** and **Stephen Wright** are:

    i.   **Stuart Benjamin Wright,** b. May 04, 1969. He is a physician and began medical practice in Oneida, New York.

    ii.   **Stephanie Lee Wright**, b. October 25, 1974. She married **Christopher Randall Miller.**

Children of **Stuart Benjamin Wright** are:

    i.   **Lindsey Elaine Wright**, b. April 25, 1996.

    ii.   **Paul Robert Wright,** b. January 25, 2002.

    iii.   **Evan George Wright**, b. August 19, 2004.

Child of **Stephanie Lee Wright** and **Christopher Randall Miller** is:

    i.   **Grace Lee Miller**, b. April 22, 2010.

STEBBINS FAMILY HISTORY

The first Stebbins ancestor who merits mention appears in articles and books about the Battle of Hastings on October 14, 1066 between the French army led by William, Duke of Normandy, and the English army led by King Harold. Although there are several historical accounts about the invention of stirrups, perhaps early in China or later in Germany, the decision to use stirrups on horses belonging to the French victors is attributed to a Frenchman named Stebbins. This is one of the reasons for the victory, enabling the French horsemen to best the English.

Like many of his fellow officers, this Stebbins was among those who stayed in England and acquired land doled out by William to his friends and associates. He probably settled in the county of Essex where his descendants appear in countless church and country records dating back to the early 16th century. A village named Stebbing is the site of a very old parish church several miles from Bocking Parish where the earliest recorded ancestor, William Stebbins, died. Edward Stebbins who married Sarah Ann Atkinson, daughter of Thomas Atkinson, is a direct descendant of this family.

Note about STEBBINS family history.

This book covers only the Stebbins line running directly from the early ancestors to Edward Stebbins of

Meadville, Crawford County, Pennsylvania via Rowland Stebbins, one of the first immigrants to America. Those interested in more extensive records should access the STEBBINS CUZ-FILE compiled by CaptRod@gte.net. It incorporates thousands of Stebbins descendants in both England and the United States.

Generation No. 1

1. William Stebbins was born Abt. 1521 in Essex County, England, and died May 15, 1561 in Bocking Parish, Essex County, England.

Generation No. 2

2. Child of **William Stebbins** is:

i.	**William Stebbins**, born 1540 in Black Notley, Essex County, England.	

Children of **William Stebbins** are:

i.	**Thomas Francis Stebbins**, b. Bocking, Essex County, England; d. October 16, 1660, Bocking, Essex County, England.	
ii.	**William Stebbins**, b. 1567, Black Notley, Essex County, England; d. Black Notley, Essex County, England.	
iii.	**Elizabeth Stebbins**, m. **John Leavens**, June 16, 1602, Bocking, Essex County, England; b. Abt. 1565.	

Generation No. 3

3. **Thomas Francis Stebbins** (William 2, William 1) was born 1565 in Bocking, Essex County, England, and died October 16, 1660 in Bocking, Essex County, England. He married **Ellen** (?) 1591 in Bocking, Essex, England. She was born Abt. 1570 in Bocking, Essex County, England, and died 1612 in Bocking, Essex County, England

Children of **Thomas Stebbins** and **Ellen** (?) are:

i. **Dennis Stebbins**, b. Abt. 1590; d. November 1590.

ii. **Rowland Stebbins**, b. October 1592, Bocking Parish, Essex County, England; d. December 14, 1671, Northampton, Hampshire, Massachusetts.

iii. **Martin Stebbins**, b. April 28, 1594, Bocking Parish, Essex County, England; d. November 1659, Boston, Massachusetts.

iv. **Elizabeth Stebbins,** b. May 07, 1598, Black Notley, Essex County, England.

Generation No. 4

4. **Rowland Stebbins** (Thomas Francis 3, William 2, William 1) was born October 1592 in Bocking Parish, Essex County, England (probably in the village of Stebbing), and died December 14, 1671 in Northampton, Hampshire County, Massachusetts. He married **Sarah**

264

Whiting November 30, 1618 in St. Mary's Church, Bocking, Essex County, England, daughter of **John Whiting** and **Sarah Smith**. She was born November 30, 1591 in Boston, Lincoln County, England, and died August 04, 1649 in Springfield, Hampden County, Massachusetts. He and his family first appear in "The Original List of Persons of Quality," a book commonly known as Hotten's List of Emigrants.

Notes about Rowland Stebbins:

      He and his family departed Ipswich, England in 1634 on "Good Bark Francis" last of April 1645 and landed at Boston, Massachusetts. The shipping list gives Rowland's age as 40, wife Sarah 43, and children Thomas 14, Sarah 11, John 8, and Elizabeth 6. They settled first in Roxbury. Rowland Stebbins was one of the early settlers of Springfield, moving there about 1649. Sarah Whiting Stebbins was buried at Springfield 04 October 1649. Rowland had a seat in the meeting house at Springfield in 1663. Sometime after February 1664-65, Rowland moved to live with his son John at Northampton, Massachusetts, where he died 14 December 1671, leaving a will dated 01 March 1669/70.

Children of **Rowland Stebbins** and **Sarah Whiting** are

    i.   **Thomas Stebbins**, b. Bet. 1619-1620, Ipswich, Suffolk County, England; d. September 15, 1683, Springfield, Hampden County, Massachusetts; m. (1) **Hannah Wright**, November 16, 1645, Springfield, Massachusetts; b. August 1626, Wright Bridge, Essex County, England; d. October 16, 1660,

Springfield, Hampden County, Massachusetts; m. (2) **Abigail Burt,** December 14, 1676, Springfield, Hampden County, Massachusetts; b. 1623, Harbeton, Devonshire, England; d. February 03, 1691/92, Springfield, Hampden County, Massachusetts.

ii. **Sarah Stebbins,** b. Abt. 1623, Bocking, Essex, England; d. October 04, 1649, Springfield, Hampton County, Massachusetts. She married **Thomas Merrick** September 14, 1639 in Springfield, Hampden County, Massachusetts. He was born Abt. 1620 in Wales, and died September 07, 1704, in Springfield, Hampden County, Massachusetts.

iii. **John Stebbins** b. 1626, Bocking, Essex, England, d. March 29, 1679, Northampton, Massachusetts. He married (1) **Mary Ann Munson** May 15, 1646 in Springfield, Hampshire County, Massachusetts. She was born Abt. 1623, probably in England, and died 1656 in Northampton, Massachusetts. He married (2) **Abigail Bartlett**, November 17, 1657. She was born 1630 in Hartford, Hartford County, Connecticut, and died October 11, 1710, South Hadley Falls, Hampshire County, Massachusetts.

Note for John Stebbins:

Several references, including The Stebbins Genealogy by Ralph Stebbins Greenlee and Robert

Lemuel Greenlee (Volumes I and II, Volume 1, pages 1 through 59, The First Generation), say that the manner of his death was regarded as "mysterious, in some way connected with witchcraft, but nothing was proved.

    iv.   **Elizabeth Stebbins**, b. Abt. 1628, Bocking, Essex, England; d. October 28, 1700 Springfield, Hampden County, Massachusetts.

Generation No. 5

5. **Thomas Stebbins** (Rowland 4, Thomas Francis 3 William 2, William 1) was born 1619-1620 in Bocking, Essex, England, and died September 25, 1683 in Springfield, Massachusetts. He married (1) **Hannah Wright** November 16, 1645 in Springfield, Massachusetts, daughter of **Samuel Wright** and **Margaret Stratton.** He married (2) **Abigail Burt Munn**, daughter of **Henry Burt** and **Eulelia (?)** and widow of **Benjamin Munn**. She was born Abt. 1623 in England and died November 23, 1707 in Springfield, Massachusetts.

Children of **Thomas Stebbins** and **Hannah Wright** are:

    i.   **Samuel Wright Stebbins,** b. September 19, 1646, Springfield, Hampden County, Massachusetts; d. July 13, 1708, Springfield, Hampden County, Massachusetts.

    ii.   **Thomas Stebbins**, b. July 31, 1648, Springfield, Hampden County, Massachusetts; d. December 07, 1695,

Springfield, Hampden County, Massachusetts.

iii. **Joseph Stebbins**, b. May 18, 1650, Springfield, Hampden County, Massachusetts; d. November 09, 1650, Springfield, Hampden County, Massachusetts.

iv. **Joseph Stebbins**, b. October 24, 1652, Springfield, Hampden County, Massachusetts; d. October 15, 1728, Springfield, Hampden County, Massachusetts.

v. **Sarah Stebbins**, b. June 18, 1654, Springfield, Massachusetts; d. November 06, 1721, Springfield, Massachusetts.

vi. **Edward Stebbins**, b. April 14, 1656, Spring, Hampden County, Massachusetts; d. October 31, 1712, Springfield, Hampden County, Massachusetts.

vii. **Benjamin Stebbins**, b. April 11, 1658, Springfield, Hampden County, Massachusetts; d. October 12, 1698, Springfield, Hampden County, Massachusetts.

viii. **Rowland Stebbins,** b. August 01, 1660, Springfield, Massachusetts; d. April 24, 1661, Springfield, Massachusetts.

ix. **Hannah Stebbins**, b. August 01, 1660, Springfield, Massachusetts.

Generation No. 6

6. **Joseph Stebbins** (Thomas 5, Rowland 4, Thomas Francis 3, William 2, William 1) was born October 24, 1652 in Springfield, Massachusetts and died October 15, 1728 in Springfield, Massachusetts. He married **Sarah Dorchester** November 27, 1673 in Springfield, Massachusetts, daughter of **Anthony Dorchester** and **Martha Kritchwell.** She was born October 16, 1653 in Springfield, Massachusetts and died August 18, 1746 in Springfield, Massachusetts

Children of **Joseph Stebbins** and **Sarah Dorchester** are:

i.   **Joseph Stebbins**, b. October 07, 1674, Springfield, Massachusetts; d. September 29, 1722, Springfield, Massachusetts.

ii.   **Benjamin Stebbins,** b. January 23, 1675/76, Springfield, Massachusetts; d. October 17, 1748, Springfield, Massachusetts.

iii.   **Thomas Stebbins**, b. July 13, 1679, Springfield, Massachusetts; d. June 29, 1713, Springfield, Massachusetts.

iv.   **John Stebbins**, b. September 22, 1681, Springfield, Massachusetts; d. November 17, 1686.

v.   **Mehitabel Stebbins**, b. November 27, 1683, Springfield, Massachusetts; d. March 03, 1761, Northampton, Massachusetts.

vi. **Ebenezer Stebbins**, b. November 20, 1686, Springfield, Massachusetts; d. July 17, 1765.

vii. **Sarah Stebbins**, b. June 08, 1688, Springfield, Massachusetts; d. February 06, 1725/26, Springfield, Massachusetts.

viii. **John Stebbins** b. November 08, 1690, Springfield, Massachusetts; February 23, 1732/43, Springfield, Massachusetts.

ix. **Hannah Stebbins,** b. November 09, 1692; m. **Michael Tonslay**, March 11, 1712/13.

x. **Martha Stebbins**, b. June 28, 1697, Springfield, Massachusetts; d. March 03, 1737/38, Springfield, Massachusetts.

Generation No. 7

7. **John Stebbins** (Joseph 6. Thomas 5, Rowland 4 Thomas Francis 3, William 2, William 1) was born November 08, 1690 in Springfield, Massachusetts, and died February 23, 1742/43 in Springfield, Massachusetts. He married **Sarah Warriner** December 22. 1715 in Springfield, Massachusetts, daughter of **James Warriner** and **Sarah Alvord**. She was born April 01, 1694 in Springfield, Massachusetts, and died August 25, 1734 in Springfield, Massachusetts.

Children of **John Stebbins** and **Sarah Warriner** are:

i. **Sarah Stebbins**, b. April 08, 1717; d. November 1778.

ii.   **Amy Stebbins**, b. Augusts 06, 1724,
       Springfield, Massachusetts; d. October
       07, 1760, Springfield, Massachusetts; m.
       Jacob White, February 02, 1774/75,
       West Springfield, Massachusetts; b.
       November 13, 1716; d. January 10, 1762,
       West Springfield.

iii.   **John Stebbins**, b. December 30, 1726,
       Springfield, Massachusetts; d. October
       16, 1760, Springfield, Massachusetts.

iv.   **Lydia Stebbins**, b. September 08, 1728,
       Springfield, Massachusetts; m. (1) **Moses
       Merrick**, February 02, 1743/44; m. (2)
       Samuel Brooks, July 1759.

v.   **Edward Stebbins**, b. September 26,
       1729, Springfield, Massachusetts; d.
       April 10, 1816, Springfield,
       Massachusetts; m. **Elizabeth Burt**,
       February 19, 1761; b. April 08, 1740,
       Springfield, Massachusetts; d. September
       08, 1821, Springfield, Massachusetts.

vi.   **Asaph Stebbbins**, b. February 03,
       1731/32, Springfield, Massachusetts; d.
       July 20, 1806, Granby, Massachusetts; m.
       Lucy Bardwell, Abt. 1759; d. February
       18, 1826, Granby, Massachusetts.

vii.   **Lois Stebbins**, b. February 03, 1732/33,
       Springfield, Massachusetts; m. **Thomas
       Goldwaithe**.

Generation No. 8

8. **Edward Stebbins** (John 7, Joseph 6, Thomas 5,
Rowland 4, Thomas Francis 3, William 2, William 1)
was born September 26, 1729 in Springfield,
Massachusetts, and died April 10, 1816 in Springfield,
Massachusetts. He married **Elizabeth Burt** February 19,
1761 in Springfield, Massachusetts, daughter of **Joseph
Burt** and **Thankful McRanny**. She was born April 08,
1740 in Springfield, Massachusetts, and died September
08, 1821 in Springfield, Massachusetts.

Children of **Edward Stebbins** and **Elizabeth Burt** are:

    i.   **Amy Stebbins**, b. October 09, 1761,
        Springfield, Massachusetts; d. January
        22, 1840, Springfield, Massachusetts; m.
        Earl Cooley, November 28, 1781,
        Springfield, Massachusetts; b. Abt. 1758.

   ii.   **Bathsheba Stebbins**, b. December 26,
        1762, Springfield, Massachusetts; m.
        Remembrance Smith, February 19,
        1781, Springfield, Massachusetts.

  iii.   **Elizabeth Stebbins**, b. October 16, 1764,
        Springfield, Massachusetts; d. June 16,
        1841, Springfield, Massachusetts.

  iv.   **Warham Stebbins**, b. December 07,
        1765, Springfield, Massachusetts; d.
        November 09, 1840, Springfield,
        Massachusetts.

    v.   **Elam Stebbins**, b. March 23, 1768,
        Springfield, Massachusetts; d. October
        05, 1842, Springfield, Massachusetts.

vi.   **Edward Stebbins**, b. February 20, 1770, Springfield, Massachusetts.

vii.   **Levi Stebbins,** b. July 11, 1772, Springfield, Massachusetts; d. May 30, 1856, Williamsburg, Massachusetts.

viii.   **Ithamer Stebbins**, b. March 26, 1776, Springfield, Massachusetts; d. December 22, 1861, Springfield, Massachusetts.

ix.   **Luther Stebbins**, b. March 27, 1778, Springfield, Massachusetts; d. March 28, 1868, Caldwell, New York.

x.   **Lois Stebbins**, b. January 01, 1781, Springfield, Massachusetts; m. **Luther Russell**, February 14, 1801.

xi.   **James Stebbins**, b. January 28, 1783, Springfield, Massachusetts.

Generation No. 9

9. **Edward Stebbins** (Edward 8, John 7, Joseph 6, Thomas 5, Rowland 4, Thomas Francis 3, William 2, William 1) was born February 20, 1770 in Springfield, Massachusetts. He married **Anna Taylor** June 11, 1792 in Springfield, Massachusetts. She was born in Springfield, Massachusetts, and died 1860.

Children of **Edward Stebbins** and **Anna Taylor** are:

i.   **Nathaniel T. Stebbins,** b Aft. 1793; d. August 16, 1872, Nebraska City, Nebraska.

ii.   **Ann Stebbins,** b. Aft. 1793, Springfield, Massachusetts; m. **Theodore Sykes**.

iii.   **Edward Stebbins**, b. October 26, 1793, Springfield, Massachusetts; d. November 06, 1846, Meadville, Pennsylvania.

iv.   **Harriet Stebbins**, b. December 01, 1804; d. Ludlow, Massachusetts.

v.   **Mary W. Stebbins**, b. March 16, 1807, Longmeadow, Massachusetts; m. **Israel Markham** May 30, 1827, Longmeadow, Massachusetts; b. October 07, 1797, Enfield, Connecticut; d. Enfield, Connecticut.

Generation No. 10

10. **Edward Stebbins** (Edward 9, Edward 8, John 7, Joseph 6, Thomas 5, Rowland 4, Thomas Francis 3, William 2, William 1) was born October 26, 1793 in Springfield, Massachusetts, and died November 06, 1846 in Meadville, Pennsylvania. He married (1) **Delila Ellis** June 24, 1823. She was born in Chester, Massachusetts, and died August 04, 1823 in Meadville, Pennsylvania. He married (2) **Sarah Ann Atkinson** 1829 in Meadville, Pennsylvania, daughter of **Thomas Atkinson** and **Sarah Sommers**. She was born January 04, 1812, and died April 01, 1871 in Meadville, Pennsylvania.

Children of **Edward Stebbins** and **Sarah Atkinson** are:

    i.   **Edward E. Stebbins,** b. November 13, 1830, Meadville, Pennsylvania.

    ii.   **Thomas Atkinson Stebbins,** b. October 25, 1832, Meadville, Pennsylvania; d. January 26, 1921, Meadville, Pennsylvania.

    iii.   **Ann Elizabeth Stebbins,** b. December 11, 1834, Meadville, Pennsylvania; m. **James Stuart,** October 1857, b. Abt. 1831; d. Erie, Pennsylvania.

    iv.   **James Henry Stebbins,** b. March 05, 1837; d. July 16, 1895, Meadville, Pennsylvania.

    v.   **Delila Ellis Stebbins,** b. October 24, 1839l n, (1) **William Frey;** m. (2) **Dewitt Harrington.**

    vi.   **Frederick Wallace Stebbins,** b. May 08, 1842, Meadville, Pennsylvania.

    vii.   **Mary Jane Adelaide Stebbins**, b. October 24, 1844; d. June 30, 1910; m. **Henry Laycock,** April 07, 1872.

    viii.   **Henrietta Atkinson Stebbins**, b. February 10, 1847; d. September 16, 1848.

Generation No. 11

11. Edward E. Stebbins (Edward 10, Edward 9, Edward 8, John 7, Joseph 6, Thomas 5, Rowland 4, Thomas Francis 3, William 2, William 1) was born

November 13, 1830 in Meadville, Pennsylvania. He married **Elizabeth Linegar** December 25, 1852 in Cleveland, Ohio, daughter of **(?) Linegar** and **Mary Walters.** She was born June 28, 1837 in Weisenstine, Switzerland. She died Abt. 1900 in Mount Dora, Florida. He died in 1919.

Child of **Edward Stebbins** and **Elizabeth Linegar** is:

    i.   **William Stebbins**, b. 1856, Cleveland, Ohio; d. 1857, Cleveland, Ohio.

12. Thomas Atkinson Stebbins (Edward 10, Edward 9, Edward 8, John 7, Joseph 6, Thomas 5, Rowland 4, Thomas Francis 3, William 2, William 1) was born October 25, 1832 in Meadville, Crawford County, Pennsylvania, and died January 26, 1921 in Meadville, Crawford County, Pennsylvania. He married **Caroline A. Coburn** November 06, 1858 in Meadville, Crawford County, Pennsylvania. She was born December 11, 1836, and died August 11, 1891 in Meadville, Crawford County, Pennsylvania. Both were buried in Meadville.

Children of **Thomas Stebbins** and **Caroline Coburn** are:

    i.   **Edward Ellsworth Stebbins**, b. April 01, 1861, Meadville, Crawford County, Pennsylvania; d. November 21, 1941, Meadville, Crawford County, Pennsylvania.

    ii.   **Henrietta Stebbins**, b. October 15, 1864, Meadville, Crawford County, Pennsylvania; m. **Edward Eiler**.

iii.   **Gertrude Stebbins**, b. November 06, 1867, Meadville, Crawford County, Pennsylvania; d. November 21, 1869, Meadville, Crawford County, Pennsylvania. She is buried in Meadville.

iv.   **Thomas Burton Stebbins**, b. April 20, 1862, Meadville, Crawford County, Pennsylvania; d. 1951, Meadville. Crawford County, Pennsylvania.

13. Elizabeth Ann Stebbins (Edward 10, Edward 9, Edward 8, John 7, Joseph 6, Thomas 5, Rowland 4, Thomas Francis 3, William 2, William 1) was born December 11, 1834 in Meadville, Crawford County, Pennsylvania, and died March 1897 in Meadville, Crawford County, Pennsylvania. She married **James Edward Stuart** May 06, 1858 in Meadville, Pennsylvania, son of **Thomas Stuart** and **Margaret Forster**. He was born December 26, 1811 in Erie, Pennsylvania, and died 1881 in Meadville, Pennsylvania.

Children of **Elizabeth Stebbins** and **James Stuart** are:

i.   **Otto K. Stuart,** b. 1858, Meadville, Crawford County, Pennsylvania

ii.   **Margaret E. Stuart**, b. 1862, Meadville, Crawford County, Pennsylvania.

iii.   **William F. Stuart**, b. 1864, Meadville, Crawford County, Pennsylvania.

iv.   **Sarah Stuart**, b. 1865, Meadville, Crawford County, Pennsylvania; m. **Andrew W. Mulrainey,** Meadville,

277

Crawford County, Pennsylvania; b. December 1865.

v.   **Albert Edward Stuart**, b. March 14, 1865, Meadville, Pennsylvania; d. January 26, 1920, Grafton, Taylor County, West Virginia.

vi.   **Harry S. Stuart**, b. 1869, Meadville, Crawford County, Pennsylvania.

vii.   **James Henry Stuart**, b. Aft. 1870, Meadville, Crawford County, Pennsylvania.

14. **Delila Ellis Stebbins** (Edward 10, Edward 9, Edward 8, John 7, Joseph 6, Thomas 5, Rowland 4, Thomas Francis 3, William 2, William 1) was born October 24, 1839 in Meadville, Crawford County, Pennsylvania, and died Bet. 1897-1910 in Meadville, Crawford County, Pennsylvania. She married (1) **William Frey** January 06, 1858 in Meadville, Crawford County, Pennsylvania. She married (2) **Dewitt Clinton Herrington** December 29, 1868 in Meadville, son of **Edward Herrington** and **Nancy Burchfield**. He was born April 1837 in Pennsylvania, and died July 31, 1910 in Meadville, Crawford County, Pennsylvania.

Children of **Delila Stebbins** and **William Frey** are:

i.   **Maggie Louise Frey**, b. Aft. 1858, Meadville, Crawford County, Pennsylvania.

ii.   **Mary Adelaide Frey**, b. Bef. 1864, Meadville, Crawford County, Pennsylvania.

278

Child of **Delila Stebbins** and **Dewitt Herrington** is:

    iii.   **Edward Augustus Herrington**, b. Aft.
        1868, Meadville, Crawford County,
        Pennsylvania.

15. **Frederick Wallace Stebbins** (Edward 10, Edward
9, Edward 8, John 7, Joseph 6, Thomas 5, Rowland 4,
Thomas Francis 3, William 2, William 1) was born May
08, 1842 in Meadville, Crawford County, Pennsylvania,
and died in Cleveland, Ohio. He married **Martha
Catchall** Abt. 1867.

Children of **Frederick Stebbins** and **Martha Catchall**
are:

    i.   **Harry Stebbins,** b. 1867.
    ii.   **Maud Stebbins,** b. Aft. 1867.

Generation No. 12

16. **Edward Ellsworth Stebbins** (Thomas Atkinson
Stebbins 11, Edward 10, Edward 9, Edward 8, John 7,
Joseph 6, Thomas 5, Rowland 4, Thomas Francis 3,
William 2, William 1) was born April 01,1861 in
Meadville, Crawford County, Pennsylvania, and died
November 21, 1941 in Meadville, Crawford County,
Pennsylvania. He married **Mary Elizabeth Stafford**
October 27, 1885. She was born June 23, 1864 and died
November 01, 1949.

Children of **Edward Ellsworth Stebbins** and **Mary Stafford** are:

i.   **Edward E. Stebbins**, b. August 26, 1886, Meadville, Crawford County, Pennsylvania; d. September 06, 1886, Meadville, Crawford County, Pennsylvania.

ii.   **Carrie Elizabeth Stebbins**, b. December 13, 1891, Meadville, Crawford County, Pennsylvania; d. May 31, 1963; m. **Parke Grismore**.

iii.   **Edna Henrietta Stebbins,** b. July 12, 1894, Meadville, Crawford County, Pennsylvania; d. April 01. 1968, Pittsburgh, Allegheny County, Pennsylvania.

iv.   **Charles Stafford Stebbins**, b. March 02, 1896, Meadville, Crawford County, Pennsylvania; d. June 01, 1976, Akron, Summit County, Ohio.

v.   **Frank Marvin Stebbins**, b. August 21, 1897, Meadville, Crawford County, Pennsylvania; d. May 29, 1907, Meadville, Crawford County, Pennsylvania.

vi.   **Robert Lewis Stebbins**, b. February 20, 1903, Meadville, Crawford County, Pennsylvania; d. March 25, 1903, Meadville, Crawford County, Pennsylvania.

vii.   **Thomas Atkinson Stebbins**, b. March 07, 1904, Meadville, Crawford County, Pennsylvania; d. July 02, 1985.

viii. **Harold Burton Stebbins**, b. May 31, 1907, Meadville, Crawford County, Pennsylvania; d. September 09, 1976, Wadsworth, Summit County, Ohio.

ix. **Edward Ellsworth Stebbins, Jr.**, b. July 04, 1909l Meadville, Crawford County, Pennsylvania; d. October 10l 1969; m. **Catherine (?).**

17. **Albert Edward Stuart** (Elizabeth Ann Stebbins 11, Edward 10, Edward 9, Edward 8, John 7, Joseph 6, Thomas 5 Rowland 4, Thomas Francis 3, William 2, William 1) was born March 14, 1865 in Meadville, Crawford County Pennsylvania (See pages 200-203, #46 and 249 #27.)

18. **Margaret E. Stuart** (Elizabeth Ann Stebbins 11, Edward 10, Edward 9, Edward 8, John 7, Joseph 6, Thomas 5 Rowland 4, Thomas Francis 3, William 2, William 1 Stebbins was born 1962 in Meadville, Crawford County, Pennsylvania.

19. **Mary Adelaide Frey** (Delila Ellis Stebbins 12, Elizabeth Ann Stebbins 11, Edward 10. Edward 9. Edward 9. John 7, Joseph 6. Thomas 5, Rowland 4, Thomas Francis 3, William 2, William 1) was born Bef. 1864 in Meadville, Crawford County, Pennsylvania.

Generation No. 13

20. **Edna Henrietta Stebbins** (Edward Ellsworth 12. Thomas Atkinson, 11, Edward 10, Edward 9, Edward 8,

John 7, Joseph 6, Thomas 5, Rowland 4, Thomas
Francis 3, William 2, William 1) was born July 12, 1894
in Meadville, Crawford County, Pennsylvania, and died
April 01, 1968 in Pittsburgh Allegheny County,
Pennsylvania. She married **Lear Markel**, 1922.

Child of **Edna Stebbins** and **Lear Markel** is:

    i.   **Gordon Allen Markel,** b. March 09,
               1934.

21. **Charles Stafford Stebbins** (Edward Ellsworth 12,
Thomas Atkinson 11, Edward 10, Edward 9, Edward 8,
John 7, Joseph 6, Thomas 5, Rowland 4, Thomas
Francis 3, William 2, William 1) was born March 02,
1896 in Meadville, Crawford County, Pennsylvania, and
died June 01, 1976 in Akron, Summit County, Ohio. He
married **Matilda (?)** 1923.

Child of **Charles Stebbins** and **Matilda** is:

    i.   **Lois Stebbins,** b. Aft. 1923; m. **Robert**
               Augstadt.

Note for Lois Stebbins:

    In 1984, Lois Stebbins Augstadt was living at
500 S. Kensington, Le Grange, Illinois.

22. **Thomas Atkinson Stebbins, Sr.** (Edward
Ellsworth 12, Thomas Atkinson 11, Edward 10 Edward
9, Edward 8, John 7, Joseph 6, Thomas 5, Rowland 4,
Thomas Francis 3, William 2, William 1) was born
March 07, 1904 in Meadville, Crawford County,

Pennsylvania and died July 02, 1985. He married **Inez Brand** 1929. She was born December 28,1907 and died March 02, 1987.

Children of **Thomas Atkinson Stebbins Sr.** and **Inez Brand** are:

  i.   **Thomas Atkinson Stebbins, Jr.,** b. June 01, 1932; m. **Shirley Watson.**

  ii.   **Dolores Stebbins,** b. October 02, 1937.

  iii. **William Edward Stebbins Sr..** b. June 30, 1942.

23. Harold Burton Stebbins (Edward Ellsworth 12, Thomas Atkinson 11, Edward 10l Edward 9, Edward 8, John 7, Joseph 6, Thomas 5, Rowland 4, Thomas Francis 3, William 2, William 1) was born May 31, 1907 in Meadville, Crawford County, Pennsylvania, and died September 09, 1976 in Wadsworth, Summit County, Ohio. He married **Muriel Alice Sharrock** July 03, 1932 in Akron, Ohio. She was born April 22, 1905 in Galion, Crawford County, Ohio.

Children of **Harold Stebbins** and **Muriel Sharrock** are:

  i.   **Carol Ann Stebbins,** b. November 24, 1933, Akron, Summit County, Ohio.

  ii.   **Kathleen Stebbins** b. May 11, 1944, Wooster, Wayne County, Ohio.

24. Virginia Stuart (Albert Edward 12, Elizabeth Ann Stebbins 11, Edward 10, Edward 9, Edward 8, John 7, Joseph 6, Thomas 5, Rowland 4, Thomas Francis 3,

William 2, William 1) was born July 10, 1893 in
Marietta Ohio, and died July 17, 1982 in Chicago,
Illinois. (See pp. 210-211, #55 & 254-55, #38.)

25. **Adelaide Elizabeth Stuart** (Albert Edward 12,
Elizabeth Ann Stebbins 11, Edward 10, Edward 9,
Edward 8, John 7, Joseph 6, Thomas 5, Rowland 4,
Thomas Francis 3, William 2, William 1) was born
March 20, 1900 in Marietta, Washington County, Ohio.
(See pp. 211-212, #56 & 255-256, #39.)

Generation No, 14

26. **Gordon Allen Markel** (Edna Henrietta Stebbins 13,
Edward Ellsworth 12, Thomas Atkinson 11, Edward 10,
Edward 9, Edward 8, John 7, Joseph 6, Thomas 5,
Rowland 4, Thomas Francis 3, William 2, William 1)
was born March 09, 1924.

Children of **Gordon Allen Markel** are:

    i.   **Steve Markel.**

    ii.   **Judy Markel**.

27. **Dolores Stebbins** (Thomas Atkinson Stebbins 13,
Edward Ellsworth 12, Thomas Atkinson 11, Edward 10,
Edward 9, Edward 8, John 7, Joseph 6, Thomas 5,
Rowland 4, Thomas Francis 3, William 2, William 1)
was born October 02, 1937. She married **Fred D. Long**
1958.

Children of **Dolores Stebbins** and **Fred Long** are:

    i.   **Larry Leland Long.**

    ii.   **Paul A. Long**.

28. William Edward Stebbins, Sr. (Thomas Atkinson Stebbins 13, Edward Ellsworth 12, Thomas Atkinson 11, Edward 10, Edward 9, Edward 8, John 7, Joseph 6, Thomas 5, Rowland 4, Thomas Francis 3, William 2, William 1) was born June 30, 1942. He married **Rena L. Tippens** 1966. She was born May 1949.

Children of **William Stebbins** and **Rena Tippens** are:

    i.   **William E. Stebbins, Jr.**

    ii.   **Amy L. Stebbins.**

    iii.   **Carrie E. Stebbins.**

29. Carol Ann Stebbins (Harold Burton 13, Edward Ellsworth 12, Thomas Atkinson 11, Edward 10kl Edward 9, Edward 8, John 7. Joseph 6, Thomas 5, Rowland 4, Thomas Francis 3, William 2, William 1) was born November 24, 1933 in Akron, Summit County, Ohio. She married **John Harold Moss** September 13, 1958 in Medina, Medina County, Ohio. He was born February 18, 1934 in Chloe, Braxton County, West Virginia.

Children of **Carol Ann Stebbins** and **John Moss** are:

    i.   **Jean Elizabeth Moss**, b. November 23. 1939.

ii.   **Lois Kay Moss,** b. January 17, 1951,
        Wooster, Wayne County, Ohio; m. (1)
        Scott Cowan; m. (2) **William Charles
        Nixon**, May 30, 1981; b. August 17,
        1939.

iii.   **James Harold Moss,** b. November 17,
        1962.

iv.   **David Scott Moss**, b. November 17,
        1962

30. **Kathleen Stebbins** (Harold Burton 13, Edward
Ellsworth 12, Thomas Atkinson 11, Edward 10, Edward
9, Edward 8, John 7, Joseph 6, Thomas 5, Rowland 4,
Thomas Francis 3, William 2, William 1) was born May
11, 1944 in Wooster, Wayne County, Ohio. She married
James Charles Thompson September 02, 1967 in
Wadsworth, Summit County, Ohio. He was born
November 01, 1942 in Akron, Summit County, Ohio.

Children of **Kathleen Stebbins** and **James Thompson**
are:

i.   **Christine Louise Thompson**, b.
        September 17, 1969, Wooster, Wayne
        County, Ohio,

ii.   **Paul Andrew Thompson,** b. June 20,
        1973, Wooster, Wayne County, Ohio.

31. **Joseph Stuart Goode** (Virginia Stuart 13, Albert
Edward 12, Elizabeth Ann Stebbins 11, Edward 10,
Edward 9, Edward 8, John 7, Joseph 6, Thomas 5,
Rowland 4, Thomas Francis 3, William 2, William 1)
was born 1920 in Auburn, Ritchie County, West

Virginia. He married **Kay Bolt**. (See p. 214-215, #62, and pp. 258-259, #45.)

32. **Adelaide Goode** (Virginia Stuart 13, Albert Edward 12, Elizabeth Ann Stebbins 11, Edward 10, Edward 9, Edward 8, John 7, Joseph 6, Thomas 5, Rowland 4, Thomas Francis 3, William 2, William 1) was born 1923 in Auburn, Ritchie County, West Virginia. (See p. 215, #63, and p. 259, #46.)

33. **Emily Marshall Pritchard** (Adelaide Stuart 13, Albert Edward 12, Elizabeth Ann Stebbins 11, Edward 10, Edward 9, Edward 8, John 7, Joseph 6, Thomas 5, Rowland 4, Thomas Francis 3, William 2, William 1) was born September 06, 1931 in Pittsburgh, Allegheny County, Pennsylvania. (See p. 215, #64, and pp. 259-260, #47.)

34. **Jean Elizabeth Moss** (Carol Ann Stebbins 13, Harold Burton 12, Edward Ellsworth 11, Edward 10, Edward 9, Edward 8, John 7, Joseph 6, Thomas 5, Rowland 5, Thomas Francis 3, William 2, William 1) was born November 23, 1959. She married **Brian Charles Lundquist** September 12, 1982 in Medina, Medina County, Ohio. He was born August 28, 1960.

Children of **Jean Moss** and Brian **Lundquist** are:

  i. **Megan Jean Lundquist**, b. September 28, 1989.

  ii. **Briana Jean Lundquist**, b. March 03, 1993.

35. **Christine Louise Thompson** (Kathleen Stebbins 13, Harold Burton 12, Edward Ellsworth 11, Edward 12, Edward 10, Edward 8, John 7, Joseph 6, Thomas 5, Rowland 4, Thomas Francis 3, William 2, William 1) was born September 17, 1969 in Wooster, Wayne County, Ohio. She married **John David O'Hara** April 09, 1994 in Barberton, Summit County, Ohio. He was born October 19, 1969 in Greenfield, Highland County, Ohio.

Child of **Christine Thompson** and **John O'Hara** is:

    i.   **Elizabeth Kathleen O'Hara**, b. October 08, 1996, Akron. Ohio.

36. **Diana Lee Grimm** (Adelaide Goode 13, Virginia Stuart 12, Albert Edward 11, Elizabeth Ann Stebbins 10, Edward 9, Edward 8, John 7, Joseph 6, Thomas 5, Rowland 4, Thomas Francis 3, William 2, William 1) was born May 6, 1944 in Auburn, Ritchie County, West Virginia. She married **Stephen Edgar Wright**. He was born March 20, 1942. (See pp. 260-261, #49.)

BIBLIOGRAPHY

ATKINSON, BELL, STEBBINS, and STUART private letters and papers.

Cox, Ethelyn. Historic Alexandria, Virginia, Street by Street. Alexandria Foundation, 1976.

THE CRAWFORD MESSENGER, 1805-1835.

Genealogy of the Atkinson, Weidner, and Sommers Families, compiled by Mrs. Lovett Frescoln for Adelaide Stuart Pritchard D.A.R. membership, 1951.

Journal of the Pennsylvania House of Representatives, 1826-1827, 1835-1836.

Klein, Philip Shriver. Pennsylvania Politics, 1817-1832, A Game Without Rules. Historical Society of Pennsylvania, Philadelphia, 1940.

Photograph of the Old Court House. The Peale Museum. Baltimore, Maryland.

Reynolds, John Earle. In French Creek Valley. Meadville, Pennsylvania: The Crawford County Historical Society, 1938.

Williams Kenneth P. T. Atkinson, Pioneer Editor.
Crawford County Historical Society, 1953.

INDEX

Thomas Sommer, 148, 175-177; William, 26, 121; Wilton, 135-136.

AUGSTADT, Robert, 209, 282.

BAILEY, Allyson Kay, 259; Angela Marie, 259, Douglas Wilson, 214, 258-259.

BAIRD, Jonathan, 239; Juliet Bell, 239-240.

BALDWIN, Mr., 121.

BARDWELL, Lucy, 171.

BARR, Mary, 241-242.

BARTLETT, Abigail, 266.

BAUMAN/BOWMAN, Mathias, 128; Samuel, 141.

BEISSEL, Johann Conrad, 127-132.

BELL, Dorcas, 226-227; Elizabeth, 224; Jane, 227; Samuel Whitaker, 201, 249; Uda Dietta, 200-203, 249; William (Captain) 226-227.

BEMIS, Annie, 197; Cora, 197; Dudley, 250-251; Ella Sophia, 197; Fitz-Henry, 197; Frank Brooks, 209; Frank Laroy, 197, 208-209; George, 250; George Herbert, 197; Harry C., 197; Herman H., 197; John C., 197; Marvin Prendergast, 251; Samuel, 201, Stuart Hamlin, 250.

BEMUS, Juliana, 250.

BIDDLE, John, 131.

BIGELOW, Betsy, 201.

BIRCHARD, Nancy, 155-156.

BLACK, R. H., 246.

BLYSTONE, Christopher, 108.

BOLT, Kay, 214-215, 258-259, 286-287.

BOONE, John, 131.

BOSSLER, Hannah, 159-160.

BOWMAN, Harriet, 235.

BOYER, Widener William, 151, 156-157; William, 156-157,

BRAND, Inez, 210.

BRAWLEY, Charles Milton, 241, 251-252; 256; Ella, 241; Francis Roy, 241; James, 241; James Harvey, 241;

John Newton, 241; Leda Irene, 256; Lucinda, 256;
Marin Francis, 241; Ralph A., 256; Ray Martin, 256;
Roma Mary, 252; Roy Francis, 241, 251-252, 256;
Sabine Eliza, 241; Vesta, 256; 260; Walza Vera, 256;
William Roger, 233.
BRENDLE, W., 21- 22, 38.
BROOKS, Samuel, 271.
BROSIUS, Unknown, 269.
BROWN, David, 138-139; James, 138-139.
BUCHANAN, James, 38-40.
BURCHFIELD, Nancy,189, 278.
BURT, Abigail, 266; Elizabeth, 271, 272-273; Eulelia,
257; Henry, 267; Joseph, 272.
CALDWELL, Mary Agnes, 201, 249.
CARR, David, 38.
CARTER, Arthur, 208; Boyd, 208; Elizabeth, 208;
Floyd, 208; Howard, 208; Ira, 208; Jess, 208; Lydia,
208, Thomas G., 207-208.
CARY, Boyd Balford, Jr., 215, 259-260; Boyd Balford,
Sr. 215, 260; Matthew Roger, 215, 260; Roland Mylles,
215, 260.
CATCHALL, Martha 192, 279.
CHAPMAN, Daniel, 144.
CHASE, Mary Cena, 256.
CHEYNEY, Walter Lyman, 179.
CLARK, Anna, 177; Henry Clay, 178; James, 177; John,
121, 177-178; Sarah E., 177, 197; Thomas, 177, William
177.
CLAY, Henry, 113.
CLIFTON, Harry, 160.
CLINE, Hannah, 144.
CLINTON, George 23.
CLYMER, David, 131-132, George, 131-132.
COBURN, Caroline A., 185-186, 276-277,
CODY, Susan, 240;

FREDERICK, Brother John, 133.

FREMOLE, Catherine, 179; Child, 180; Johann, 157, 179-180; Matthew, 180; Mary Elizabeth, 157-158; Penelope, 157; Saloma, 180, Salome, 158; Susan, 180; William, 157-158.

FREY, Maggie Louise, 191, 278; Mary Adelaide, v-vii, 191, 203-206, 278, 281; William 189-191.

GAYLE, Amelia Ross, 166-170; John 167.

GITTER, Bernhard, 129; Elizabetha Lorenz, 129; Susanna, 129-131, 137.

GOE, Elizabeth, 237.

GOLDWAITHE, Thomas, 271.

GOODE, Alonzo, 211, 255; Adelaide, 211, 215, 255, 259, 287; Deborah, 258-259; Joseph, 210-211, 254-255; Joseph Stuart, 211, 214, 255, 258-259, 286-287.

GORGAS, Aileen Lyster, 181-182; Charles Rittenhouse, 144; Christina, 144, 164-165; Christina Amelia "Minnie", 169, 182-183; Daughter, 159; Elizabeth, 144; Jacob, 129, 141, 143, 159; Jesse, 168; John, 128-129, 159-160; Joseph, 132, 141-145; Josiah, 145, 161-162, 166-170; Maria Bayne "Ria", 169; Mary Gayle "Mamie", 168; Mary Salome, 144, 163-164; Nellie, 166; Richard Haynsworth, 169-170; Sarah, 144, 160-163, 180; Solomon Atkinson, 144, 165-166, Thomas, 144; William, 144, 159-160; William Crawford, 168, 180-182; William Rittenhouse, 166.

GRAEFFE, Sarah, 144.

GRAFF, Eliza, 175-177.

GRAY, Charles, 158; Henry, 158; James, 158; Mary, 158,

GRIMM, Earl Jennings, 215, 259; Diana Lee, 215, 216-217, 259, 260-261, 288; Linda, 215, 259.

GRISMORE, Parke, 199, 280.

GROSS, Harlan Abner, 196.

HAHN, Sarah H. 222.

LAWRENCE, Captain James, 32; Phoebe, 232.

LAYCOCK, Henry, 174-175, 275.

LEAKE, Unknown, 183.

LEAVENS, John, 263.

LINEGAR, Elizabeth, 184-185, 275-276; Unknown, 184, 276.

LONG, Fred D., 212, 284-285; Larry Leland, 212, 285; Paul A., 212, 285.

LOTHRIDGE, Stanley, 242.

LUNDQUIST, Brian, 216, 287; Brianna Jean, 216, 287; Megan Jean, 216, 287.

LUSK, Unknown, 242.

LUX, George, 5.

MACFARLAND, Malcolm, 252.

MACK, Alexander, 129; Christina, 129, 141.

MAGAW, William, 38, 83-86.

MARKEL, Gordon Allen, 209, 212, 284; Judy, 212, 284; Lear, 209, 281-282; Steve, 212, 284.

MARKHAM, Israel, 274.

MASON, Harriet Patience, 233.

MAST, Annie, 233-234.

MASTERSON, Katherine Elizabeth, 196.

MAYER (MOYER), Benjamin, 12, 14, 132-134, 137.

McCLYMONDS, Esther, 246-247.

McCREARY, John, 233.

McCULLOUGH, Mr., 121.

McELROY, George, 121, 148.

McELWEE, Elizabeth, 194-197.

McFARLAND, Archibald, 171; Frank Monroe, 178; George, 171, Georgina, 171; John 121, 170-171, 178, 226; John, Jr., 226; Malcolm, 178; Margaret, 171; Salome, 178; Sarah Atkinson, 178; Thomas, 171, William, 171.

McLAUGHLIN, Margaret, 215, 260.

McMEEN, (McMehan/MacMahan), William, 222.

McRANNY, Thankful, 272.
MEAD, Samuel, 23.
MERRICK, Moses, 271; Thomas, 266.
MINCK, Barbara, 164.
MILLER, Christopher Randall, 261; Grace Lee, 261.
MOFFET/MAFFET, James, 234; John, 219, 220, 234;
Mary Ellen, 234; Robert, 220; Robert Grier, 234;
Samuel, 220, 234; Sarah Ann, 235; Stranges, 234;
William, 220, 234.
MORRIS, Clara, 254.
MOSS, David Scott, 213, 286; James Harold, 213, 286;
John Harold, 213, 285-286; Jean Elizabeth, 213, 216,
285; Lois Kay, 213, 286.
MULLEN, Clara, 195.
MULRAINEY, Andrew, 188, 239, 277-278.
MUNN, Abigail Burt, 267; Benjamin, 267.
MUNSON, Mary Ann, 266.
NAGEL, Johann, 243.
NESTOR, Rosa Bell, 211, 255.
NIXON, William Charles, 213, 286.
OBER, Catherine, 159.
O'HARA, Elizabeth Kathleen, 216, 288; John David,
216, 288.
OLEWINE, Benjamin, 157; Mary Fremole 151.
OTTO, Rebecca, 200, 248.
PALFREY, Amelia Gayle "Minnie", 183, 198; George
Declouet, 182-183; Jessie, 183; William Gorgas, 198;
William Taylor, 183, 198.
PENN, William, 3.
PERRY, Martha, 224; Commodore Oliver Hazard, 32.
PFEIFFER, Israel, 193; Judith C., 121-122, 192-194.
PHILIPPE, Elizabeth, 118, 145.
PHIPPS, David, 224.
PINCKNEY, Charles, 23.
PINKS, Jane Sophia, 122, 179; John, 179,

POLLOCK, Patton, 224.
PRITCHARD, Emily Marshall, 212, 215, 256, 259-260, 287; Ernest Markwood, 211-212, 255-256; Rev. Millard Fillmore, 211-212, 255-256.
QUIGLEY, Jane, 230-233.
REAM, Curtis, 140.
REDIC, Sara Melzina, 254.
REEMSNYDER, Unknown, 158.
REUBENDORF/RABENTHAL, Caroline, 149-153.
REYNOLDS, Rebecca, 237-238.
RICHEY, Mary, 235-236.
RIDDELL, Frances Ferguson, 222.
RITNER, Governor Joseph, 119.
RITTENHOUSE, Sytje (Psyche), 129.
RUNDLE, Alice P., 248, Mary Stuart, 248; William B., Jr., 248; William B. Sr. Honorable, 248.
RUSSELL, Luther, 273; Mary, 223-225.
SALTZMAN, Hannah, 222.
SARTWELL, Mary, 179.
SCHLEIGH, Sarah L., 244.
SCHLOSSER, Frances E., 164; George, 163-164; John, 164.
SCHNEIDER, Frederick, 128; Johannes Heinrich, 128.
SCHULZE, Governor John Andrew, 106, 110.
SCRIVINS, Harriet, 206-207.
SERGEANT, John, 113.
SHANK, Charles Wallace, 250; Robert Taylor, Jr., 250; Robert Taylor, Sr., 249-250.
SHARROCK, Muriel Alice 210, 283.
SHIPPARDSON, H., 177.
SHIRK, Madalena, 159,
SMITH, Columbia, 211, 255; Remembrance, 272; Sarah, 265.
SNAVELY (SHIVELY), Mary, 144.
SNIDER, Henry, 128.

Anna, 232, 253; Archibald, 233; Cassius Kirk, 242, 252-253; Charles, 233; Charles Samuel, 242, 252; Chauncey Leeroy, 242, 253; Clark Addison, 242; Eleanor Donaldson, 233; Eliza H., 233; Elizabeth Ann, 242; Florence Merilla, 242; Flossie, 262; Hazel Kirk, 253; Herbert Harper, 242, 253; Herberta Chearer, 253, 257; James S., 233; Jane, 233; John, 229-234; Lili, 242; Lulu, 256-257; Margaret, 234, 252; Marie, 232; Mary, 233; Melinda, 233; Otto Barr, 242; Ralph Ray, 242; Russell, 253; Samuel, 232, 234. 241-242; Sara Lucinda, 233; Walter Scott, 242; William, 230-233; William Quigley, 232.
STRATTON, Margaret, 267.
STUART, Adelaide Elizabeth, 202, 211-212, 249, 255-256, 284; Adelaide Lucy, 250; Albert Edward, 188, 200-203, 239, 249, 278, 281; Alfred Clark, 240; Aldo M., 247; Andrew Armstrong, 221; Andrew Jr., 224; Andrew Sr., 219, 237; Anna Mary, 236, 243; Archibald, 218-220, 222, 223, 224, 236. Archibald Forster, 237-238, 248; Carrie Benton, 240, 250-251; Carrie Elizabeth, 243; Charles, 220, 222, 224, 225, 230-231, 236, 253-254; Charles C., 237; Charles Robert, 254, 257-258; Charles Samuel, 242; Charles Wallace Jr., 240, 250; Charles Wallace Sr, 229, 239-240; David, 224; Donald Edward, 258; Doreen Linda, 258; Edward Ellis, 240; Edward Reynolds, 238; Eleanor, 228; Eleanor Donaldson, 220, 229-234, 241; Eleanor E.. 237; Eliza, 228, 236; Eliza Bell, 240; Ellen, 224; Esther Ellen, 254, 258; Frank, 240; George Runyon, 238; George Wallace, 250; Georgiana, 240; Harold Albert, 202, 249; Harry S., 188, 239, 278; Henry, 248; Herbert T., 247; Hugh Elmer, 247; Hugh Kenneth, 254; James, 219, 220-222, 224, 235, 237, 240; James Dallas, 246-247, 254; James Edward, 186-191, 229, 238-239, 277-278; James H., 243; James Henry, 189, 239, 278; James Leonard, 237, 246-247;

301

Jane, 219, 220, 236, 244-246; Jane E.. 237; Jennie
Forster, 240; John, 223, 236; John Andres, 243; Joseph
B., 206; Joseph Kelsey, 240; Juliet, 238; Juliet Bell, 250;
Levi, 236; Lily A., 237; Louise, 248; Lucy Catherine,
239, 249-250; Luella M., 243; Margaret E., 187, 200,
224, 237, 239, 248-249, 277, 281; Margaret Forster, 32,
188, 225-229, 238, 247; Marie Reynolds, 238, 248;
Marion West, 250; Mary, 237; Mary Catherine, 238;
Matthew/Matthias, 219, 222-223; Norman, 248; Otto K.,
187, 238, 277; Perry, 224, 237; Rebecca Reynolds, 240;
Reed Russell, 237; Robert Richey, 236, 242-244;
Rosanna 235; Samuel, 223; Sara, 188, 224, 239, 277;
Sofia, 222; Thomas, 186, 219, 225-229, 237, 277;
Thomas Baird, 239; Thomas Donaldson, 222; Thomas
Heron, 229, 240-241; Thomas Heron Barber, 239-240;
Virginia, 202, 210-211, 249, 254-255, 283-284; William,
188, 223, 224, 230-231; William Bell, 228-229; William
F., 239, 277; William Watson, 244.
STYGER, Unknown, 136.
SULLIVAN, Mary, 233; William, 234.
SWEITZER, Mary, 140.
SYKES, Theodore, 274.
TAFT, Frances E., 164; Unknown, 164, 198; George,
198.
TAYLOR, Anna, 171, 273-274.
TEWKSBURY, James, 227.
THOMAS, Unknown, 222.
THOMPSON, Caroline, 235; Christine Louise, 214,
216, 286, 288; James Charles, 214, 286; Paul Andrew,
214, 286; Sarah Ellen, 208-209, 214.
THORNBURY, Margaret, 135.
THRAPPE, Bennett Scott, 232.
TIBBETS, Unknown, 257, William, 257.
TIMBERLAND, Richard T., 227-228
TIPPENS, Rena, 213, 285.

TOMB, Hannah, 234; Matilda, 234.
TONSLAY, Michael, 270.
WALKER, J. F., 236.
WALTERS, Mary, 184, 276.
WARD, Eunice, 232; Daniel, 233.
WARRINER, James 270; Sarah, 270-271.
WASHINGTON, George, 20.
WATERHOUSE, Dr. Benjamin, 67.
WATSON, Shirley, 283.
WEBB, Dr., 159.
WEED, William, 233.
WEIDNER, Catherine, 128; Mary, 130-132; Peter, 128-130; Peter Jr. 129-131; Salome, 3-13, 128-136; Sophia, 130-131.
WHITE, Agnes Ann, 246; Archibald Park, 246; Howard, 246; Jacob, 271; Jenette, 246; John Stewart, 246; Margaret Jane, 246; Matilda K.D., 246, Rebecca Jane, 246; William Snodgrass, 244-246; William Vance, 246.
WHITEHEAD, Elizabeth, 131; James, 131-132; Penelope, 131.
WHITING, John 265; Sarah, 264-267.
WRIGHT, Evan George 261; Hannah, 267-268; Lindsey Elaine, 261; Paul Robert, 261; Samuel, 267; Stephanie Lee, 217, 261; Stephen Edgar, 216-217, 260-261, 288; Stuart Benjamin, 217, 261.
VIER, Marie Frances, 165-166;
YOUNG, Unknown, 158;
ZERBE, Ella, 165; Ida, 165; Jonathan, 164-165, Rome, 165.

www.ingramcontent.com/pod-product-compliance
Lightning Source LLC
Chambersburg PA
CBHW070600270326
41926CB00013B/2379